Praise for *Therapy with Tough Clients*

As Gafner takes the reader through the therapy of two of his most challenging clients, he presents what he calls directed unconscious therapy and often transcends the "translucent membrane" between hypnosis and non-hypnotic therapy. This book is intended as a hands-on resource and is replete with clinical wisdom. Wonderful-Serious-Wise, this is the work of a true master, *Therapy with Tough Clients* should be required reading for all entry level therapists and most seasoned therapists as well.

Stephen R. Lankton, MSW,
author of *Tools of Intention*

Therapy with Tough Clients was primarily written to be of help to the clinician by offering a variety of approaches to treating challenging cases. But the book does much more than this: Gafner challenges us to recognize and transcend our own limitations, encouraging a personal growth that will no doubt spill into performing more creative and effective psychotherapies. Read this book and you will be better in more ways than one!

Michael D. Yapko, Ph.D., author of
Trancework* and *Depression is Contagious

When searching the bookshelves it is evident that there is virtually no literature available devoted to exploring the tricky subject of handling challenging clients, especially from a hypnotherapy perspective. Not afraid to meet this difficult aspect of the therapeutic relationship head on, George Gafner has written a thought-provoking book that admirably fills this glaring void. Espousing a refreshing pluralistic approach to therapy he explores working with overt and covert resistance, whilst openly discussing the often taboo subject of the therapist's personal cognitive and emotional reactions.

One of the many highlights of this engaging book is that approaches are illustrated through on-going case studies, which are constructively dissected, affording the reader the opportunity to fully get to grips with every nuance. Ostensibly based around PTSD, there is much to learn for those not versed in the treatment of trauma as each approach is adaptable to any client that presents a challenge to the therapeutic process.

Gaffner is an expert in therapeutic story telling and therefore this book is unashamedly based around metaphor. That said, other aspects of hypnotherapy, including the use of paradox, are effectively demonstrated in situ in the abundant therapy transcripts. The author also includes informative discussions on the potentials and pitfalls of using cultural metaphors, whilst reviewing hypnotic language and hypnotic phenomena for those new to hypnotherapy. With therapists from every background in mind, the author discusses how approaches can be applied both hypnotically and non-hypnotically. He also explores their application in a diverse range of settings, from couples therapy to those working with people held in correctional facilities.

This is a well-rounded book that holds something for everyone, irrespective of their therapeutic background.

Peter Mabbutt FBSCH, CEO/Director of Studies
London College of Clinical Hypnosis

Fans of Milton Erickson and his work with metaphors will love George Gafner's new book, *Therapy with Tough Clients*. From the very beginning, it is obvious that the author has mastered the use of metaphors as he discusses different categories of metaphors: darkness, weight, captor, and descent. In addition, he refers to "overused metaphors" as well as misunderstood cultural metaphors and he also listens to his clients' metaphors even before the hypnotic experience begins.

The book focuses on two case histories, Maggie and Charles, both veterans who are suffering from a number of problems since their return from combat. They are introduced in the first chapter, and we get to follow their progress throughout the book, but the book is not limited to only Maggie and Charles. One interesting case was how he successfully handled a potentially volatile situation when an angry spouse burst into the middle of her husband's session.

Although the book is filled with various metaphors, the author also believes in the value of ego strengthening, and devotes an entire chapter emphasizing it. At the same time, he shows his human side by sharing a couple of "ooops" comments to let us know that he also makes mistakes. Gafner says, "therapy is more of an art than science," and I totally agree. It is obvious that he is a master of the artistic use of metaphors in therapy, and his book is easy to read.

Roy Hunter, FAPHP, DIMDHA,
author of *The Art of Hypnotherapy*

George Gafner is a seasoned clinician who provides a variety of creative ways to use hypnotic procedures and storytelling to treat diverse clients. He uses case vignettes effectively to illustrate the process of therapeutic decision-making. Anyone who is a follower of the Milton Erickson mode of intervention will find this book engaging and informative.

Donald Meichenbaum, Ph.D., Distinguished Professor Emeritus, University of Waterloo, Ontario, Canada and Research Director of the Melissa Institute for Violence Prevention, Miami, Florida

George Gafner has devoted his professional career to refining his approach to hypnosis to benefit the clients with whom he worked. This book provides a distillation of years of exploration, study, and clinical practice that George shares with us in an engaging and highly readable manner. He presents interesting and complex cases and aptly demonstrates how hypnosis is often the treatment of choice due to the wide variety of options it provides. The book is clear and comprehensive, insightful and illustrative. Readers will find a depth of knowledge and analysis in these pages that will stimulate valuable ideas that can be utilized in their own work.

Brent B. Geary, Ph.D., co-editor of
The Handbook of Ericksonian Psychotherapy

THERAPY WITH TOUGH CLIENTS

The Use of Indirect and Unconscious Techniques

George Gafner, MSW, LCSW

Crown House Publishing Limited
www.crownhouse.co.uk
www.crownhousepublishing.com

First published by

Crown House Publishing Ltd
Crown Buildings, Bancyfelin, Carmarthen, Wales, SA33 5ND, UK
www.crownhouse.co.uk

and

Crown House Publishing Company LLC
6 Trowbridge Drive, Suite 5, Bethel, CT 06801–2858, USA
www.crownhousepublishing.com

First printed 2013

British Library Cataloguing-in-Publication Data
A catalogue entry for this book is available from the British Library.

ISBN
ISBN: 978–184590–878–2 (print)
ISBN: 978–184590–882–9 (mobi)
ISBN: 978–184590–883–6 (epub)

LCCN: 2013942529

Printed and bound in the USA

To Sam Atterbury

Foreword

George Gafner is a storyteller and all of his clients know this. It is not unusual for his clients to ask him to tell them stories during a session. He is also a hypnotist, and has had many years of experience as a therapist. Storytelling and hypnosis seem to go seamlessly together for him (as they do for me). When the story is sufficiently engaging the listener goes into a kind of reverie state, there is focused attention, and most therapists would recognize that their client is in what can be described as a natural everyday trance. This interaction between therapist and client is comfortable and provides a useful instantaneous rapport. What better way for a therapist to help a client work through difficulties?

George has worked with many clients during his professional career in institutional settings such as the Veterans Administration (V.A.) system and jails. These settings and clients are amongst the most difficult to help with psychotherapy. Many of the veterans have PTSD; prisoners and others in institutional settings may be sociopathic and abuse themselves with drugs and alcohol. Yet, somehow, stories and the metaphors embedded within them are so universal that they become the "royal road" to establish a productive therapeutic alliance. People appear to be more receptive to suggestions when listening to stories. In that sense the therapist is communicating directly with the client's unconscious or inner mind. The more possibilities the therapist builds into the story, the more likely it will be that the listener will latch onto one or more of the embedded suggestions, and use them to reframe themselves out of their stuckness. George is well aware of this, and especially the need to put into the storytelling sufficient pauses so that the listener can process information in his/her own unique way. He also understands that in the interpersonal interaction time in his office that he has to be himself and from time to time share some personal things. (The latter, of course, is done cautiously and with conscious design!)

In this volume, there are many clients whose concerns are discussed in detail. They illustrate George's experience in working with a diverse population and the ways he chooses to help them. As a kind of leitmotif he focuses on two clients—Maggie and Charles—who appear repeatedly in the book. Most therapists would regard them as being difficult to work with, and George illustrates this in detail, including his own mistakes. He worries about these sessions and mistakes, and we all learn along with him as he freely lets us participate in his progress with Maggie and Charles. It is almost like looking over his shoulder as he ponders what to do next—stories seem to come to the rescue time after time! And he is not afraid to be directive from time to time.

This book is strewn throughout with gems of wisdom and practical things to do, and it is well worthwhile studying. As an added bonus, Chapter 14 contains a number of useful story transcripts which can be adapted to many different circumstances.

Rubin Battino, MS
Yellow Springs, OH

Contents

The client's response should always be our guide.

seeding p48

Toclip 117

38 ambrosia
40 dissociation
41 catalogue
43 - observe space lead
51
5b - IBS Gonsalkorak

Introduction

An enduring teachable moment

When we do unconsciously-directed work with clients we are privileged, as they open for us that window to the deepest part of them. When we direct therapy through that window—with story, anecdote, hypnotic language, pacing of ongoing response, or various other techniques—I call this an *enduring teachable moment*, as it is a time of heightened receptivity. But this is not a one-way glass like we used in the 1970s to view trainees doing therapy. We, as therapists, also have an ongoing process, much of it unconscious, reflected back through that window, and in this book I try to capture both sides of that window as I take you through therapy with two engaging and multidimensional people, Maggie and Charles. They represent two of the most complicated and challenging clients I ever had, and by working with them I demonstrate a host of techniques that you may find useful in doing therapy with your toughest clients.

Once I heard someone say that a delight in poetry is "discovering something I didn't know I knew." Now, recalling that discovery is an example of this enduring teachable moment, and I'd bet that whatever that person read that day in a poem continues to sit there deep within, waiting to be triggered in the future by a like association. So, too, an enduring teachable moment is evident when I run into a client I saw 15 years ago and she mentions, "You know, that old woman in the woods you told me about, I still think about her." Something triggers the memory of the woman in the story. It may be mention of a cold day, a forest, or of some other aspect of The Three Lessons story she heard from me years ago, all inextricably linked to the meta-message of the story, that people have resources within to help themselves with their problems. That memorable tale, which I adapted from a story of the same name by Lee Wallas (1985), is an example of what *you* can do in your practice, borrowing from a story or technique in this book, adapting it to your needs, and fashioning it for whatever clinical scenario you encounter.

Luis, back from Afghanistan

As the unconscious is certainly the aegis of hypnosis, and as this book deals in part with hypnosis, let me share a clinical example that opened up this window to me as much as the client. Around 2005, I was referred a young Hispanic soldier, Luis, who had recently returned from Afghanistan. His problem was erectile dysfunction. He was in perfect health, on no medications, did not have depression or PTSD—despite months of harrowing combat—and like many hypnosis referrals, it came out of frustration after all else had been considered. Luis was married, of average intelligence, spoke good English, and said he didn't drink or use drugs. He was calm, in no distress whatsoever, and said he wasn't bothered at all about the war. His only concern was that he was impotent.

The next session we began hypnosis. He responded with deep trance and amnesia to a conversational induction and The Three Lessons story, which embeds the suggestion that people have resources within to help with their problem. The next session I employed a similar procedure but added an ego-strengthening story and set up finger signals for unconscious questioning. Using age regression, I asked him to go back in time to "any time in the past that might have to do with the problem ... and when you're there, Luis, you may let your 'yes' finger rise." After about a minute his index finger twitched and he began to mutter some words that were unintelligible to me, but I did glean a fragment of a phrase, "I-U-D, I-E-D."

I re-alerted him and discussed today's session. It soon was apparent that his unconscious mind had mixed up the improvised explosive devices (IEDs) in the war with his wife's new intrauterine device (IUD), and impotence resulted. Discussion normalized and integrated this phenomenon, the problem immediately resolved, he was seen one more time in a month and was doing fine, end of story.

Now, how many sessions of talk therapy might have been needed to resolve that problem?

Peter in jail

Therapy with Luis was during a scheduled appointment in a comfortable office at the Veterans Affairs (V.A.) Medical Center. The conditions were optimal. But such conditions aren't always necessary to elicit a similar response within unconsciously-directed therapy. For example, I am now retired, for the most part, but I used to work about four days a month at the local jail. The other day one of the psychiatrists grabbed me as I was walking by and asked me if I would see this very anxious client I'll call Peter, a Black male being treated for bipolar disorder. I sat with Peter for a few minutes in a busy hallway outside the exam rooms in the medical section of the jail. The first thing I noticed was Peter's very fast and shallow breathing.

I showed him deep breathing and asked him if I could tell him a little story while he practiced this better way to breathe. "You can close your eyes or keep them open, whatever you wish," I told him He chose to close his eyes and I told him The Three Lessons story, which I often use early on. People continued to walk by in handcuffs and chains, doctors and nurses were talking, and it was business as usual while Peter responded highly favorably to the story. In two minutes we were done, his anxiety was allayed, and he left with some tools to help him in the future. I have had similar responses in even worse conditions there, like talking to them through the food trap in the door in segregation, or standing in the corner of a busy day room with the curious walking by, straining to hear what was being said. In other words, a nice office with a recliner and wind chimes music is nice, but if you don't have it, you can improvise, even in the midst of rapists and murderers.

Standing on broad shoulders

In my years in this business I have learned from many, from my family, colleagues, people in the field, and my trainees, who came from divergent backgrounds and theoretical perspectives. However, my clients probably taught me more than anyone. For 38 years I worked at clinics and hospitals, and for 28 of those years I directed a program in family therapy and hypnosis training in the V.A. in Tucson, Arizona.

I learned from people who had extraordinary experiences, like the men who had been prisoners of war in World Wars I and II, as well as in later wars in Korea and Vietnam. I learned from the reactant and hostile, like the spouses and children who involuntarily attended family therapy, or those who were directed to attend one of the two anger management groups I conducted for 20 years. One Vietnam veteran with florid PTSD said he was eager to attend because "this is my 12th marriage and I intend to keep it." He did well in the group and his wife was eternally grateful. Years after the group, when I encountered that man or many others, I asked them what they remembered about the group, and invariably they answered, "To take a deep breath or a time-out ... but what I liked best was the stories you told." Indeed, stories and anecdotes, both indirect, or unconsciously-directed techniques, have been my allies for many years.

I learned from my long-term therapy clients and I learned from the ones I saw only once or twice, like the paranoid personality disorder who defied me to try and help him. The V.A. is a fascinating place to work because you encounter a wide diversity of people with every kind of clinical problem. The youngest veteran I saw was 19 and the oldest 102. The oldest couple I saw had been married 76 years. Their recipe for a successful marriage? "Always talk things out and never go to bed angry." I learned from the elderly schizoid woman whose eyes I never saw because of her mirrored sunglasses. I learned from the overly compliant and passive, the therapy addicts who lived in their heads and were resistant to all change however small. I learned from the 200 trainees I had over the years in psychology, psychiatry, nursing, social work and other disciplines. I estimate that over the years I had to do with some 10,000 clients that I either saw directly or whose cases I supervised. In this business we quickly learn that some we help, some we don't, and some we never know because they just fade away.

Trying new things as we counter resistance

For years on Tuesday evenings I was a volunteer therapist at the refugee clinic of the University of Arizona where I saw victims of torture. These people from Central America, Africa and the Balkans had experienced all manner of cruelty, loss and humiliation. I've always done therapy in either English or Spanish, but sometimes at this clinic an interpreter was employed, usually a French-speaking medical student who had done a rotation in Africa. From those in the refugee clinic I learned how fleeting and precious life is, and how we need to make the most of those few minutes or hours we are with any client. Seeing people who were able to overcome the most awful circumstances somehow made it easier for me to help the majority of my clients, people whose problems were understandably dear to them but which paled in comparison to those of survivors of the Bataan Death March, or the lone survivor in a village where all were killed.

Along the way I learned patience. With patience you don't give up on clients and you keep trying new things in order to make an impact. As we try new approaches and techniques we discover what may work in certain situations, but we especially learn what may work for *us*. From these successes we build confidence, and this confidence is immediately apparent to others. I intended this book to be not only an aid to your practice, but also an impetus for the growth and development of the clinician.

Scientifically supported treatments

Currently, in many quarters there is a strong push to practice only one modality for most disorders. Of course, this means some variant of cognitive-behavioral therapy (CBT). I support CBT as a front-line approach. However, I know many seasoned psychologists and other practitioners—not only those new to the field—who disdainfully throw up their hands and are at a total loss when the client says, "I already had CBT and it didn't work," or "I believe my problem resides in my unconscious, and I want therapy directed at *that*." I had many clients who in the first few minutes said, "Please don't ask me to list my dysfunctional thoughts; I already did that both in group and individual therapy." So what does one do with those clients? Well, please read on.

A hands-on resource to assist with the toughest of clients

I make the assumption that you have been trained in one of the major disciplines, that maybe you are licensed, and that in your counseling or therapy practice you are guided by a generally accepted therapeutic approach. You've heard the saying, "When you buy a new hammer everything looks like a nail." Well, I know clinicians whose average day consists of EMDR or hypnosis sessions, hammering one nail after another. I asked them, "What if they have acute grief or a crisis?" You guessed it, EMDR is good for everything, they know because every client looks like a nail. I'm not denigrating EMDR, as I've used it for many years, but almost all the time *for everyone*?

For you, perhaps you practice some version of CBT, or a mindfulness-based therapy, or maybe your theoretical orientation is psychodynamic, NLP, or some other popular approach. Perhaps you employ meditation or relaxation and stress management with your clients. If you could use an extra hand with your toughest clients, I encourage you to read on.

When first conceiving this book I thought, "What kind of resource can best assist clinicians irrespective of their approach?" As such, I intended this book to be a hands-on resource that offers you ideas, choices, and opportunities to employ as an *add-on* to your approach. I'm very familiar with clients who, early on, would set off alarm bells in my head, you know, where the hair on your neck stands up and your gut response is, "Oh, no, not another one!" With such clients, you know you have your work cut out for you and maybe you even say to yourself, "They don't pay me enough to try and help people like this, let me think … hmm, how can I ensure that they WON'T return?" Believe me, I've thought those thoughts, but I kept them to myself, not wanting to be mean-spirited or disrespectful, and went ahead and did my best with people who were, as we say in the U.S., "a sharp stick in the eye." Now, that type of client is an obvious example of a person whose resistance and overall presentation are worse than challenging. Even with them there are techniques that can help.

Building a foundation before advancing to corrective measures

With many people, the challenges are more subtle. You think therapy is progressing well and all of a sudden they start canceling, or just don't show up. Something is operating beneath the surface—the issues are too dear, or you failed to put your finger on something important. In any event, you need to identify and rein in resistance so that therapy can move forward. For sure, I realize that there are some clients who simply aren't ready to address vital issues. They bolt from therapy early, but hopefully they learned something from a session or two so that this foundation can propel them to successful therapy in the future.

One thing I emphasize in this book is how we can "till the soil before planting the seed" by building a firm base of ego-strengthening before moving on to corrective techniques. I explain this to clients as "doing a mental building up first," likening it to a debilitated medical patient who requires major surgery (Hammond, 1990). That patient can first benefit from rest and good nutrition, strengthening her ahead of time. In psychotherapy, I believe that far too often the client comes in and says, "I need help with this problem," and we unwittingly jump in with corrective measures. The client isn't ready, we lose them, and once again we're left ruminating on the old maxim, "Be careful what you ask for." With a few sessions of ego-strengthening such treatment failures can be avoided. I always emphasized to trainees that early on they concentrate on one thing:

Ensuring that the client will return. "If they don't come back you can't help them," I reminded them.

Two other major pitfalls for therapists are 1) low-grade blocks to treatment during the course of long-term therapy, and 2) therapist burnout. You've seen this person (or multiple persons, if it's family therapy) for a good deal of time, progress is slow but steady, but you've grown weary. And if you feel weary or bored, believe me, it will show! With both these scenarios there are various techniques that you can add to both energize treatment and yourself. Doing therapy is damn hard work and you need to keep adding tools to your toolbox. Even with working part-time now I make sure my toolbox stays heavy. I keep adding tools to it and I haven't burned out yet.

This client is 'treatment resistant'

I always tired of colleagues who surrendered at the least resistance, saying they couldn't help so-and-so because the client lacked motivation, or was "treatment-resistant." To be sure, those are accurate terms for some clients, but certainly not all. If people say they want help, they show up and participate as best they can and nothing happens, they may indeed be resistant, but on an *unconscious* level. Consciously they're on the same page as you, but something is holding them back. That *something* usually resides in the unconscious, and that's where your efforts should be directed. In a workshop once someone asked, "George, does unconscious resistance mean they can't help it?" I would argue, in effect, yes, for many, this process lies outside of awareness and thus outside of voluntary control. No, I'm not talking about secondary gain, like the auto accident victim whose PTSD or neck pain won't improve until the lawsuit is settled. (If I were the accident victim I wouldn't improve either!) I'm talking about the others who have average or above intelligence, no organic cognitive problems, and no apparent secondary gain. They just can't get with the program, something is holding them back, and they simply can't let go. It's like any other barrier in therapy that needs to be cleared from your path so you can proceed. However, because we're talking about the unconscious here, you need to proceed by getting in *underneath* the radar, by hitting the ball *beneath* the net.

The therapist can make something happen in the session

Jay Haley said that it was the job of the therapist to *make something happen*, and I've always taken those words to heart. We have a panoply of techniques at our disposal to help motivate and to bypass barriers in the unconscious, and many of them I'll cover in this book. You, kind reader, may already have an ample tool box. My intent in this book is to augment that tool box many-fold so you can better instigate behavior change in your clients, or at least effect a critical reframe to make life more tolerable. Most approaches to psychotherapy avoid or pay lip service to unconscious process, even though convincing psychological literature indicates that a greater portion of our mental functioning is governed by automatic or unconscious process, by forces that lie outside of voluntary control (Bargh & Chartrand, 1999; Mlodinow, 2012). Milton Erickson demonstrated the indirect approach beginning in the 1930s when psychodynamic treatment ruled the day, when the unconscious was viewed as a primordial ooze of negative impulses. Erickson showed us that the unconscious can be a highly employable resource, and in this book I try to tap into the ways we can access this vault of opportunity, the therapist's as well as the client's.

Therapy is art informed by science

I'm a strong supporter of evidence-based treatments but I also believe that in much of real-world mental health treatment we can't simply follow a manual. We must adapt treatment to the unique needs of the individual, and the more skills and tools we can bring to bear, the better for both us and our clients. I've written extensively on hypnosis—and the application of hypnotic techniques within standard talk therapy—and this book builds on that work. As such, it is a synthesis of many years of seeing difficult clients, and teaching and writing about the things we can do to amplify our skills in further helping those clients. In this book I draw on science, but therapy is more art than science. I believe that the science informs the art rather than the other way around.

Maggie and Charles

In this book I take you on an excursion involving the treatment of two people, Maggie and Charles. Maggie suffers chronic problems, irritable bowel syndrome and PTSD, and to date she has failed all interventions. Charles' problem is acute. A clinical psychologist as well as a Vietnam veteran, he is distraught, primarily from the guilt of a romantic attachment to one of his own clients; however, as therapy goes on, something deeper and more pervasive is revealed. For both people, problem resolution resides in one place, the unconscious. Through therapy transcripts I demonstrate the range of indirect techniques that you can bring to bear on the problems of your clients. The ongoing therapy process is punctuated by chapters that further explicate these techniques. I demonstrate the use of hypnotic language and similar devices through "call-outs," where italicized principles or techniques in the text are defined in the right margin, thus providing an ongoing explanation of technique and process. At intervals in the transcript dialogue I critique both the ongoing content and process. Therefore, the reader is continuously attuned to the thoughts and reactions of the therapist. People are hard-wired to appreciate variety, and to this end I attempt to hurl at the reader a vast array indirect techniques, all employed to bypass resistance and move therapy forward.

Key components in the book

It may be intriguing to some that these "hypnotic techniques," formerly thought to reside exclusively in the sphere of formal hypnosis, can also be employed within standard talk therapy. In this book I like to think I am intentionally poking a finger into the translucent membrane separating hypnosis from not-hypnosis. In the didactic chapters that punctuate the therapy transcripts, I discuss concepts and techniques seldom addressed previously, such as the therapist's voice, subtle vocal shift, the pause, the strategic inter-val of silence, and seeding, along with the use of these techniques in non-traditional settings, such as correctional facilities. The use of story and anecdote are developed, both for ego-strengthening and to initiate unconscious problem solving, along with story techniques, such as story without an ending, story within a story, and alternat-ing stories. I discuss steps for therapists to write their own stories, and where the therapist can locate source material to this end.

I try to make the case for integrating ego-strengthening into stand-ard talk therapy. I advocate it as a "shovel-ready project," in other words, akin to "first picking the low-hanging fruit," as the therapist builds a firm foundation with ego-strengthening before progressing to remediative measures. These clinical accounts are true; however, I have sufficiently altered details to protect the privacy of the clients. Nevertheless, the techniques discussed, along with the incidents described—however strange they may seem—actually occurred.

I enjoyed putting this book together. I hope it can serve as a ready-to-use reference for you in your practice and help you grow in the process. Don't give up on those difficult clients, as there's always something else you can try!

CHAPTER ONE

Initial sessions with Maggie and Charles

The Case of Maggie: a referral for individual therapy

Perusing Maggie's V.A. medical record before the first session, I glimpsed a 33-year-old Mexican-American woman who had become discouraged and hardened after 12 years of treatment in the U.S. Veterans Affairs system. In the past two years she had had three brief, voluntary psychiatric hospitalizations for suicidal thought, had been tried on various SSRIs, mood stabilizers and other agents, and had been in and out of individual therapy with a series of psychology interns. She continued to decline offers to participate in the PTSD women's therapy group. Diagnostically, she was classified early on with depression and chronic PTSD, and the recent assignment of borderline personality disorder seemed to reflect staff frustration. Medically, she was followed in a primary care clinic as well as the GI Clinic for irritable bowel syndrome.

First session with Maggie

Maggie had someone with her, a short, rather shriveled up Mexican woman.

Maggie: This is my mother. I didn't have anybody to watch her. She's pretty deaf and doesn't speak much English.

Therapist: Buenos días, señora.

The woman smiled politely, sat down in a chair in the corner of the office and folded her hands on her lap.

Maggie: I have IBS and I hear you tell stories, so that's why I'm here. I know you also do hypnosis, but I don't think I need that.

She spoke in a soft but firm voice that had the huskiness of a smoker. She was tall and lanky and wore a black tank top, shorts and sandals and reeked of marijuana smoke. I could not see her eyes behind mirrored aviator glasses. Her long, black hair framed what was possibly an attractive, olive-skinned face. Actually, little of her face was visible with the sunglasses and an Arizona Diamondbacks baseball cap. The profile of her face yielded a pronounced narrow nose seen in some Mexican-Americans in the U.S. Southwest, considered by many as aristocratic or Aztec. I asked her to remove the sunglasses and when she did I observed eye contact that was steady, even intense. Her face remained expressionless as she spoke, except for a slight puffing of her lips that served as a perfunctory smile. "This woman is in control," I thought.

Therapist: So, you like stories, huh?

Maggie: Sometimes. Just so you know, I don't like to tell much about myself. I get a copy of my record every six weeks. Half of what the doctors write is all wrong.

I thought about how some clients routinely request a copy of their record. This can mean they have filed a claim for service-connected compensation and are monitoring ongoing documentation on which a determination on benefits is based.

(In the V.A., clients may be paid for any problem or condition that occurred or was exacerbated by their time in the military. From nearly 30 years in this system I knew that if a claim was extant, the "green poultice" could be at work and the client might not

make much effort to get better. If I were in their shoes I probably wouldn't get better either.) I made a mental note to ask about a claim. And then the story. She mentioned stories right at the beginning, so that's what I needed to embrace and employ right from the start and not be distracted by her problematic history and provocative presentation.

Therapist: So, Maggie, you get any money from the V.A.?

Maggie: Fifty percent for IBS.

Therapist: So, that's about 500 dollars a month.

Maggie: A bit more—and tax-free thankfully. I get by on that plus an odd job now and then. I'm not taking any classes now. My mom is taking up a lot of my time.

Therapist: So, you have IBS. Constipation-predominant? Got a claim in now?

Maggie: Constipation big time, Doc! And no, I haven't filed any claims for a long time.

Therapist: Please call me George, I'm not a doctor. And when did the gastrointestinal problem begin?

Maggie: It started in 1991 when I was in Kuwait in Desert Storm, we were huddled behind a berm with our gas masks on and a SCUD missile zoomed over my head and it literally scared the shit out of me.

Therapist: So, you *do* talk about yourself sometimes.

Maggie: Yeah, when I feel like it.

I could see this might be a fairly brief session, which I didn't mind, as I appreciate any extra time for the paperwork. I verified a bit more of her history. Early on, I never ask about substance abuse. If they bring it up, fine. If I act interested in that at the start they sometimes don't return.

Therapist: Okay, now is the best part, my story for you today. You can sit back in that recliner, close your eyes or keep them open, whatever feels better … (in a slightly lower volume) as I've learned over the years that a person doesn't even have to pay attention because the unconscious mind can glean anything important, as you *slow down your mind, or your body*, become *absorbed* on the outside, become attuned to the inside, *amuse* yourself inwardly, or simply *experience* relaxation and comfort in your own unique way, as I tell you a little story.

Suggestion covering all possibilities

The story is about Pandora and her box, have you heard it before?

Maggie: Ancient Greece is all Greek to me.

She elevated the recliner's foot rest and sat back. She crossed her arms on her chest and let the sunglasses fall to the floor. Her mother remained impassive but had now closed her eyes.

Pandora's Box
Therapist: This story was first heard around an olive press …

Maggie: Olive oil makes me itch.

Therapist: … or maybe at bedtime, who can know for sure?

Maggie: Bedtime for sure. Pandora is her name, right?

She had now relaxed her hands on her lap.

Therapist: Maggie, just sit back and listen to the story, okay?

Maggie: You call the shots, Doc.

Therapist: Pandora was about 15 years old, toiling in a small garden next to the family home. She was alone and it was late in the afternoon. Suddenly a blinding light appeared. She blinked once, twice, and then through the diminishing brightness she glimpsed someone she'd heard about all her life. Yes, it was Zeus, king of the gods. Pandora shrieked in fear *[Transit-time-can-speed up]*. "You need not be afraid," he said as he took a step closer. In his hand he held something and her eyes were drawn to this object.

Interpersonal suggestion

Maggie removed her cap and shifted in the recliner. Her mother stirred briefly.

Therapist: That's the way, Maggie, *doing anything* you need to do to feel comfortable, knowing that sometimes a little *movement* can allow you to *deepen* your experience …

Pacing

Leading

Maggie breathed deeply and as she exhaled she coughed briefly. I got another whiff. Marijuana and cigarettes, I decided. Her mother's chin was on her chest, probably sleeping, I thought.

Therapist: Zeus thrust the object toward her. She could see it was some kind of box. "Pandora, take this special box and keep it all your days, it is my gift to you," he said. She needed two hands to hold the box, as it was very heavy. "Never, ever open this box, Pandora," he commanded. "Yes," she mumbled. Then, Zeus ascended, quickly disappearing into the sky.

Pandora hid the box in a cave and thought about it every day. Once a month she would sneak into the cave, dig up the box, and examine it very closely. The box was covered in gold and silver and studded with jewels, the most beautiful thing she had ever seen. After a few years, Pandora's curiosity got the better of her and one night she sneaked out of her house, walked up to the cave, unearthed the box, and brought it out into the moonlight. She said to herself, "I know I shouldn't but I'm going to peek inside real fast." She grasped a sharp rock, pried open the lid an inch and just then it happened—a deep whooshing sound that quickly rose in volume.

She screamed and dropped the box. The lid broke off and the whooshing continued, now as loud as a cyclone. Pandora shrank back and covered her eyes. She looked through her fingers and saw many things, terrible things, flying out of the box. Hunger, fear, cruelty, war, sickness, sadness—all the evils of the world were rushing out of that box. The whooshing continued for several minutes, and then all was quiet. She stole over to the box, picked it up and peered inside. Something remained in the box, yes, something was gleaming down there in the bottom. Do you know what that was shining down there in that box, Maggie?

Maggie slowly collected herself, licked her lips and swallowed. Her mouth was very dry. Her eyes remained closed.

Maggie: Nope, no idea what it was. I could sure use a cigarette right about now.

Therapist: It was *hope*. Yes, *hope* gleamed brightly down there in the box.

I ceased speaking and waited. Several seconds passed before Maggie stirred. She opened her eyes, looked over at her mother, glanced quizzically at me, and then lowered the footrest.

Maggie: So, now's when I tell you what that transparent story means, right?

Therapist: Au contraire, Maggie, we'll talk about it next time after it's *percolated* in your unconscious. Also, please remember this: You *never want* to read too much into any story.

Seeding
Restraint

Maggie: Okay, better give me another appointment then.

Therapist: You sure? Sometimes it's good to *think* a while first. This "story therapy" isn't for everybody.

Restraint

Maggie: Nah, let's do it. I heard that most people you don't see 'em any more often than two weeks, that works for me. So, story therapy is the same as hypnosis?

Therapist: Here it usually is. Not all the time. You appeared to show a good hypnotic response today, slowing way down, relaxing, all that stuff.

Her mother's eyes were now open. She leaned forward in anticipation of leaving.

Maggie: She has to pee, I can tell.

Therapist: See you next time.

Notes for practice

I employ restraint as an overall posture with reactant clients. Now, that may seem counter-intuitive to you. Aren't we supposed to encourage clients to embrace therapy? Restraint here also includes *not* commenting on, or reinforcing, what appeared to be a fair response. With a non-reactant client I would have readily scheduled a follow-up appointment and ratified her cataleptic response (lack of movement and swallowing, "facial mask," etc.), relaxation and general cooperation, and asked her how much time had passed since she entered the office (to ratify time distortion) however, I know she's tried and failed therapy other times, so I'm going to hold her back from change and encourage her to go slow with this process. By doing so, she's more likely to believe that therapy will help her, and when she makes gains they are more likely to hold because of continuing restraint.

Another thing that may seem counter-therapeutic is *not* verbally processing the story. After all, aren't we supposed to talk about content so it can be integrated? With this case as well as the case of Charles, I advocate *not* immediately discussing the story. By doing so, I'm not restraining as much as utilizing the naturally occurring process of percolation, or incubation. I say to clients, "Let's hold off on discussing it right now. My reason for this is so that the metaphor can sit in your unconscious mind and continue to process without conscious interference. First thing we'll do next time is talk about the story."

I believe that 10 days to two weeks is a critical time for unconscious processing. Why? I base this on clinical observation of client behavior. Unconscious processing of a metaphor, like a story, may be similar to the unconscious processing of a paradoxical directive in therapy. In their meta-analysis of paradoxical interventions, Shoham-Salomon & Rosenthal (1987) determined that one month is the critical time frame for the directive to take effect. Shoham-Salomon and Rosenthal stated, "The superiority of paradoxical interventions over other treatments at follow-up may indicate the better durability or, alternatively, a surge in their effectiveness one month after the intervention. In other words, we may have encountered a sleeper effect in which paradoxical interventions require an incubation period before they can produce a superior effect" (1987, p. 26).

Now, some writers believe that the story can be discussed and explained immediately. Michael Yapko (personal communication, 2007) noted, "Let's remember that Aesop explained his fables." I recommend you try both ways to see what works for you.

I interspersed a suggestion directed at her IBS, said it quickly in the midst of the story. I watched her as I said it and no change in facial expression followed it, so I was reasonably assured that no conscious attention was drawn to it. That's good, as I'll build on it next time. A full discussion of hypnotic techniques, including literature review on the efficacy of hypnosis, and various types of hypnotic induction and sample scripts, can be found in my volume, *Techniques of Hypnotic Induction* (Gafner, 2010).

The Case of Charles, another referral for individual therapy

I don't know about you, but nothing gives me pause like a client who is also a therapist. I feel pressure, first, the perceived scrutiny of the client, and second, the felt need to prepare more than I do with other clients, as "I better get it right." A wise psychiatrist I worked with once told me, "Forget about all that stuff, the client is hurting just like every other client, just give 'em your best shot like you always do." That advice helped a lot with Charles, a client who was more challenging than most.

First Session with Charles

Charles strode smoothly and confidently into my office. He was a practicing clinical psychologist and had been combat medic in the Vietnam War. He sought treatment for Generalized Anxiety Disorder (GAD) and insomnia. He told me that in his practice he regularly relied on hypnosis and metaphor. I don't like to make hasty judgments based solely on one's appearance, but everything about this man screamed incongruence, telling me, "Something isn't right here." He was neatly dressed in a short-sleeved shirt, tan Dockers slacks and light brown penny loafers. He wore a bola tie, basically a string tie with a clasp, a tie generally accepted for formal dress in the southwest U.S. He was tall and had a sinewy muscularity. With his long hair in a ponytail and a bushy gray mustache he looked younger than his 64 years. He had high, arching eyebrows that gave the impression of asking a question, and his eyes were mere pale blue slits as they were heavily lidded, appearing languorous and indifferent. His voice was both leathery and slightly nasal. Looking at him and listening to his voice was disconcerting to me, which I tried not to show.

Therapist: I saw in your record that you were awarded the Distinguished Service Cross after your tour in Vietnam. The only one higher is the Congressional Medal of Honor.

Charles: Yeah, they had a big ceremony with my family there. I was just a kid then. I got shot twice during all that. I took a round in the buttock, that doesn't bother me, but the shrapnel in the shoulder, that gives me more and more trouble as I get older. If you want, I can tell you all about it some time. Or you can read about it in Wikipedia and other places. It was 1969, ancient history now.

Therapist: Well, still, you're a real war hero. I don't see many of them here. Anyway, what do you like to do now when you're not at work, leisure time, that kind of thing?

Charles: I have three Bentley convertibles and I like to go out on long drives in the desert. And also I help out my wife with her gems and jewelry. She's got a real good business with that.

I thought, "Hmm, three Bentleys. His wife must have a very good business. Certainly most psychologists aren't wealthy. Well, none of my business, get back to why he's here." In the record it said he took Celexa for a chronic, low-grade depression; drank two shots of expensive bourbon before bed; his hypertension was controlled by two medications; and his general health was good. As he described his anxiety and insomnia he appeared anguished, maybe guilty, and I got the feeling that something important was not being revealed. Midway through the session I asked.

Therapist: Charles, I may be way off base here, but I get the feeling that there is something important that you're not telling me.

Charles: No, I have this vexing *nervousness now and then* that's *hard to describe* and I can't sleep worth a damn most nights as far as I can recall when I get up in the morning, that covers it all.

Vagueness

Therapist: Okay, then, try and *give me some* specifics, tell me *exactly how* you've been feeling, in your *mind*, in your *body, generally* or *precisely*, at *work*, *relationally*, or in *any other* way …

Suggestion covering all possibilities

He responded with vague generalities, talking in meaningless circles, digressing into the circumstantial, while his body language conveyed defensiveness.

Therapist: So, then, it's like looking into a mud puddle on a *foggy* evening and you see something — is that a coin shining down there in the mud puddle? It's becoming clearer to me now.

Meeting vagueness with vagueness produces clarity

His body jerked and words reflexively sprang from his mouth.

Charles: I have a romantic attachment to one of my women clients.

He glanced around the room as if looking for allies, and then put his head in his hands and sobbed.

Charles: I feel beaten down, beaten to a pulp.

I wrote down the metaphor he had just provided. Doesn't it happen so often, when there's nearly no time left they drop a bombshell in your lap? The first thing I thought of was, "How can processing actively continue between now and the next appointment in two weeks?" But I needn't assume that he wanted to come back. I hoped that I hadn't alienated him by pressing for specifics.

He had already blown his nose and cried into about 10 tissues. After handing him the waste basket I tried to wrap this up.

Therapist: Charles, I'm glad you made it in today. It takes *courage* to reveal what you did today to someone you only knew from his books … you arrived perhaps with *trepidation* … knowing deep down you needed to get something *off your chest* … walking down that hall *coming* in here … beginning to *express* important feelings … this processing needs to continue … *and* between now and next time I'd like you to *write down* what is bothering you the most about all this … it can be typed, handwritten, long or short … I'll quickly read it, then give it back to you to destroy, if you wish … how does that sound?"

Reframe

Truisms

Linking word
Directive

No forethought was required.

Charles: I'll do it!

Commitment

Therapist: Good, I'll look forward to that next time. Now, before we end I want to tell you a little story called The Three Lessons. Have you heard of this story?

Charles: I don't think so.

The Three Lessons
Therapist: It has to do with a young man growing up in another state, I forget just which one, but somewhere it gets cold in the winter. This young man heard about a wise woman, someone who could help him with his problem …

Charles kicked off his shoes, sat back in the recliner, and closed his eyes. The tension was beginning to drain from his body.

Therapist: Now, after getting directions to the wise woman's house he set out through the woods. It was very chilly, he could see his breath, and passing by an icy cold stream he knelt down and thrust one hand into that cold, cold water. He didn't know if he was there with *that* hand in the water for a *short time* or a *long time*, but by the time he pulled it out that hand had become very *numb*. That's the way, Charles, doing just fine. Isn't it *in*triguing to explore deep *in*side?

Dissociative language
Time distortion
Anesthesia
Seeding

Charles: (inaudible)

Therapist: Finally, the young man rose to his feet and continued on through the woods. He saw the wise woman's house in a clearing, approached and knocked on the door. A voice from inside said, "*You may come in,*" which was lesson number one. Inside, before he could speak, the wise woman came up to him, gazed deeply into his eyes and said, "Everything you *need to know* you already know deep inside, even though you may not yet know that you *already know*," which was lesson number two.

Activate seed

Suggestion

And the third lesson occurred when he realized it was time to go, and off he went. And everything *worked out* just fine for him.

Ego-strengthening suggestion

Notes for practice

Charles was hurting badly, which was excellent from my perspective, as it gave me a lot to work with, very different from clients who come in with chronic, low-grade distress from which I can get little traction. I almost always start both my hypnosis and talk therapy clients with The Three Lessons story (Wallas, 1985), whose primary embedded suggestion, or meta-message, is obvious and simple but extremely important, as it sets the tone regarding one's unconscious resources as well as *my* expectations about change. In other words, he can do it with some assistance from me. Any brief story is a good, healing way to end any session. The first session is critical, so I will say things that are likely to ensure they will return for a second session.

A word on homework. Some therapists have told me that insurance companies want and expect between-session assignments, as supposedly this contributes to briefer therapy. I agree with homework; however, I think that often we prescribe it too often and in knee-jerk fashion before the client is invested in the therapy process. Also, many times the homework is unrealistic or too complex, and then when they return and say, "Oh, I forgot," some therapists follow it up with even more homework! If they don't complete it, all of a sudden you have a big problem on your hands.

I'm serious about therapy and if my client is not, I'll immediately wonder aloud about the wisdom of continuing. My clients almost always follow through with homework because 1) I'm confident they've bought into a collaborative process ("We're working together on this and I'm your guide on this journey ..."), and 2) the assignment "fits" and is realizable. Therapy is hard enough without causing a power struggle over homework. That said, I realize that some clients expect homework the first session, and you can't go wrong with very general directives, like (in marital therapy), "Between now and next time I would like both of you to notice what is good about the relationship," or (in individual therapy) "I would like you to *notice* times when you don't feel quite so depressed. I don't know if that might be in the morning or evening, when you're alone or with others, but when you *notice* these times—it may be only seconds or minutes—that is something to be *appreciated*." Notice and appreciate are two words I rely on. They can focus attention on key behaviors and reinforce their response. Any exception to the problem can be revealing, and they usually occur but are not noticed by the client.

I normally don't assign homework the first session, but intuition told me that this was something I needed to pounce on early. Had

Charles prevaricated on my request to elaborate on his problem in writing, or said, "No," I would have backed off and probably revisited the issue next session. If more "no" responses followed my request for a realistic assignment, I would ask him, "Well, Charles, what's going on here? If we can't work together on this there is no need to reschedule."

Now, what I did in the first session with Charles, was it hypnosis? Some would say yes, but I say probably not. Certainly Charles responded hypnotically in that he evinced facial mask and other characteristics of catalepsy, or suspension of movement, one example of hypnotic phenomena. Had there been time to thoroughly debrief him, I would have likely seen evidence of dissociation, time distortion, and other hypnotic phenomena; however, because I employed no induction (suggestions for hypnotic phenomena, or going into trance) and a story alone, it may be a stretch to call it hypnosis. With Maggie, though, I did employ trance-inducing words as a segue to the story, and therefore Maggie's session could be deemed hypnosis. Again, this may be splitting hairs, as therapists could argue yay or nay.

I know many clinical psychologists who do progressive muscle relaxation (PMR) with lots of their clients. During the procedure some clients may evince catalepsy, dissociation, time distortion, age regression and other hypnotic phenomena even though the practitioner gives no suggestions for same. I would bet that, if asked, 90 percent of the psychologists would answer, "No, that was not hypnosis, it was PMR," and technically speaking, they're right. Psychologists often say, "PMR is only to relax the body." I don't think it's that simple. I'm quick to recommend to practitioners of PMR that they capitalize on the procedure with indirection—anecdote or story—as these precious moments of drifting off are truly teachable ones.

Usually, it's hypnosis when you call it hypnosis, and although it can be done in many ways, often a hypnosis session will, first, be labeled hypnosis, and second, be delineated by a formal induction (inducing of trance), deepening, and a therapy component, such as a story.

Then, the person is re-alerted and a debriefing follows. With train-ees, I teach hypnosis with these discrete components, as I think it makes the process easier. However, many practitioners effect trance quite briefly with a directive induction, such as the hand levita-tion, or roll the components into one with a conversational induc-tion. These identifiable components were absent with both Maggie and Charles. In 1993 the American Psychological Association (APA) defined hypnosis as "A procedure wherein changes in perceptions, sensations, feelings, thoughts, or behavior is suggested." To me, this would include even indirect (unconsciously directed) suggestions on which I rely heavily in this book. A few years back the APA came up with another definition which has drawn much criticism for its lack of completeness and clarity, and I prefer the old one.

Hypnosis has also been defined as guided daydreaming, believed-in imagination, controlled dissociation; a relaxed, hyper-suggestible state; a half-way point between sleep and consciousness, and a nar-rowing of conscious attention and facilitation of unconscious recep-tivity. Unless it's self-hypnosis, hypnosis occurs within a structured social context, and many definitions ignore or diminish the role of the therapist. That's why Yapko (1990) called hypnosis "a meaning-ful interaction in which the client and clinician are responsive to each other."

When clients come to me for hypnosis, I pretty much follow the stages, or components, cited above. There's no problem, we're on the same page. In most other cases, I practice hypnotically, as described with Charles and Maggie. Later on, Maggie asks me if what we're doing is hypnosis, and I answer yes. Charles never asks me because he knows, as he is accustomed to practicing hypnotically with his clients, too.

CHAPTER TWO

Metaphor, story and other invaluable devices

Metaphors are all around us

We only have to tune into the news on TV and we witness politicians trying to out-duel each other with metaphor. In the U.S., one Congressman says that if a budget isn't passed, "we will be kicking the can down the road one more time," only to be outdone by a Senator who says that the problem is worse than that, "a snowball rolling down the mountain, gathering size and momentum ..." In earlier years in Russia, the notorious Josef Stalin offered a distasteful metaphor to explain his genocide: "When you make an omelet, it's necessary to break some eggs." A few years back heavyweight boxer Mike Tyson, known for his fights inside and outside the ring, informed us that he really wasn't that bad a guy, couching the notion for us in metaphorical terms: "I'm not Mother Teresa but I'm not Jack the Ripper either." What's the main facet of these metaphorical expressions? Not the elegance or beauty, but the *sheer economy*. So much is conveyed with sparse words, and the same thing happens in therapy, when we communicate with clients, or when clients reveal vital information to us. Where else can we witness this refreshing, minimal expenditure of words?

Clients' expressing themselves metaphorically

Metaphor, or understanding or experiencing one thing in terms of another, pervades daily life, in the news as well as in books and film. I point this out to underscore the idea that many clients are accustomed to metaphor and its various nuances, and employ them—often with sophistication—as spontaneous, unconscious expressions, and therapists should pay close attention to these vital communications. I always tell interns, "Listen very closely to their words. Much of what you'll need to help your clients you'll hear in the first two minutes of the session, and usually there's a metaphor in there." Let's say I'm in a first session with a couple and they say, "There's a *wall* between us." I seize this piece of gold, regarding it as a gift-wrapped therapeutic invitation. Thereafter I can use this *wall* as an index of progress, no need for lengthy marital satisfaction inventories. As therapy progresses I'll periodically ask, "How's that *wall* doing?" and they may let me know that it's not so tall, maybe some boards—or bricks—have fallen out, or maybe the wall has completely disappeared. In addition to assessment I can employ the wall in intervention, for example, "Okay, we worked on communication last time and now we'll talk about steps you can take to rebuild trust. Will that mean we've loosened some mortar between the bricks over here, or maybe blown a hole through it over there, or maybe someone's able to stand on a stepladder and peek over it?"

Facile, overused metaphors

In the first chapter, Charles let me know that he felt "beaten to a pulp." Had he said, "I feel like I've been through the wringer" (an old device used to squeeze excess water from washed clothing), that's a bit vague and I would need to ask him if that means he feels flattened, worn down, discouraged, or something else. A beauty of metaphor is its elegant economy, but sometimes we need more information. If my feedback to a client who is discouraged about therapy includes "this is a marathon, not a sprint," I'll monitor his non-verbals, which will convey acceptance or rejection of the metaphor long before he answers with words. That metaphor, like many, is trite, facile, overused and could turn a client off, just the opposite of the emotional connection that occurs with an apt metaphor. Now, in your practice, how do you do that, connecting with clients via metaphor? If you haven't, take a risk and try one out. So, you toss one out there next session and it doesn't connect with the client? I've missed the mark plenty of times, no big deal, and I learned from it. In my eagerness to connect with Charles, early on I loosed a metaphor--I forget what it was—and I missed. He had been in my situation himself and let me know with an omniscient smirk when he said, "Nothing ventured, nothing gained." Clients are always our best teachers.

Siegelman (1990) notes that metaphor represents the need to articulate a pressing inner experience. However, not all metaphors flow from meaningful affect. Koetting & Lane (2001) advise us to listen for well-worn metaphors, such as "I'll never get to first base with my father-in-law," as these clichés may herald resistance in therapy. The authors advise countering with similar language, e.g., "Let's examine how you can *step up to the plate* with your father." In marital therapy, when I heard "The man is king of his castle," I didn't expect role change any time soon.

Cultural issues: Missing the point

I found in my work with people from Central America that sometimes they would not endorse psychological symptoms, such as depression or sadness, but would note "a pain in my heart" instead. Indeed, in many cultures people's metaphors for psychological conditions will be somatic. Hispanics in the southwest U.S. may say, "I have a heavy heart," which could express sadness among other things. American Indians often express depression as darkness or soul loss. In my work at the refugee clinic, I found that people from various countries in Africa may not share our Western up-and-down orientation, e.g., feeling "low" or "on top of the world," but may express it instead in terms of not feeling one with nature, or cut off from their interdependence with others. A woman from Uganda explained her depression most poignantly: "I'm a solitary person now, alone on a road that goes by nobody's house."

I've made more than a few mistakes with metaphor. One woman from Guatemala was successfully acculturating and trying out new behavior. I told her a story about a Monarch butterfly that emerged from its cocoon and then flew from Canada to Mexico and back again. She politely reminded me that it's the fourth *generation* of Monarchs that makes the migration. I was seeing an agrarian man from El Salvador for whom Spanish was a second language. I told him about an iceberg to represent the unconscious mind. Iceberg? He'd never heard of such a thing. I then mentioned the ice in his drink from the convenience store and began to extrapolate on that.

His quizzical expression made me think, "Dumb George, why do you insist on digging an even deeper hole here?" I then switched to "the part of your mind that dreams during the day or night." His smile of recognition was wonderful, but my real reward was what I learned in that interaction. We *never* need to reinvent the wheel.

Research on metaphor

Sopory & Dillard (2002), in an exhaustive study of metaphor, concluded that *metaphorical messages are more persuasive than literal ones*. Stalin broke those eggs, we get the point. When I would scold my interns for going over 50 minutes I would include, "Mussolini made the trains run on time," and they'd ask, "Who was Mussolini?" The same interns didn't know if World War II came before or after Vietnam.

The sooner the metaphor is introduced, the more persuasive it is. It's always been fascinating to me how *clients* introduce a metaphor very early in the session, and when I hear it I write it down because I'll be using it, possibly in this session, and certainly in later ones. So, too, therapists can be persuasive early on if we recognize client suffering with "you have a heavy weight on your heart," "a full plate," or something else that fits the situation.

The more novel the metaphor, the more persuasive it is. I guess this means that my tired and boring stories about nature indicate that my burden is heavy! Seriously, the beauty of metaphor is that we can draw on the rich and vast material available in books, film, music, art and other aspects of human experience, not to mention the plant and animal world.

Vividness can undermine a metaphor. You may notice that in my stories in this book I provide just enough detail to describe the situation. I think that too much detail may serve to distract the person from the larger metaphor. Many people, especially those with good imaginations, may be insulted by excessive descriptors, perhaps resenting—on an unconscious level—that the therapist doesn't think they have the capacity to fill in the blanks themselves. In asking the client to spontaneously generate a metaphor of their own, we may be tempted to say, "... see yourself by a nice tranquil lake on a bright, sunny day with billowy clouds in the blue sky ...," when we could simply ask the person "to see yourself in a pleasant place, it can be any place at all." Neither framework nor adjectives are needed, as we can trust most clients to fill in the details.

What about the imagination-challenged?

I believe it is important to ask people to imagine or visualize whatever your target is. Doing so both draws on their unconscious and asks them to *do something*. However, some people have a hard time doing this. Let's say I'm working with somebody and I want them to search for past competency, and I ask them to "... see yourself, in your mind ... sometime in the past when you felt good about yourself ... notice the context, what you were doing ..." And nothing comes up, they can't generate the image. Next, I might ask them, "... I'd like you to hear the voice of somebody in the past, someone you liked and trusted ...," for example. Too often we rely solely on the visual. Now, say they still can't, even after I've prompted them with examples. By this time it might start to feel like a power struggle, so I'll just back off. I believe the inability to generate anything (image, voice, feeling, etc.) is a poor prognosticator, but clients don't need to know that. I'll move on to an anecdote or story and see how they respond to that. If they say, "That was a very nice story but I can't see it applying to me or anybody else," I may have just plumbed their creative depths.

Metaphorical examples

Metaphors for depression

Two linguists in Canada, McMullen & Conway (2002), followed the course of therapy of 21 clients, audio-taping 471 therapy sessions to learn about client metaphors. Four main categories were present in the data: *darkness*, *weight*, *captor*, and *descent*. Now, from my experience, I would have thought that weight or darkness would have predominated, as I don't know how many times over the years I've heard people say things like "the weight on my shoulders," or how their depression is a dark cloud or a black dog. Nevertheless, *descent* accounted for 90 percent of metaphors reported. They found examples that included "spiraling down," "having a downswing," "going through a nosedive," "sinking low," and "getting mired down." I felt crestfallen and downcast just reading it.

Hackneyed metaphors and Easy Street

Sometimes people take our words too much to heart. Once I was working with a veteran who had gotten both legs blown off above the knee in the invasion of Normandy in WW II. I forget just what story I told him, but afterward I restrained him with, "Don't make too much of my *hackneyed* metaphors," and a couple days later his wife called and demanded, "What did you say to him? He hasn't had *phantom limb* pain for 20 years and suddenly it's back!"

Sonja Benson (co-author of two of my books) and I were conducting a workshop, and after a discussion of the advantages of metaphor, someone said, "Oh, so metaphor is the *easy way*," and another chimed in, "Yes, with all due respect, you're taking the *easy road* in therapy." I answered, "Of course, therapy is hard enough, why NOT make it easy?!" I can see those two knocking themselves out with elaborate, overly detailed metaphors, building the Golden Gate Bridge when a pontoon bridge would do just fine.

Concrete metaphors

In my office I had a three-foot long rib of the saguaro cactus, you know, those tall green titans with arms that can live for 200 years. I would hand it to the client, ask them if they knew what it was, and ask them to describe the stick's qualities, leading them to the fact that the rib was "strong but flexible." Then I took it back and moved on to something else, no need for more discussion. I also used the radiator caps formerly on automobiles, where you could lift up part of it to "release all that pressure building up in there." Sonja Benson likes to use modeling clay, all the things you can make with that. Concrete metaphors, I believe, are more likely to be remembered than some of our lofty verbal ones. Of course, sometimes, just like waiting until next time to process a story, it may be appropriate to discuss the meaning of the radiator cap as they clench it in their sweaty hands. I usually don't, simply my preference, as I believe that generally it is good to let any metaphor percolate in the unconscious. And I can say that even though I've had a few people yell at me and slam the door on the way out, over many years no one ever threw a radiator cap at me or whacked me with a saguaro stick.

The Story and the anecdote

I find the story—actually an extended metaphor—to be the most versatile vehicle for both delivering key suggestions and for moving therapy forward. Clients come to expect a story as a natural part of the session. I have stock stories with general themes such as ego-strengthening, growth, strength, discovery and acceptance. Some I can remember and others I must read. In the following chapters, I'll address anecdote and story in detail, along with story techniques, such as alternating stories and story without an ending. First, let's look further into the *easy* way. In a session, when you need to grab a metaphor, tell them about *somebody else*. A short anecdote, "*... let me tell you about someone else, she had a problem much like yours, and here's what helped her.*" Simple, quick, and like any metaphor, it can't be defended against, as it slips in beneath the radar. Anecdote is just a very short story. Later on we'll get into two major categories of anecdote, ones for ego-strengthening, and others for instigating, or perturbing the unconscious to promote problem solving.

Hypnotic language

Like story and anecdote, hypnotic language is a major vehicle that can aid your therapy. Certain words are considered "hypnogogic," or producing trance-like effects, such as eye fixation or suspended movement. When words that contain *in*, like imag*in*ation and *intui*tion, are mentioned, the *in* receives a slight vocal emphasis. This encourages an internal focus. Words like *wonder, story, explore, discover, intriguing,* and *curious* are also hypnogogic, as are *notice*, especially combined with *appreciate.* We refer to them as "power words," as they may arrest attention and stimulate internal search.

Apposition of opposites is a suggestion that juxtaposes opposites, like up-down, slow-fast, inside-outside, hot-cold, and left-right. This opposite phenomenon is also trance-inducing. There are other examples of hypnotic language, but for now let's mention one more, *truisms*. A truism simply describes an undeniable fact, and several truisms produce a "yes-set;" in other words, the person is more likely to agree to something after hearing truisms. (Okay, maybe you're thinking, "I heard this the last time I bought a car." Hey, therapy is part selling, too!) Let's say I'm nearing the end of a session and I'm going to ask Maggie to take a walk every day. I could just ask her, or, because I sense reluctance, I might say, "Maggie, this is our *third session*, each time we've met at *3:00*, and so far you've explained how *IBS* has affected your life, and you've told me a little of your experience in the *Persian Gulf* (all truisms), *and* (the most important word in therapy because it links and leads) between now and next time I want you to take a 15-minute walk once a day, something that can help you a lot. How about it?" Try it out on your partner before you try it on your boss.

Not knowing/not doing in Dr. Tracten's office: A suggestion I use frequently is *not knowing/not doing*. "Not *what*?" you may ask. Yeah, it could have a better name, I know, but that's what they call it. Basically, this suggestion is one of the most important ones because it sets the stage for all else that follows. It is the most liberating of all of them, as it frees up the person to do whatever they wish—and then, they often let go and relax, which is the whole reason you're stringing all these words together in the first place. Throughout this book the problematic client, George, visits the redoubtable Dr. Tracten, and George is in his office now. The doctor says, "George, just sit back and relax. There's *nothing* at all that you need to *know*, or *do*, or *think about* or *change*. *Nowhere* you need to be, *no one to please*, *no meeting* to attend. In fact, you don't even have to *listen* to these words, as the back part of your mind can pick up anything important to know. Yes, George, nothing at all to do except to just sit there and breathe."

How often in life do you hear, *"Do whatever you want, anything is okay?"* I use this suggestion in hypnosis, but also in talk therapy, for example, an abbreviated version of not knowing/not doing before a story, but I also use it at other times. Let's say I'm seeing a client and she just described a very emotional and difficult situation. She is tearful and pauses to collect herself before getting to a most painful part of her story. At that moment, I might softly interject something like, *"That's the way, just letting it happen, there's nothing at all that you need to know or do, anything is just fine."* Those are not restraining words, nor are they intended to neutralize affect; I simply want to convey to her that she not worry about "getting it right," or embarrassing herself, or anything else—that however she responds, or doesn't respond, is okay.

Hypnotic phenomena and elegant indirect techniques

Notice the hypnotic phenomena in the following account.

A woman observes her young children at play. She recognizes that their behavior is primarily unconscious, as they are absorbed in fantasy while they color, build with Legos, or watch *The Lion King*. The kids' 13-year-old brother is upstairs, immersed in a video game, but his behavior remains generally unconscious. None of the kids share mom's conscious contemplations, like making the next house payment, or the absence of her husband who should have returned two hours ago.

Dissociation is evident in the boy's playing his video game. Deep in trance, he is *outside* his body, inside the screen driving the race car, his hand *separated* from the rest of him, operating the control *independently, autonomously*, the hand with a life of its own. *Catalepsy* is evident in his *unmoving* face, motionless head, with mouth agape. The boy also experiences *time distortion*, where a *minute is an hour, an hour a minute*, losing all sense of time.

Mom experiences *positive hallucination* when she thinks she hears the phone ring. The teenage boy suddenly materializes on the staircase and as mom looks at him *age regression* occurs, as she remembers years ago when he was young. The doorbell rings

once, twice, but due to *negative hallucination* she does not hear it.
"Mom, the pizza is here," yells the boy on the stairs.

Throughout the session, but especially during and after I tell a story,
I monitor the client's words and non-verbals for evidence of hypnotic phenomena, naturally occurring responses that often become
accelerated and even exaggerated during therapy. These responses
are diagnostic—indicating how much the person has responded to
suggestions embedded in the hypnotic language, for example—but
they can also be employed therapeutically, which we'll get into later
on. The major phenomena:

Time distortion

"So, Maggie, without looking at the clock on the wall, how much time
do you think has passed since you came in here?" I ask. She looks at
the clock anyway and says, "Oh, seemed like a lot longer than that."
I then point out that she experienced time distortion, thus reinforcing her response. Time expansion was experienced by Maggie, and
had it appeared like *less* time had passed, that's time contraction.

Amnesia

I often embed suggestions for amnesia within a story or anecdote,
e.g., "and that woman, I forget her name, she said to me, 'George,
you can forget to remember or simply remember to forget;'" or,
"Anything you may have intended to remember you can conveniently
forget," or, "I woke up from a dream and couldn't remember any of
that dream." Such suggestions may foster amnesia and I sometimes
employ them at the end of a story.

Amnesia occurs spontaneously with some people and I know
that suggestions for it are not necessary if the client remarks, for
example, "Gee, that story, most of it I can't remember, I don't know
where my mind was." The primary reason for fostering amnesia is
so that the material can continue to be processed unconsciously
without the interference caused by conscious contemplation or discussion. Is there research support for this notion? Nope, anecdotal
reports only. And plenty of people much wiser than me would argue

for discussing any and all content of a session during the session. They liken trusting the percolation of the unconscious to magic or fantasy, like "when I wish upon a star."

Well, lichen and mossy ideas remind me of fishing, and I'll grant them that, that it's a fishing expedition. But isn't there a sense of wonder and discovery in something like fishing, where you get *surprised* now and then? Let me give you an example where employing amnesia worked like a charm.

Sonja and I used the videotape in workshops and we called it *Beard/No Beard*, and you'll see why. The tape shows Billy, a 60-year-old veteran of the Korean War, who was referred for hypnosis. Billy had been a tough guy, a paratrooper, two-fisted drinker and barroom brawler, who had now been sober for 20 years. He had an intriguing problem. In a small New Mexico town where he lived the newspaper had mistakenly printed that he wrote bad checks. The paper retracted and apologized, but that didn't matter. "Everybody looks at me," said Billy, and he couldn't sleep because of the ruminations. *At the start of the incident he began to grow a beard*, and now the beard was long and shaggy.

He had been prescribed various medications by the psychiatrist and been through a course of talk therapy. Eventually, he was referred for hypnosis. I saw him for three sessions of ego-strengthening, which did not impact the problem. One thing I noticed, though, was deep trance and a *complete amnesia* for content of the session. The next session, we did some brief trancework, but for most of the session I gathered from him his typical daily driving route in this small town. "Okay, Billy, so you start out on Main Street, go down Lincoln to the highway, do I have it right so far?" "You got it, Doc," he said as he scratched flakes from that scroungy beard. So, the next session, he was deep in trance and, before a story, I said it once and then repeated it: "*When you cross Lambert Lane, something will come to you that will help you with your problem.*" I knew suggestions for amnesia weren't needed. I re-alerted him and sure enough, he could remember nothing.

Three weeks later he was back and I turned the camera back on. He was *clean-shaven*, neat and clean. He showed a bright mood and was relaxed, looked years younger, a different person. "So, you do anything new that helps these days?" I queried. "Well, I finally started doing that deep breathing you always talk about," he answered. "Oh, really, when did that start?" I inquired innocently. "I dunno, I just started it and now I don't have those thoughts anymore," he said.

I checked on him in a couple months and he was fine. So, I ask you, how do I know if it was the suggestion that worked? I'll never know. Billy had no conscious recollection of something happening when he crossed Lambert Lane. Nevertheless, I'll gladly take credit for it. I've done this maybe a couple dozen times and it's worked about half the time. If you try it, remember this: The key thing is that you *tie the suggestion to something naturally occurring*. Erickson would say, "When you see a flash of light." I like roads and streets, especially the rural ones that lead to lakes where you … fish!

Dissociation

In the book I use dissociative language, e.g. *that* hand, not *your* hand. It is especially effective with people who pathologically dissociate, like PTSD clients. Also, I say things like,

"it is highly *interesting*, even *curious* how in trance, which is like an *entrance into another state*, a person's hand or foot may feel *detached*, way off, over there, *truncated*, which has nothing to do with the G.O.P.*, *and* beginning now, you can *imagine*, just imagine, that problem of yours *out there*, in the next room, around the corner, on another planet …"	Power words Pun Dissociation Pun/linking word Suggestions Dissociation

Can we use dissociative language too much? Yes. If we say anything too often it may be counter-productive in that conscious attention is drawn to it. So, in an induction or story, I may say *that* hand (with a slight vocal emphasis on *that*) two or three times, and then the rest of the time I'll say *your* hand without any emphasis. Mix it up,

---

* The G.O.P. is the Republican political party in the U.S. and its symbol is the elephant.

contrasts are our ally: up-down, loud-soft; dissociation in one sentence, catalepsy in the next, and back to dissociation again.

Catalepsy   *Stillness*

Catalepsy is a suspension of movement. Behavioral markers of catalepsy are sitting still with little or no movement, "facial mask," and little or no swallowing. A cognitive equivalent, such as slowed thoughts or overall slowed internal experience, may accompany bodily markers. I may offer the client direct suggestions for catalepsy combined with the *not knowing/not doing* suggestion:

"Isn't it nice to know that everything, especially *movement* and *(suggestions) thinking*, can really slow down, as there's absolutely *nothing* at all that you need to *know* or think about or change, *nowhere* to *(not knowing/not doing)* be, nothing to attend to; in fact you *don't even* have to listen to the words, all that's needed is to just sit there and breathe."

I might also offer suggestions for catalepsy by describing somebody else's experience in a story or anecdote, or even more indirectly: "The Athabasca glacier near Lake Louise *slowly* advanced until 1843, and has been receding several inches every year since then."

Taking advantage of hypnotic phenomena in the session

To me, these phenomena, also known as trance phenomena, are not just a diamond in the rough; they are far and away the biggest underused asset in the world of psychotherapy. Erickson, Rossi and Rossi (1976) defined hypnotic phenomena as the dissociation of any behavior from its usual context. We can observe trance phenomena in our clients during a moment of concentrated attention, or when it seems like their attention is focused on something of great meaning or interest. As we go about our day, minute to minute, our attention is geared to interpreting events occurring around us on the social, psychological and biological levels. Dissociation from that state occurs perhaps hundreds of times every hour. But when it happens in therapy, when therapists have the opportunity to notice it, that is the time when therapeutic change may have the greatest potential.

In order for us to take advantage of that potential we must carefully observe our clients, especially the minimal cues, such as a slight reddening in the cheeks, increased vitreous fluid in the eyes, a nostril flaring, or a tensing in the neck or back, to mention a few. I include among non-verbals the vocal alterations we observe, a slight cracking of the voice, a rising intonation, a breathlessness at certain times, a brief stutter, and countless other deviations from the person's normal conversational voice. Before I started doing hypnosis I never really paid much attention to all these subtle behaviors. An excellent discussion on employing hypnotic phenomena in therapy can be found in Edgette & Edgette (1995). How about if we examine hypnotic phenomena in a therapy session?

Back in Dr. Tracten's office

The problematic George is back to see Dr. Tracten. In the first session Dr. Tracten mentions something like "one's unfulfilled dreams of childhood." As soon as those words are spoken, Tracten notices George's eyes glaze over as his head turns slightly, as if glimpsing something from afar. Now, that is a highly charged therapeutic opportunity for Dr. Tracten and he must seize it. He doesn't know the meaning of George's response but he makes a mental note of when it occurred. If Dr. Tracten were intrusive and maladroit, he could interrupt with the following.

"George, at this moment are you showing me the thousand-yard *stare*, the glazed-ham *look*, the being-in-Kansas-and-just-emerging-from the-dark-root-cellar-after-a-tornado-*look*, or *some other* meaningful response?"	**Suggestion covering** **All possibilities**

Or, he could stop talking and merely observe until George reorients, which many therapists might do, but that misses the therapeutic opportunity. Dr. Tracten knows that in the deepest stage of sleep clients show a spike on the EEG when their name is mentioned. So, he would do well to just pace or match the response: "That's the way, *George*, doing fine." It's always comforting for a client to experience a gentle, permissive, and respectful pacing, or commenting on, ongoing behavior.

Fast forward to the fourth session. Dr. Tracten knows that in 1937 in Germany at age five, George's parents dumped him in an orphanage and ran off to join the Nazi party (you're getting to know all my secrets here). So, the good doctor mentions "unfulfilled dreams of childhood," he sees George drift off, and knowing that a double negative equals a positive, he figures this is a perfect time to be clever.

"Doing fine, George … your parents could *not not see* what they were doing.	Double negative and pun

But a better response would be

"Doing fine, *just let it happen that's the way* things *out there, way back* then should be dear to you always, *and* stirring up old memories is a *good thing* because inside you important *change* is occurring."	Pacing Dissociation Linking word Leading/reframe

If it were the tenth session Dr. Tracten would be in a position to tailor his response even more therapeutically. So, the take-home message here is *pay attention to the subtle non-verbals*, always pace, pace and lead when you can, and take a stab at a positive connotation (reframe) if the opportunity is there. If you guess wrong in your interpretation, the client will show it immediately non-verbally. I've guessed wrong plenty of times, no big deal, no harm done, just move on. (Oh, just so you know, I wasn't born until 1947.)

Integration through discussion?

If people are curious and want to dissect process at the end of the session, I'm glad to discuss what went on. If the client can't remember that he drifted off, that's your cue to *not* draw attention to it the next time it happens, and you just let it percolate. It's a good idea in general to reinforce—consciously, in your feedback near the end of the session—their response, e.g., "You did a good job here today ... however you respond in here is highly positive." You're letting them know that they don't have to maintain social rapport. Many clients strive to "get it right" and fear losing control and embarrassing themselves, so you need to neutralize that. I remind clients of the overarching purpose of this: "What we did here today, the whole idea is to help you reorient your inner reality so you can meet the demands of external life and be happier." For Dr. Tracten's spacey client, he would need to explain it in simpler terms.

Moments of dissociation in a session

We all dissociate—for brief periods—all day long. Your clients, who perhaps dissociate problematically and have trouble holding it together, they dissociate off and on all day long, too, and when they do it in your office, just remember, it's probably a bigger deal for you than it is for them. Many of us have been led to believe that dissociation is something rare, negative, and indicative of poor prognosis in therapy. For sure, in some cases of dissociative identity disorder (DID) such may be the case; however, I believe that in 99 percent of clients, including people with PTSD who chronically space out, dissociation—more than the other hypnotic phenomena—is something that can be paced and utilized. I had one client with DID who spaced out often. I quickly learned that she was very receptive to suggestion during these moments, which I then encouraged her to experience because those times were the most fruitful part of any session. Once you start to anticipate brief dissociative moments in your clients, you'll recognize them as opportunities to intervene.

Embedded suggestion

Matt Weyer, a psychologist in Phoenix, Arizona, came up with the wok story for Bill, who was 80 pounds overweight and rejected the idea that he should get some physical exercise. I think this is an exquisite example of embedded suggestion.

The Wok

The following story was taken from *Hypnotic Techniques* (Gafner and Benson, 2003).

> Someone once told me about a man named Bruce, the best cook he ever knew. Bruce went to different schools to be a chef, and he even worked at several fine restaurants, though he never quite cooked up to his potential. But things began to change for him one day when he *discovered* something. To his great surprise, way back in the cupboard among the various pots and pans, he found his old *wok*.
>
> The *wok* was covered with rust and had not been used for many years. He remembered the trouble he always had with Asian dishes, but at the same time his classmates at chef school had become quite adept at *wokking*. "You notice a lot of things about cooking when you get lost in *wokking*," they told him.
>
> In his kitchen, Bruce began to experiment with his wok, first with one kind of oil, and then another; first on low heat, then on medium heat, and eventually on high heat. He did a lot of thinking while he *wokked*, but mostly he contemplated, deep inside, "I can do this, really I can." And the results were absolutely marvelous.
>
> A week or so after Bill heard this story, there was a change in him. He never did prepare food any differently, but he started to *walk*. He walked and kept on *walking* until he lost those 80 pounds and kept them off.

Waterfalls and enormous soft drinks

Dr. Tracten sees his client, George, standing in the line to the toilet. George is obviously uncomfortable and eager to use the facilities. Dr. Tracten says to George, "Wait, don't go in yet, let me tell you about my trip last year to Niagara Falls."

A few minutes later, George, now anguished, still hasn't made it in but is next in line. Dr. Tracten approaches again, this time with a

64-ounce cup of Coke, and directs his client, "George, wait a minute, watch while I drink this down."

So, not exactly therapeutic embedded suggestions, but examples of the technique just the same. If George were nervous about a rock concert this weekend, Dr. Tracten might offer him an anecdote about a similar concert he attended recently:

Security anecdote

"It was curious, George, maybe even intriguing, that all the *security* personnel they had there, *security* in front of the stage and back-stage, but also in the audience and even outside before you went in, *security* everywhere."

But George didn't listen to him because he planned to take a handful of Valium out in the parking lot when he arrived at the concert.

Balloons everywhere

I have always loved using balloons to convey letting go. In addition to the Balloons story in this book, we have Tony's Balloons and Frankie's Balloons, previously published in *More Hypnotic Inductions* (Gafner, 2006). I have used them with both children and adults. Both of these flowed from the adroit pen of Ingrid Jacobs (2005), a retired elementary school teacher in Tucson.

Tony's Balloons

Not long ago I went to the county fair. I saw a young child eight or nine years old holding what looked like a huge umbrella of colorful balloons by a tangle of strings. There must have been hundreds of those balloons.

I said, "Hi there, what's your name?" The child smiled brightly and replied, "Morning, my name's Tony. I'm in third grade and I'm selling balloons." Tony was wearing some faded, holey jeans, a T-shirt with a school logo on the front, and some Nike sneakers. It was still early in the morning and there weren't many people at the fairgrounds yet. I watched Tony as he wandered around with his huge canopy of colorful balloons.

Every once in a while he'd ask someone, "Hi, wanna buy a balloon?" Most people said no, and others said they'd buy one later. I could tell he was getting discouraged. He looked longingly at the other kids enjoying the different rides, and eating cotton candy and hot dogs. After a while, I saw him by one of the tents. He was carefully pulling out the string of an orange balloon. He held it at arm's length, admiring it for the longest time, watching how the breeze played with it, and then he *let it go*. It rose slowly at first, like it didn't want to leave, but then the wind caught it and it lifted off, up into the sky. At first, it looked like Tony was sad to see the balloon go, but after a moment a smile came on his face, and just then he separated another balloon. This one was rainbow colored. He *let it go* quickly and watched as it was carried away out of sight. This was fun!

Next, he pulled out five more balloons, a blue one, a pink one, and other colors. He *just let them go*. They floated up and seemed to play tag with each other, and then drifted away. Some grown-ups and children noticed what he was doing and they gathered close for a better look.

All of a sudden an idea came to Tony. He opened up his hand and he released all the rest of the balloons. He laughed with glee. He had *let them go*, every last one.

Frankie's Balloons

It was a warm spring evening at the State Fair and Frankie's job there was to sell balloons to make money for a special project for the 10th grade at Central High School. Frankie had a large fistful of strings, and attached to each string was a balloon. On each balloon was written a word. On a red balloon was "Happiness." On a green one was "Disappointment." Other balloons of various colors contained words like "anger," "joy," "doubt," "hard work," "fun," and "fear."

Frankie had walked around the fair for three long hours, and so far he had sold only one balloon. Did that balloon have "Happiness" on it? He couldn't remember. He was getting so tired, and his hand hurt from holding on to all those balloons. It felt like the balloons were fastened to his fist with Superglue. Frankie heard in his head the voice of a trusted friend. *"You can let those balloons go,"* said the voice. He opened his hand just a little and one balloon flew up in to the air. Then his hand opened all the way and all the remaining balloons, he *just let them go.*

Never underestimate the value or utility of "children's stories" with adults; in fact, with a highly reactant adult, stories designed for children, like fairy tales, are more likely to sneak beneath the radar. Think of *The Princess and the Pea* or *The Ugly Duckling*. You know any adults who could benefit from those fairy tales? As far as stories about balloons go, you may find that these are highly employable in a variety of contexts, and can be easily fashioned into your own stories. Our original Balloons story can be found in the appendix.

Seeding

In a movie you might hear thunder and see a dark sky. This foreshadows something dramatic a while later. In a play, there is a pistol above the mantelpiece in Act I, so you know by Act 3 there'll be some shooting. In psychology it's called priming. In a priming study they used word-pairs to influence one's choice of laundry detergent. The group that was primed with *ocean-moon* selected … yes, *Tide* (Geary, 1994).

In therapy, we use seeding by mentioning something early (the seed) and then mention it again later (to activate the seed). Let's say in my next session with Charles, I'll be telling him a story about *slowing down*. So, I casually mention early on that traffic was *slow* coming into work today, and that the janitors *take a long time* to empty my wastebasket. Then, later in the session the seed is activated when in a story I mention *slowing down*. I could also seed the concept non-verbally by *slowly* getting up to grasp my cup of tea, and *slowly* returning to my chair.

This is an elegant, highly effective technique and, of course, it works well outside the person's conscious awareness. Sure, it takes a little preparation, but it's well worth it.

Sound seed and split suggestion

This may be the equivalent of mining for unobtanium. I came up with it one day when I wasn't darning socks, and I've used it a few times with modest success. A sound seed is precisely that, seeding the sound of the target to be activated later on. Gloria's clinical issue is insomnia due to ruminations.

Gloria loved Indian food, actually anything with *curry*, and she also loved *furry* animals, anything that *purred*.	Sound seed
After the sun went down she could stop *worrying/ hurrying* because approaching slumber was to be deeply appreciated.	Seed activated with misspeak

Wouldn't it be so much easier to just tell Gloria to turn on a white noise machine when she goes to bed, take a pill, or to just lighten up? Well, she's already tried many things and she won't take pills unless they're really necessary. I've had a lot of clients like that. Sometimes we have to try different things to slip beneath the radar.

Split suggestion is just that:

Gloria revved up her *slow/sewing* machine, and later, she drifted off, dreaming about *pace/lace*.	Misspeak Split suggestion with misspeak

You with me here? *Slow pace* is the suggestion. Is this any better than just throwing in *slow pace* as an interspersal suggestion? Probably not with the average client. But with the highly reactant, it may hit home. How do we know if it worked? By the client's subjective report, objective measure, new behavior, lots of ways. The problem with using more than one technique at one time is obvious, but in the real world of therapy we do that all the time. Many times they get better and I'm really not sure why, and it really doesn't matter, as long as they get better. The corollary of that is they *don't* get better and then we look back and see what *didn't* work, which is always very instructive. The client's response should always be our guide.

So, this misspeak thing was used twice in the above examples. A handy little device.

Misspeak

 "What?" you may say. "I thought this was about clarity and purpose in language, not about intentionally making mistakes in speaking." Well, let me explain.

- In a class by itself as an unconsciously-directed technique, *misspeak* is seldom used, perhaps because it is barely referred to in the literature. Furthermore, few practitioners avail themselves of this effective technique, possibly because it doesn't lend itself to spontaneous employment and usually requires a modicum of preparation prior to the session.

- To be used sparsely, this can be eminently useful in communicating a suggestion to the unconscious. For example, "... she ceased the *umbilical/unbiblical* behavior with her daughter," or "The man changed his behavior across the *board/border* down in Mexico." The therapist appears to misspeak, the first word is the suggestion and the second word serves to distract or lead away. For the overly-analytical, maybe you'll want to lead away further:

- Vic Timrod was indeed able to *extricate/explicate* his special problem, but all he could think about was the rising price of petrol.

- Barry Cade had it within himself to *seal off/feel* on a very deep level, but why did the highway workers leave just three orange cones on the road?

- It's really quite easy to ascribe mental *Valium/value* to nervousness, but Euros versus pounds never seems to add up.

- Elizabeth had *forgive/fortitude* to endure many things, but the ads they have on TV these days.

- I appreciate that you can *heal/feel* and still discern the nuances, but all the rain last July.

- She said once, "If my problem were a boil, I could *laugh at/lance it*, but when, tomorrow?"

- I occasionally notice unhelpful emanations from deep within, and *deflecting/detecting* them doesn't mean I'll be a private detective anytime soon.

- That nagging symptom, he couldn't help but *modify/mollify* it, but then, why do dogs bark?

Misspeak may be indicated if straightforward or indirect measures have failed, or if the client mobilizes defenses around a particular issue. In either case, in pondering the case prior to the session, I examine the target behavior or attitude and then write down similar sounding words that I could fashion into a word pair, and then place it in a phrase, or as part of a story or anecdote. *Cooperation-corporation*, *acceptance-exception*, letting go—*bacon, let go/lettuce* and tomato sandwich. Are you with me so far? Remember, the first word is the suggestion and the second word keeps the listener from mulling over the "mistake" or trying to analyze it.

I say the first word fast and slide right into the second one. Other examples: "It's the *shame/same* burden others carry, and casting that off is usually a good thing, or "she discovered, to her delight, some resources in the dark *allies/alleys* of her mind." This one is a bit of a mouthful, though I have used it: "Concerning beverages, coffee, tea … you may find yourself *sitting peacefully/sipping tastefully* in those fearful situations." Usually, shorter is better unless you need to lead away.

When you're talking to the unconscious it doesn't have to make conscious sense, be a complete sentence, or be stated cogently. You're tossing in these little bomblets or seeds and the unconscious takes it from there. Do we have any scientific evidence that this works? Of course not! Can you see academic psychologists designing a study around this creature?! With recalcitrant clients, I have used this along with other indirect techniques and have seen results. And ... (you may be ready to ask ...), no, in all my years of doing this I have never had one person say, "Ha, I caught what you were doing there with that slip of the tongue." Not even clients who are themselves therapists and who use indirection in therapy. That's why it's called an *unconsciously*-directed technique. Employing misspeak once or twice in a session will do.

Interspersal—another elegant indirect technique

What is it?

To me, only metaphor, in all its remarkable aspects, ranks ahead of interspersal as a serviceable and effective technique in therapy. Think of having a brainstorming discussion with family or colleagues, and you *toss in* an idea. The same thing in therapy, you interject a suggestion or idea during the session. So, "Maggie, you've made progress with your constipation—*you can do it*—and I bet your doctor is pleased."

The more tangential or oblique the better. When employed with Maggie above, interspersal is much like the non sequitur used in the short-burst type of ego-strengthening described in Chapter 4. Both aim to insert suggestions underneath the defenses' radar, hitting the ball beneath the net of critical analysis.

Although interspersal was alluded to in Erikson's writing as early as the 1930s, the technique was first described in-depth in 1966. In that article (Erickson, 1966), the author demonstrated: (1) the interspersal of various durations of time to cure intractable urinary frequency, and (2) the control of cancer pain by interspersing suggestions for comfort within a meandering story about growing tomatoes. Even though Erickson did not employ a formal hypnotic induction in these cases, the clients' response was clearly deeply hypnotic.

Indications for use

As a general rule in therapy, the more reactant, well-defended, rigid or analytical the client, the more indirection of all types is indicated. As such, interspersal joins hypnotic language, metaphor, story, anecdote, seeding, confusion, and other techniques in this regard. Although interspersal is indicated for the reactant, its use certainly is not limited to those clients. Once I became familiar and comfortable with it I began to employ it with all clients, reaching into my toolbox for it probably once or twice in most sessions of individual, family and group therapy. Clients then came to anticipate its use along with anecdote and story. Any more than a time or two in a session and it may become a distraction and draw conscious attention to it along with needless analysis.

We'll be revisiting these terms and concepts as we continue, but for now, let's get reacquainted with Maggie and Charles.

CHAPTER THREE

Irritable bowel syndrome (IBS) and continued therapy with Maggie and Charles

Irritable bowel syndrome

Maggie's chief medical complaint is not rare. Prevalence rates for IBS are 13.6% in the U.K., and an estimate of 8–17% in the U.S. Women are twice as likely as men to be diagnosed, and it is believed that most individuals with the disorder *do not* seek medical help (Blanchard, 2001). If you're not currently seeing IBS among the problems in your practice, look closer, especially among your women clients. There may be someone you can help.

IBS is a *functional* disorder of the lower intestinal tract. This means there is no structural abnormality, just disordered large bowel function. No one knows *why* one gets IBS. It's like when my physician told me I have *essential* or *idiopathic* hypertension. He doesn't know why, I just do. Clients with IBS have a variety of unpleasant symptoms, the cardinal one being abdominal pain. They may be diarrhea-predominant or constipation-predominant, like Maggie. We should never agree to treat IBS in the absence of concurrent medical treatment. At this time, gastroenterologists' medications and other treatments are generally ineffective, and most of these doctors welcome the mental health clinicians' adjunctive treatment. Indeed, psychological measures can be highly effective.

Treatment of IBS

Very briefly, CBT has a strong track record (Blanchard, 2001), bested only by hypnosis. Leading the field of hypnosis treatment is England's Manchester group of GI doctors and other staff (Whorwell, 2008). In these programs, relaxation and hypnotic ego-strengthening play a vital role in a multifaceted approach. If you're interested in a step-by-step description of Manchester's treatment, I highly recommend the article by Gonsalkorale (2002).

Noncardiac chest pain study

Another disorder treated by GI doctors is noncardiac chest pain of esophageal origin, NCCP for short. A few years back I administered the treatment protocol in an unpublished GI study (Fass, no date) to treat NCCP. After a fairly invasive medical work-up, clients were randomized to either wait-list or the treatment condition, which consisted of six sessions of ego-strengthening stories within trance. Clients listened to a CD three times a week. On the CD was a brief induction followed by the Molasses Reef story (used on Maggie's CD in this chapter). Before this study was terminated for administrative reasons, all 12 subjects showed improvement in the target symptom.

My recommendation to clinicians is this: Arm yourself with CBT and hypnotic skills, along with knowledge of IBS, and generate referrals from GI doctors. You'll have a prosperous and interesting practice.

Maggie second session

In the interim, I'd been thinking of Maggie's cataleptic response to the story last time. Catalepsy is a useful phenomenon to employ in therapy with anxious clients, as the slowing down and suspension of movement can be used, for example,

"Before you give a report in front of your class you can imagine, just imagine, this *slowing down* as a soothing balm embracing both your body and your mind ... initiating this feeling with your anchor and one deep breath ... and those eyes out there that seem to be boring into you can soon become very *boring ...*"

The anchor, or associational cue, I assign is "a little circle you make with your thumb and index finger." However, as one of my main targets with Maggie is her IBS constipation, the last thing she needs is suggestions for more slowing down.

Maggie's mother went right to her chair in the corner. She nodded politely when I greeted her, and then folded her hands on her lap. Before closing her eyes, she said in Spanish, "Thank you for all your help." Maggie's sunglasses were nowhere to be seen this time. She said she felt "just fine" about last session. I could smell no marijuana this time, just cigarettes. She provided further background information and concluded (quite correctly) that the meta-message of Pandora's Box is that "You can let go of stuff and still be okay." Regarding her IBS, she noted, "I eat everything, I don't care anymore." She'd had CBT, kept a stool diary ("My Yule-time stool log," her humor again), ate a high-fiber diet, and drank plenty of water, none of which she did currently. Her daily activity consisted of general coursework at the community college and visiting her mother. Socially, she had no close friends and had had no boyfriend for a long time. I asked her about this.

Maggie: I'd like a steady relationship, but it has to be a man with all his parts, not like the ones I meet at the V.A.

Therapist: Oh, I meant to ask you last time. IBS discomfort, constipation and all, the way you feel right now, how would you rate it on a scale of increasing severity from one to ten?

Maggie: Right up there, maybe an eight.

Therapist: Do you have any questions or comments from last time?

Maggie: Well, it was very curious, maybe enjoyable is the right word. I'm just glad you're not beating me up with my dysfunctional thoughts.

She settled into the recliner. I prepared the material I'd be using today.

Maggie: Oh, a psychologist I ran into out here said your "story therapy" isn't at all scientific.

Therapist: Well, you've failed CBT—that's scientific—more than once, what we're doing here could work, and knowing you a bit, I can say that unconsciously-directed therapy—hypnosis, or "story therapy," if you will—is highly indicated. No guarantees, but if you keep coming, this could definitely help.

I didn't mention that yes, indeed, there is strong scientific support for treating IBS with formal hypnosis. I've found that it is the rare client who wants a detailed explanation or literature citations, though I have provided them to a rare few who asked. Most want some assurance that they're not wasting their time. These days, consumers can find most things on the internet, but less so in the early 2000s. I told her that today I would be telling her a healing story and adding in some GI-specific anecdotes and interspersal suggestions, all of which I'd be audio-recording. By next time I'd have a CD for her so she could listen to it at home. As this would be an important part of therapy, I jotted myself a note to ask her if she's listening to it at least two times a week. Why two? I ask for two and am happy if they do it once. I asked for three times a week in the GI study I mentioned, and those people were paid research subjects, not veterans, for the most part, and had little psychopathology.

Maggie: Sounds like a winner, let's do it.

Therapist: Okay, Maggie, just settle into that chair and let that feeling of relaxation and comfort begin to develop ... that's the way, knowing on good authority that there's absolutely *nothing* at all that you need to know, or do, or think about or change, *no* class to attend, *no* expectations to meet ... in fact, you don't even have to listen to the words,

Not knowing/not doing

which can drift *in* and drift *out* … noticing those extremities, *left hand, right* hand, warmth, *coolness*, heaviness, *lightness,* appreciating perhaps intriguing sensations and feelings on *the inside* … And you can let your comfort deepen, as I tell you a little story called Molasses Reef.

Apposition of opposites

Suggestion

Healing stories

White sand beach (Benson, 2011)

Walking along on a white sand beach in Florida, with the warm sun, the ocean breeze, and soothing sound of waves crashing, it can be quite easy to become absorbed in one's inner thoughts or musings … almost involuntarily or without consciously noticing it at all. The wind blows the grains of sand, leaving ripples of evidence that sometimes change happens so easily, and yet, imperceptibly at the same time, until a later glance shows you a new landscape and possibilities of what will come next. Staring out at the ocean, the eyes see everything while the inner mind pays attention only to those details that really matter most. If a person is not used to solitude, time might pass slowly at first, then as the mind gives way to the delightful peace and wonderful possibilities of just drifting and dreaming, time may speed up so an hour seems like a minute. And that daydreaming can unlock unknown potential, find new solutions, like so many doors opening, or so many seagulls dipping and sailing on the air currents.

The Molasses Reef story

I was on one of those beaches that day, and after walking for what must have been many minutes I sat down in the sand. I noticed a man and a woman several feet away, seated on a bench, and they were leaning toward each other, conversing in what I can only describe as a loud whisper. The man said, "I want to tell you a good story," and this immediately captured my attention, as I have been fascinated by a good story ever since I was young. I moved over closer to them so that I was within earshot, but they paid me no heed. (*Conveyances, public or private, deeply appreciate faster transit time.*)

The man was describing a beautiful marine sanctuary called Molasses Reef. He said, "It's off of Key Largo … I dove there in the 1940s … most people didn't know it existed back then." The woman seemed to know what he was talking about and the discussion of Molasses Reef went back and forth. The reef was so named because long ago a ship laden with barrels of molasses had sunk on that spot. "It covers a sizable area, maybe 5,000 square meters," said the woman. "Yes," said the man. "I still dream about it." Then, they were silent for a long time. Still, no one glanced in my direction. The man leaned forward on his cane, deep in thought, and the woman sat back and closed her eyes.

The crash of the surf seemed quieter just then, or maybe they resumed speaking with more volume. The man's eyes then opened while the woman remained in her reverie. He said, "If you can imagine the place of your dreams, that was Molasses Reef. A truly enchanted, magical place—the majestic silence, the riot of color and the movement of all that lived there."

"I've seen some wondrous things myself," added the woman. "The mouth of the Amazon, the Taj Mahal, the leaves turning in Vermont, the Lake District in England, the first steps of my grand-daughter, Lake Louise, the lights of Manhattan …"

The man interjected, "Better than all of those is Molasses Reef." The woman nodded and drifted off again in her daydream. I was further lulled by the silence and my own mind drifted to the reef and back again. I may have actually fallen asleep, as I was startled when the man's words again penetrated my consciousness. "In 1984 a freighter bound for Portugal sank right on top of the reef. It was a catastrophe. What had taken thousands of years of natural construction was suddenly and irreparably damaged. Or so it seemed, until the Reef Doctor came along." "Yes, the Reef Doctor,

I read about him," responded the woman. (*Privately, faster transit time.*)

"The Reef Doctor, I remember his exact words when he surveyed the damage. He said, 'Much of this reef is pulverized, but we have something that can give nature a jump start *so it can heal itself.*' He and his team of marine biologists proceeded to construct several dozen reef replacement structures with hidey holes for fish, limestone galleries. In no time coral attached themselves to these galleries, and after one year they saw shrimp, sea grasses, sponges, and even new fish species. The limestone galleries were a resounding success, and now the reef is *gradually healing itself*, with a little help from the Reef Doctor."

"That's a very nice story," said the woman. The man looked tired and he sat back, closed his eyes, and returned to a state of deep reflection. The woman rose and stretched and looked briefly in my direction. (Davis, 2003; Gafner, 2004)

Therapist: And now, Maggie, I'm going to mention two anecdotes, not for conscious consumption, but strictly for the back part of your mind. The first one is this:

IBS-specific anecdotes

The Burglary
One night I went to a friend's house and discovered the police there, as a burglary had occurred. The police were dusting for fingerprints and one of them told me, "We'll take your prints, just for *elimination* purposes." I said, "No, I have to go now, but before I could *exit*, they stopped me. "For *elimination* purposes only," said the police woman firmly. "You'll be helping us, but you'll also be helping yourself." As I drove home I thought, "Well, I *better* be *eliminated* as a suspect."

Suggestions

Therapist: And the second one is this, called the Great Vowel Shift.

The Great Vowel Shift

Historians of language development have noted that the Great Vowel Shift happened *roughage/ roughly* around the time of Chaucer. *Exit* discussions with textbook editors may leave us with various impressions.

Misspeak
Suggestion

Interestingly, Maggie's eyes remained open during the stories and anecdotes; however, her gaze was fixed on a spot on the wall. She appeared very relaxed, having displayed an overall response similar to last time, though perhaps deeper. The first thing I did was check for amnesia.

Therapist: What do you remember from what I was talking about?

Maggie: Not much, someone walking on a beach.

Therapist: Good, amnesia, we like that! It's not necessary to read too much into metaphors.

Maggie: You may have said that last time, something about a coffee pot.

Therapist: Percolation. Let it percolate in the back part of your mind.

Maggie: I guess I'll be listening to this beach story again.

Therapist: Twice a week, please, we'll talk about that.

Notes for practice

Therapy appeared to be progressing well. So far she had required a minimum of restraint. I was glad she was seeing her GI doctor for her IBS. For specific progress, I can check her notes from that clinic in the computer; however, for my purposes, a subjective 1–10 scale is sufficient. I watched her today as interspersal suggestions were delivered, along with misspeak in the anecdotes. She stirred slightly during those, which could have meant that these departures drew conscious attention to the suggestions.

Charles' second session

I leafed through Charles' long, handwritten statement—a confession, really—on yellow legal paper, then sat back and read it carefully. Charles' current fantasy about his woman client, Belle, had been preceded by several affairs with women—none clients—and all married, dating back 20 years, though there had been no affairs in the last five years. His children from his first marriage had disowned him. The pages contained admissions of pornography, compulsive masturbation, gambling, and equal measures of remorse and anguished guilt. His current wife, Bernadette, had immersed herself in her bead and jewelry business and "we have some conflict, not a lot of communication," said his account. I handed the papers back to Charles.

Therapist: It's hard for me to believe that Belle is only a fantasy.

Charles: Well, you'll just have to believe me.

My mind was swimming and I thought, "Am I obligated to report these egregious breaches of ethics, however historical?" This was followed by the thought, "Reporting? He hasn't said he had affairs with clients. Get a hold of yourself here!" I regarded Charles, a miserable looking ball of suffering, and tried to put myself in his shoes.

Charles: Well?! What else do you think about what I spent hours writing?

Therapist: Well, if it were me, I'd transfer Belle to another therapist—unless you think you can control your fantasies. It seems like you might not be too far from physically crossing the line with Belle. What do you think?

Charles: Fine, whatever.

Therapist: I know you know this, but you need to do this tactfully, keep the client's best interests in mind. Maybe to do it right you need to contact a lawyer, I don't know.

Charles: Don't worry about it, I'll take care of it.

I was feeling very frustrated with this discussion. I wanted to cease my advice-giving or scolding and get back to therapy here. It seemed like everything about this case so far was very provocative. Charles' face suddenly turned as red as a beet and his breathing became rapid. I thought, "Don't have a stroke on me here!" I observed him for several seconds. No stroke, he was just losing it emotionally.

Therapist: Damn it, Charles, get a hold of yourself. You've taken some important steps here and I'm confident you'll feel better in time. Take some deep breaths now and settle yourself down, man!

He sat back in the recliner, his breathing slowed, and soon normal color returned to his face. He closed his eyes for several seconds and then opened them again. Strangely, he started to hum a song to himself. I watched and waited. In no time he had resumed his standard composure. I observed something in him that puzzled me. Then he did it again. He circled his eyes as if searching for a target, and after a few seconds this circling heralded a twinkling delight. The delight was followed by a pursing of his lips and immediately a defensive, cynical comment followed. His first such comment had been, "I wonder if you really know what you're doing here," and after the second pursing of lips he said, "Is that what they taught you in social work school?"

He had exhibited some sarcasm last time, but now he had cranked it up a notch. If he was hurling insults in the second session, what could I expect down the line? I felt defensiveness from him, but also an aggression. I'd had many clients who were defensive and hostile, but never one who made me feel so uncomfortable. I regarded his eyes and thought of a bird of prey. I wondered how he acted around his clients, or his wife. I wondered what kind of clinician he was, as no warmth at all emanated from him; however, he had a good name in Tucson and was recognized as a competent therapist. There was a long waiting list to get in to see him and he accepted no insurance, just private pay. His eyes had now been closed for a minute or more, he suddenly opened them, sat up erect, and I was taken aback by what followed.

Charles: Hey, how about a story, you know, I tell YOU a story? Not a juvenile one like The Three Lessons.

I looked at him. If his aim was to knock me off balance, he had certainly succeeded. He wanted to tell ME a story? Did I hear that right?

Therapist: Well, sure, go for it.

I sat back in my chair, and appearing in what looked like a reverie, he began.

The Garden, a story by Charles

Charles: It's called The Garden, you may have heard of it. In a small Mexican village lived Eufrasia, a vigorous young woman, and the joy of her life was her garden. She loved spending every spare minute there amidst the mesquite and desert willow trees, and the wonderful flowers and bubbling fountains.

The garden attracted wildlife from the countryside, rabbits, lizards, snakes, javelinas, and even the occasional bobcat. But what mostly frequented her garden were birds of all color and song. She saw red-breasted cardinals, wrens, finches, dusky doves, sleek roadrunners, and many Gambel's quail, bobbing and clucking with their hatchlings. They enjoyed the warm breezes playing through the leaves and the steady rain of blossoms, and, of course, they liked the seed she fed them.

I had now closed my eyes, enjoying the respite. I had not heard this story for some time, having used it myself. It was originally written by a psychology intern, Richard Bissett, in the early 1990s, and I later adapted it and it was one of many stories distributed as a handout over the years at the V.A. and elsewhere, and eventually included in one of my books (Gafner, 2004) after therapy with Charles concluded. This was not the first time a client had told me a story during a session, but definitely the first under such circumstances. In family therapy with children, I have employed Richard Gardner's mutual storytelling technique (Gardner, 1971). My mind was now thinking ahead. Perhaps down the road other story techniques could work with Charles, especially a story without an ending, where the client's unconscious generates the ending. My contemplative state was broken as Charles resumed speaking.

Charles: Eufrasia reveled in her visitors. She planted the most succulent plants for them, and she spread seed in the path three times a day to go with the sugar water for the hummingbirds and cumquat chunks and pomegranates for the cactus wrens. Her garden was the paragon of perfect harmony. As she sat in her yard the visitors were oblivious to their benefactor, how tranquil and invigorating it was! Every ripple of water in the fountains seemed to course through her; indeed, during these timeless moments she was part of the fountain, or was she one of the birds? Oh, it didn't matter. Nothing mattered, as time passed and present and future did not exist.

While spreading seed early one morning she was distracted by something. It was a pigeon, a common city pigeon, dull, dirty, gray and horribly pedestrian. "A rodent with wings fouling my garden," she thought, and she immediately rose to her feet and tried to shoo it away. But the pigeon only flew a few feet and then returned. Who could blame it for being lured to this wonderful garden? "I'm surprised it never showed up before," she thought.

Day after day she awoke to find the pigeon defiling her garden. Bathing noisily in the marble bowl intended for finches, pecking at the other birds and soiling the jasmine. All this was very discouraging to Eufrasia. Soon, her garden ceased to provide the joy she had known for so long. Why set out feed if it will be eaten by that rotten pigeon? She spent less time in her garden, staying inside, and sighing loudly. "I am 'sighing' my life away!" she screamed in desperation one day.

One morning she awoke to a strange premonition. Something was different. Perhaps it was the sound of the garden. She closed her eyes and listened. She heard music, the music of her garden, the fountain bubbling, the cooing of the doves. She looked around. No pigeon! "Oh, I mustn't get my hopes up, it could return," she mused. Then, the weeks passed, as once again she immersed herself in her garden. But something deep inside was occurring, something outside of her awareness, and then one night in a dream it surfaced, painful and palpable. She *missed* the pigeon.

She didn't just miss it, she longed for it. Once again she caught herself sighing. She would bake some sweet nut cakes and spread them on the path, maybe then it would return. But it did not. She moved into the garden, slept there at night, and washed in the fountain. "Why am I doing all this?" she thought. The weeks passed and still no pigeon. But just as quickly as it had disappeared, there it was again! It wasn't dull gray, but luminescent and beautiful. As the bird preened its feathers she felt a sense of peace, an inner contentment. She returned to her bed at night. Maybe it would still be there tomorrow. She fell into a deep sleep and drifted and dreamed.

I opened my eyes. Charles' eyes were closed. I thought how impressed I was that he could recite the story from memory, whereas I had to read it.

Therapist: Now, I'm not supposed to ask you the meaning of the story, right?

Charles: As if you don't know. The original author wrote this for chronic pain.

I tried to reorient myself to the basics.

Therapist: Charles, you're not suicidal, are you?

Charles: Of course not.

Therapist: And last time I mentioned the importance of using your anchor and a deep breath when you're feeling anxious, right?

Charles: Is this the mental health clinic or the Alzheimer's clinic? Your other clients may need reminders, but I don't.

Therapist: You may be more like my other clients than you realize.

Charles: I know I'm not. No need to insult me.

Therapist: Wash out my mouth with soap, then. I'll see you next time.

Charles: The pleasure was all yours.

Notes for practice

This client had turned out to be more wily than I could have imagined. I needed to be vigilant about clinical boundaries, stay in control, and stick to my treatment plan. I found it most intriguing how Charles had spontaneously recovered from acute distress only to tell *me* a story that had many interpretations. I was glad that this appointment was my last of the day. Ringing in my head was the old maxim, "The map is not the territory."

I was also just plain fatigued, not accustomed to work, as I had been home for six weeks recovering from prostate cancer surgery. Little did I know at that time that two years later I would need to undergo 40 sessions of external beam radiation when the cancer came back. At this writing, 10 years out from seeing Maggie and Charles, I have a clean bill of health. Still, I think back on then and realize how those two cases were more consuming than 20 other clients.

CHAPTER FOUR

Ego-strengthening

Albert Bandura

Albert Bandura (1997), regarded in the U.S. as the father of self-efficacy, famously noted that psychotherapists may bestow the greatest benefit, *not* by giving them specific remedies for their problems, but by helping clients build self-efficacy. (In this book, I use self-efficacy, self-esteem and ego-strength interchangeably.) Bandura's idea of building self-efficacy—defined as the belief that one's behavior will lead to successful outcomes—included such things as assertiveness training, anger management training, social skills training, role play and other rehearsal, aimed at building people's self-confidence and competence, especially in interpersonal situations. By addressing what he termed "socio-cognitive skills," he included what we now recognize as cognitive-behavioral therapy (CBT).

Some contemporary clinicians who employ CBT pay little attention to things like role play or assertiveness training, believing that if they help anxious or depressed clients modify their negative beliefs and automatic thoughts, clients will in turn view themselves more positively, shed anxiety and depression, and new-found functional behavior will follow. Were it only so simple! Of course, some people may respond readily to any mode of therapy, or to CBT alone. These folks are likely to be motivated, employed, educated and with sufficient income, and not personality disordered. But clients who go to public clinics are usually a different story. Burdened by years of chronic pain, PTSD, depression, schizophrenia and other problems, these people often have trouble getting to first base in any therapeutic regimen. They could certainly benefit from the socio-cognitive. However, let's consider something else that can influence both staying in therapy and making changes down the road: ego-strengthening.

Direction versus indirection within hypnosis

In Hartland's (1971) seminal article on hypnotic ego-strengthening, he offers therapists various ways in which they can help clients overcome long-term problems. For the smoker, he commands, "You can do it." For the obese, "You *can* lose weight." In trance, the client is given repeated authoritarian, highly directive suggestions. Nothing indirect or permissive, just unadorned straight suggestion, plain and simple.

For the better part of the last century, and continuing into the present, this is the way hypnotic suggestion has been delivered by many therapists, and is presumably what clients want and expect from hypnosis. In Jay Haley's *Uncommon Therapy* (Haley, 1973), he introduced Milton Erickson's work to the world, which heralded a fork in the road, and since then many practitioners of hypnosis have come to favor indirection over a highly directive approach. To this day, some continue the traditional ways, especially those who rely on hypnotizability tests, or are influenced by popular training texts from decades ago. One of those was Kroger's (1963) *Clinical and Experimental Hypnosis in Medicine, Dentistry and Psychology*. In a section on treating alcoholics with hypnosis, he recommends saying to the client in trance:

> *"Each and every time you hold a drink in your hand, you will think of rotten eggs—the horrible, violent, disgusting smell of rotten eggs."*
> *(p. 312)*

Go ahead and try that on your next substance-abusing client right after breakfast!

Those were simpler times, and I'm old enough to remember them. The term polysubstance abuse had not been invented, nor had dual diagnosis. Substance abusers were either an alcoholic or a heroin addict. There were no meth labs and you couldn't become addicted to cocaine (so it was believed). Those were authoritarian times in general, when people saw things in black and white, good and bad.

70

There was no internet or global economy, no threat from terrorists. The Cold War was on, East versus West. Psychodynamic therapy was beginning to give way to behaviorism. People's problems were deficits to be eliminated. Clients in trance were told—in no uncertain terms—to give up their symptoms.

Many tools in the toolbox

Now, I'm not denigrating directive techniques in psychotherapy in general, or in hypnosis in particular. I use directive inductions. There is no finer or quicker directive induction than the eye-roll: "I have my hand here above your head, now follow my hand with your eyes as I move the hand back over your head, and as those eyes roll back they can gently close and you can drop into a nice, peaceful state of relaxation," elegant in its simplicity. When emergency medical personnel are rescuing someone with a broken leg on a mountain slope and they need a quick trance while they stabilize the patient, they don't have time for a conversational induction. They use the eye-roll. Same with busy doctors in a clinic. I use directive inductions, like the eye-roll, hand levitation or arm catalepsy (Gafner & Benson, 2000), especially with clients who desire that approach. I strongly advocate that therapists know both kinds and be familiar with one or two inductions in each category.

"I need to know I 'went under'"

Some clients say, "I have to *know* that I went under," and for them, if they experience their hand lifting into the air of its own accord, that's the proof. One of the best ones "to prove you went under" is the ice-bath induction (Gafner & Benson, 2000), which we use in training but also occasionally with those clients who require "proof." We use a metal bowl full of ice and water. They immerse a hand and leave it in as long as they can tolerate it, while someone keeps track of the time. Then, following induction and suggestions for analgesia, the person's hand is placed again in the bowl and time is noted. Almost always the duration tolerated the second time is double or more than the first immersion. In training, we did this one time with a staff person, Donna, a consummate clinician, but also anxious and with a need to "do it right" and not embarrass herself in the process. She also considered herself "hard to hypnotize." The first immersion lasted 45 seconds, and when the second one had reached *six minutes* with no indication of stopping, *I* was the one who pulled out her hand because *my* hands were so cold from holding the bowl and balancing it next to her. Now, that was one strong convincer for Donna.

These days, more and more clients appreciate a gentle, permissive conversational or story induction (see Chapter 14) whose operative word is *may* rather than *will*, for example, instead of "you *will* drop into deep trance," "You *may* soon begin to notice a *tingling or numbness* in the extremities, perhaps a *coolness or warmth*, *heaviness or lightness, or some other* interesting sensation, and *when* you recognize these initial markers of trance, you can start to drift off into a nice, comfortable state of relaxation ..." Notice that I didn't say "*if* you recognize." but *when,* the implication being that trance will occur. Notice also that a menu of responses was offered, with the expectation that one would be forthcoming.

Many people, myself included, combine directive and indirect techniques, for example, an arm catalepsy induction with a story, or a permissive induction and a story in which one character says to another, "You *will* give up those cigarettes." There are really innumerable ways to mix and match all the techniques mentioned in this book. See what works for you and follow one iron-clad rule: Let the client's response be your guide. Employing these techniques within standard psychotherapy is discussed later in this chapter.

Influence of Erickson

The first writer to actively address building up clients was Milton Erickson. Both a psychologist and a psychiatrist, he began articulating his approach in the 1930s when Freudian approaches ruled the day. Although Erickson didn't use terms like self-efficacy or ego-strengthening, he was dedicated to enhancing clients' competence and generalizing it to all interpersonal situations. He not only regarded the social context of clients' problems; he often included family members in the session, and as such may have been the first family therapist.

He was the first to regard the unconscious as a resource to be utilized in therapy, while influential clinicians of the day viewed the unconscious as a cauldron of negative impulses to be vanquished. Erickson employed formal hypnosis only 20% of the time, but the other 80% was filled with hypnotic techniques (Beahrs, 1971). Michael Yapko, a California psychologist whose body of work argues most persuasively for employing hypnotic techniques in the treatment of depression as well as other disorders, remarked at a workshop, "If you ask me how often I use hypnosis I'll say some of the time; but if you ask me how often I work hypnotically, I'll tell you *100% of the time*" (personal communication, 2001).

Ego-strengthening within hypnosis

Like Yapko, Cory Hammond, a psychologist from Salt Lake City, Utah was heavily influenced by the work of Erickson. Hammond (1990) likened many clients' beginning therapy to debilitated medical patients in need of major surgery. First, they need rest and good nutrition to prepare them for the rigors of the operation. In other words, before jumping into therapy, build the person up with ego-strengthening suggestions. For years, major writers have advocated ego-strengthening within formal hypnosis. Stanton's (1997) research showed that ego-enhancing suggestions helped clients gain control over their lives, and Lavertue and colleagues (2002), in a study involving 224 subjects demonstrated that subjects in the relaxation and ego-strengthening treatment conditions improved in self-efficacy while lowering their depression scores. Ron Pekala (Pekala, et al., 2004), in his study of veteran alcohol and drug abusers, employed moderately directive suggestions for relaxation, self-confidence and habit mastery in the audiotape subjects listened to as part of the study. Sonja Benson and I (Gafner & Benson, 2001) reported on metaphorical ego-strengthening with victims of torture in a refugee clinic.

In the mental health clinic at the V.A. in Tucson, Arizona, my department was routinely referred clients for hypnosis. A major source of referrals was the psychotic disorders clinic, as the director of the clinic, Dr. Janine Allison, advocated strongly for her clients and was a supporter of hypnosis. The clients were stable psychiatrically but needed assistance with the angst and anxiety that accompanies schizophrenia and related diagnoses. In the first session, I would tell the client, "We're going to spend two or three times doing some ego-strengthening. Waking up every morning to the world of schizophrenia, you could probably use some 'mental building up,' don't you agree?" To a person, they agreed. The same holds true for clients with chronic pain, PTSD, depression and other disorders. They were referred for insomnia and anxiety management and an essential part of the treatment was ego-strengthening. These clients' main treatment was conducted in the department from which they were referred, and the hypnotherapy was adjunctive.

I remember one veteran, a practicing attorney, who, in the initial interview, stated, "I've had to suffer through legions of earnest helpers trying to change me." He had been refractory to several SSRIs, older antidepressants, and psychotherapy. People like that were pleasantly surprised to hear, "We're just going to do ego-strengthening for now. All you need to do is sit back and listen to some stories and you can let your unconscious mind do what it wishes with the material." The attorney's depression was kept at bay by several sessions of ego-strengthening alone and when I saw him three years later he was still listening to his CD and feeling well.

Most referrals for hypnosis were seen for 4–5 sessions, each consisting of the induction of trance followed by a story. An anchor, or associational cue, typically making a circle with their thumb and index finger, was installed as a relaxation reminder away from the office. The last session they were given an audiotape (later a CD) for continued practice at home. To be sure, this 4–5 session format was flexible and could contain different modes of induction or various remediative techniques, such as age progression or abreaction techniques, or a host of other techniques for unconscious exploration or other objectives. In this book, ego-strengthening is a major technique, especially with Maggie.

Improvement with ego-strengthening alone

We discovered that many times clients—especially those whose presenting problem was an anxiety disorder—improved with ego-strengthening alone. Was it because of the hypnosis directed at relaxation in the mind and body, or was it because of something deeper? In a relaxed and receptive state, defenses are also relaxed and all but the most "left-brain" analytical people seem to self-reference the meta-message in the story, incorporating it in their own way, and adapting it to their own unique situation. If the client's management of anxiety improves, that's one thing; but if there is also improvement in self-efficacy (on various measures), we surmise it is due to the ego-strengthening. That would be a scintillating study, randomizing subjects to wait-list, induction and deepening, and induction/deepening plus ego-strengthening. Lacking that study, years of experience by many of us at the Tucson V.A. has convinced us of the benefits of ego-strengthening, especially metaphorical ego-strengthening, or story. (For a discussion of our GI study involving hypnotic ego-strengthening for noncardiac chest pain of esophageal origin, please see Chapter 3).

But didn't Mussolini make the trains run on time?

Sometimes I'm asked, "Why practice metaphorical ego-strengthening when much of the therapy world accomplishes this with direct suggestions?" First, as I mentioned earlier, I *do* indeed employ directive techniques though for years I've leaned heavily toward indirection. All of my professional life I worked in public clinics and hospitals, places inhabited, I believe, by large numbers of the reactant. Certainly, men and women who put their lives on the line serving their country deserve our respect, gratitude, and munificent benefits. However, I've always wondered if high reactance and personality disorder are more prevalent in veterans who seek mental health services compared to the general population. I have no data to support this, only years of personal observation. Like the "green poultice" (being paid for evincing psychopathology), V.A. staff from Washington on down avoid speaking publicly on these issues, as they are controversial. Each clinical encounter there is the "elephant in the room," as both veteran and clinician know that V.A. benefits may depend on what is written in the progress note. Nevertheless, this is the culture in which I developed my ideas, so maybe indirection was adaptive behavior. However, feedback from many quarters internationally, including wealthy private practices, has shown me that most clients appreciate the respect and permissiveness inherent in a non-authoritarian approach in general.

Another session with Dr. Tracten

I am also convinced of the benefit of *not* discussing the story during the debriefing portion at the end of the session, but instead discussing it when they return next time. So, let's say client George has resumed therapy with the redoubtable Dr. Tracten. In the second session or so George listens to The Greenhouse story about a little seedling that survives adversity and goes on to endure and prevail and eventually prosper as a strong, sturdy tree. George is re-alerted at the end, he opens his eyes and remarks, "I know what that story meant!" but the omniscient Dr. Tracten puts up his well manicured hand and says, "No, not now, we'll talk about it next time after it percolates in the back part of your mind for a week. I know you want to talk about it—and we *will* discuss it—but I have my reasons for doing it next time." George may leave a bit frustrated but he is soon convinced of the percolation process, not because of Dr. Tracten's supreme confidence, but because he sees that it actually works.

A little restraint

Now, by holding off on discussion, the good doctor is not restraining George in the therapeutic sense; instead, he is taking advantage of the intervening week so that unconscious processing can occur without conscious interference. An example of restraint would be as follows. Let's say that the intractable George returns a year later for individual therapy and Dr. Tracten has observed firm reactance over time. One week the client returns feeling markedly improved. Dr. Tracten might restrain him with something like, "George, I'm pleased you're starting to feel better, but some caution is in order here. Borderline personality is a chronic disorder and you should *go slow*, test changes gingerly, and be *cautious* about embracing new-found gains." By therapeutically restraining him, any gains may more likely be maintained. Now, this might go against the grain of some of you, as our natural inclination is to give the anguished George a pat on the back and rejoice with him when he's feeling better. But don't just take this writer's word for it. In your practice, try *not* restraining and try *not* waiting to discuss the story, and see how it goes. You need to be comfortable with what works for *you*.

So, George happens to sustain his gains, and Dr. Tracten ventures forth with The Balloons story, which embeds the suggestion of *letting go*. George returns in a week and the first thing Dr. Tracten asks about is the story. George's interpretation is that he should let go of cutting on his arm and rip paper instead. Tracten knows George has never done anything more serious than cutting and he asks, "Wonderful, George, but isn't that a waste of paper?" The two talk about this interpretation for a few minutes before moving on to other things. Next week, before George's appointment, the receptionist complains that George's shredding of magazines in the waiting room is upsetting other clients. "So, you'd rather I lacerate my arm instead?" George asks. His suspicion is confirmed: Those equivocal mental health imbeciles are entirely to blame for his problems!

Different people, different conclusions

It has always amazed me how 10 people can get 10 different meanings from the same story, and whatever it is doesn't matter. The important thing is that you're reaching them at the deepest level, where change presumably happens, and that this whole process is now the currency of discussion between you and the client. Like concrete metaphors, stories are remembered by clients. Many times I've had people remark years later, things like, *"I still think about that old lady in the woods.*" (Referring to The Three Lessons story) I remember telling a stock ego-strengthening story at the end of a session to a borderline woman (not George's sister) who was very downtrodden and depressed from years of failure in everything. At the conclusion of the story she tearfully responded, "That's the first time in years that my heart has been touched, thank you so much!" Of course, I've also had a few untoward comments, such as, "That was a stupid story," or, "Do you enjoy amusing yourself with these vapid stories?" However, I've developed a fairly thick skin from occasional comments like that, or from some people in marital therapy who shake their fist at me before running out and slamming the door. And let's remember, many times the most seemingly unreceptive client may be reached by your techniques. Like a gardener, we sow many seeds. Some sprout and some get eaten by the birds.

Ego-strengthening outside of hypnosis

Group anger management

Many years back we began to add an ego-strengthening story at the end of a session of conventional talk therapy. We had learned the value of this from our group anger management classes, where we routinely told a short story at the end of each class. Some of the stories were ego-strengthening but the main intent was the mindfulness principle embedded in the story. You can imagine a place like the mental health clinic of a V.A. in the U.S., where anger management is a veritable growth industry. I had two, hour-long groups of eight sessions going year around for two decades, and the repeat attendees I could count on one hand. The participants were mostly men, some were elderly, veterans from WW II; some were from the recent wars, but the average person was from the Vietnam era, men in their 50s and 60s, many with chronic PTSD, and several real fire breathers who were not high functioning. Many attended at the behest of their wives, and some were mandated by the court for such things as road rage.

They were generally receptive to the stories and especially the mindfulness principles such as acceptance, being nonjudgmental, seeing things differently, and letting go. Just like in individual and family therapy, clients became accustomed to the story as a routine part of the session. We gave them the rationale for not discussing the story right at the start and by the second session they caught on to our purpose and were eager to discuss the story at the start of the following session. We even did some research on this (Scott & Gafner, 2007) and compared groups with story and without story (straight didactic information about alternatives to acting out, using the time-out, etc.). The results of the study were that at the conclusion of the group sessions, the subjects in the story group performed better on an anger/aggression measure, but at six months and a year both groups scored the same. There is a complete discussion of the group anger management elsewhere (Gafner & Benson, 2003). The main point is that we learned that the story technique is very adaptable to individual and family therapy as well as group therapy. (Employing a veteran as a confederate in the group is discussed in Chapter 13.)

Conveying suggestions

"We only have ten minutes left, make sure you get to the story," I was informed more than once in a session. "Thanks, you know, I forgot all about it," I answered. I would usually tell a story at the end of a session, while anecdotes are amenable to any time in the session, e.g. "that reminds me of a guy named Peter who I saw a few years back. He thought he was original in calling his depression *"my black dog."* I didn't tell him that Churchill said it earlier. Peter tried various things to "just make my black dog run away for good," was the way he put it, but I convinced him to leave that dog in the bedroom for a few minutes a day, aiming for a 10 percent reduction in sadness for starters. So, I can deliver metaphorically, via anecdote, any main therapeutic thrust, like pattern interruption or ego-strengthening. In fact, those suggestions, along with story, both conveyed beneath the radar, may be the most therapeutic portion of any session, with the listening, empathy, didactics and everything else playing a supporting role.

Major ego-strengthening techniques

Story, anecdote and "short-burst"

I have various stock stories that I either read or recite from memory. One of my favorites is the aforementioned The Greenhouse (Gafner & Benson, 2003, 2000), which I adapted from Lee Wallas' (1985) story, The Seedling, which she wrote for use with survivors of childhood sexual abuse. The metaphor in some stories is lost on people of other cultures and languages. Not so with this one, as I've used it in Spanish and with an interpreter for other languages. With this and other stories, if the listener is male we can have the protagonist be a boy. Does the listener more readily self-reference and incorporate the metaphor if the sex is matched? I don't know, but matching is commonly done. If reactance is high, I usually *don't* match, which is consistent with the tenet of the higher the reactance, the more indirection is indicated. For a very reactant individual, if the story deals with a young boy in London, for example, I'll change the protagonist to an elderly woman in New Delhi. Many of my ego-enhancing stories deal with subjects other than people, like lighthouses, animals, roads and plants. Are people more likely to self-reference the embedded suggestions if the subject is other than people? Possibly so. Yet one more thing for which there is no research support.

The Greenhouse

Once upon a time, there was this magnificent greenhouse. A boy (or girl) walked by it every day on his way to school. He always wondered what it might be like to have a job inside that marvelous greenhouse. School would soon be out for the summer, and one day the boy stopped at the greenhouse and asked if he could have a job there. The boy sat on a sack of peat moss as he waited for the boss to interview him. Soon, though it seemed like a very long time, the boss arrived. She was a large woman with very strong arms. "You can have the job," she said, but only if you work very hard and do a good job every day, all summer long. You must pay close attention and not let your mind drift off in here," she instructed.

The boy was delighted to get the job. When he reported to work the first day it was immediately evident what the boss had meant, as there was a lot *inside* the greenhouse to notice and appreciate besides the job. The greenhouse was an immense structure, its windows shining in the sun on the outside, and once *inside*, enveloped in a shaft of sunlight, he gazed up at the rays of sun slanting through the thousands of panes of glass. Inside there it was warm and humid, and you could find all varieties of plants, hanging from up above, down below on shelves, and down farther yet on the floor, every variety of plant, in various sizes of pots. Stepping from one aisle to another his nose was pleasantly assaulted by various smells, some familiar, but many that were unrecognizable odors that blended together into one extraordinary scent. It was something that arrested his attention in a most curious and pleasing way. Inside, there he was in a wondrous reverie which seemed to last forever, as time simply stood still and he forgot about the outside world.

Unbeknownst to the boy, some months earlier a little seedling had toppled off the back of a shelf, where it lay in the dark, with its broken pot and dry brown stem, seemingly deceased, forlorn and forgotten. One day while sweeping the floor the boy discovered the seedling. He examined it closely and wondered if any life existed down deep in the gnarled, dry root ball. He asked the owner if he could keep it, but she said, "No, throw it out, don't waste your time with that," but he persisted, got to keep it, and took it back to his work area. He put it in new soil in a larger pot and tended it for a week or two while he saw that it received sufficient water, nutrients and sunlight. And sure enough, soon the boy observed new green growth on top, while down below, out of sight, the root ball began to grow and expand. It continued to grow and grow and the boy contemplated how that little seedling had survived, all because of *its strong root system*.

Years later, the boy was an adult and occasionally he pondered the little seedling, how it was by now a strong, sturdy tree in somebody's yard. But mostly he thought about how that little plant had survived, endured, prevailed, and eventually prospered, all because of its *strong root system*.

Anecdotes

I keep a list of these handy for use any time in the session. For a client who especially needs ego-strengthening, I will reserve at least 15 minutes of a session for the client to listen to some anecdotes. As with stories, clients become accustomed to this and look forward to it. So, typically, I'll stop at some point in a session of talk therapy—near the end of a session is often most convenient—and say, "Okay, now for the mental building up part, so just sit back, you can close your eyes or keep them open, as I read to you the following anecdotes." I pause for several seconds after each one. Discuss them at the end? Sometimes I do. Here are some (Gafner, 2004):

245 Feet High
In 1825, David Douglas began to explore the forest south of Fort Vancouver. Local Indians noticed this man wandering through the woods, collecting plant specimens and certain seeds. Douglas was determined to find the mysterious pines with huge cones of Indian legend. He had traversed the unexplored territory for weeks when he came upon an immense sugar pine that was 18 feet thick and some 245 feet high.

Lodgepole Pine
Lodgepole pine grows on a thin layer of soil and develops a rather shallow root system. The tree's seeds are so small that it takes about 100,000 to make a pound of seeds. Often the seeds are enveloped by the branches and become completely encased in wood. In one study, the naturalist William Inskeep found seed from a 150-year-old cone imbedded in the tree. Inskeep discovered that seeds from this cone were still viable.

Strong cactus
The haageocereus tenuis cactus survives in extreme conditions in northern Peru. It grows on its side, branches splayed forlornly, its base decaying in the loose sand. The sides of the stems produce roots

that store water, which is rarely available. It may experience moisture when a fog rolls off the ocean, or when it rains only every two years.

Matchstick girl

Now a doctor with a psychiatry practice of her own, Diana feels an instant bond with her clients. She knows because she suffered immensely, and she really *knows*.

Diana said, "I used to think I had evil in my family, but now I see it for what it really was, a sickness that ran deep and affected every one of us." She died her first painful death at age four when her innocence was stolen, and this continued for many years. Her mother and sister took their own lives. She saw no sunshine. "I was the little matchstick girl left out in the cold," said Diana.

She had an imaginary friend who visited her every birthday and would ask, "Are you strong?" And Diana would answer, "*Just enough.*" *Love this* She sought help from a trusted counselor who helped her come out of the cold. At the end of the hour she asked Diana, "Are you strong?" "*Just enough*," she answered. Nowadays, Diana introduces herself to a new client. Her big smile illuminates, warms, and embraces. She will never be completely whole, but she is happy and inside her head she still hears the question from her imaginary friend, and she breathes deeply and answers, "*Just enough.*"

Short-burst ego-strengthening

Sonja Benson, my co-author and co-workshop leader on several projects, employs this technique even more than I, and with remarkable success. The technique is attributed to Brent Geary, of the Erickson Foundation in Phoenix, Arizona (personal communication, 1999). Operationally, it is essentially an interspersed suggestion. However, it differs from the traditional interspersal in that it is actually part of a confusion technique, as a non sequitur, or out-of-context nonsense statement, precedes the suggestion: *Tech*

Penelope, you may let your experience deepen as
I count backward now from 10 to one. 10, 9, *The*   **Non sequitur**
descent of an opportune mist and *you can change*,   **Suggestion**
Penelope ... 8, 7,

The non sequitur creates confusion from which the client naturally wishes to escape, and the therapist provides a way out, and in the desired direction. We typically use it within an induction or deepening during hypnosis, or during a story in talk therapy. We always tell the client ahead of time something like, "Today you may hear occasional words that don't make sense consciously. It's all part of helping you with your problem." As Peggy Papp (1983) said, "A good doctor does not prescribe bad medicine." You never want clients to think you're amusing yourself at their expense. Believe me, early on I had that happen and unforgivable damage was done.

We normally strive to make our words count; however, with a non sequitur you *don't* want to be didactic. Keep it neutral and purposeless, as it is simply window dressing to set up the suggestion. These are good ones:

They sold trinkets beside the road, or,
The shopping carts always seem to stick together,
or
There was a silence between the leaves.

Not: The Papists stormed the palace.
Never: Barking dogs may bite.
But: Why do dogs bark?

A question rivets attention. A shorter question leaves much more to the imagination, thus heightening confusion. No power words, nothing about religion or politics, nothing controversial. The non sequitur is the vehicle, the suggestion is the destination. After a long day my mind is mush and maybe I'll have to glance around the office for a non sequitur, like

The thickness of the carpet, or once there was a lamp shade

and then I have stock suggestions, no need to reinvent the wheel.

Your unconscious mind can help you now, or
You can overcome this problem, or
You can let go, or
You can do it.

Mixing techniques in a session?

We use short-burst once or twice a session. Don't be too ambitious with these techniques. Use story, anecdote and interspersal in the same session? Let's say old George has a chronic, low-grade illness, and he's tried various remedies with no improvement. The doctor says, "Try these three new medications, I bet they'll help." But George says, "Thanks, but I'll try *one at a time* so I can tell which one worked." If the doctor convinces him that they all work together and must be taken accordingly, then it's a different story.

I won't try and convince you that an ego-enhancing anecdote mixed with short-burst in the same session is the best remedy. If you do that for two sessions and you can show improvement before and after with an objective measure or new behavior, then I'm convinced that that combination was right *for that client*. For years, I always started with story, or metaphorical ego-strengthening. These days, I use story and anecdote about half and half, often reserving short-burst for the more reactant.

Don't forget Albert Bandura

Don't neglect straightforward, consciously directed interventions. I've told plenty of people that they need to drop therapy and get a life instead. If the person agrees to join a gym or attend a social club or a CBT or assertiveness training group, great! That's what you want, behavior change—especially socially—outside the office. All this other stuff is there if you need a bridge to that end. Often when

I did hypnotic ego-strengthening with people it was as adjunct, as the people were also being seen in the pain or psychotic disorders clinic, for example, or, when I finished with them, they would return to individual or group therapy.

Use your intuition, that's why you have it on call. Whether you employ ego-strengthening de rigeur to build a foundation, or as a stand-alone technique, I'm betting that you'll love the results.

CHAPTER FIVE

Maggie and Charles continued

The Case of Maggie

Over the next two months I saw Maggie four times. She reported modest improvement in her IBS ("about a six") and her mood was brighter. She reported she was listening to the CD on a regular basis and had begun jogging in the morning. Each session I told her an ego-strengthening story interspersed with IBS-specific suggestions. She said she thought therapy was going well. Her mother accompanied her each time and looked like she was continuing to go downhill.

Maggie canceled the last session, saying she had to take her mother to a medical appointment. At the end of the message she added, "this therapy is getting a bit intense." I appreciated her honesty. In my experience, many other clients would simply not show up when they thought therapy was hitting too close to home. Selfishly speaking, I didn't mind at all when people canceled as it gave me a chance to catch up on things. Besides seeing clients, training, supervision, committees and other things accounted for half my time.

Recent losses

When Maggie showed up her mother was absent. You know the saying, "Like something the cat dragged in," well, that's how she looked today. She was disheveled, anxious, distracted and appeared depressed. Furthermore, the mirrored sunglasses were back.

Therapist: Smoking any dope today, Maggie?

Maggie: I wish I had some lately.

Therapist: So, what's going on?

Maggie: My boyfriend broke up with me and my mom had to start dialysis.

Therapist: Oh, sorry about your mom … and I didn't know you had a boyfriend.

Maggie explained how Tim, a man more than 20 years older, had been in her life for the past three years. Her "sugar daddy" was her term for Tim, a man who was "good in bed."

Maggie: Maybe I didn't fit in his life anymore, maybe he found someone else, I don't know, he wasn't a big talker, I always had to pull the words out of him.

A curious development, indeed. Mostly I wondered why she had been holding back on mentioning Tim.

Making sense of it all

In a wide-ranging discussion we talked about loneliness, hurt and rejection, to name a few topics. To date, Maggie continues to decline discussion of her dreams and nightmares.

Therapist: I've bounced back from rejection, others have, and I'm sure you can, Maggie.

Maggie: Just what I need, a pep talk.

She was especially sarcastic today. Finally, she took off the sunglasses. We then explored her history of relationships with men, and I learned there had been many other men and even a couple of women lovers over the years. They were all several years her senior, usually with money. In their company, she had felt "… warm … taken care of … appreciated for who I am … no one lasts long if they're out to change me." Now, hearing all that, I wasn't about to jump into the trap of speculating on how she might get involved in a more functional relationship in the future. At least not right now.

I had planned an age progression exercise this session in which Maggie would imagine herself in the future. Typically, with this my phrasing is something like, "… I'd like you to project yourself, in your mind, to some time in the future, it can be any time at all, two weeks from now, two years or 20 years from now, where you see yourself and what you're doing … notice the context … is it daytime or night, and are there people around?" Each step is verified with finger signals. However, this would have to wait for another time, as Maggie seemed to be gearing up to tell me more.

Maggie: Tim wasn't just good in bed. At other times he'd sneak up behind me."

Therapist: And?

I was almost afraid to ask.

Maggie: He'd pinch my bum, not just pinch it, he'd grab a piece of my bum, pinch it hard, and then twist it even harder. He had big strong hands, he's a weightlifter, used to be a cage fighter.

Therapist: And that felt good, the pinching?

Maggie: You can imagine, *just imagine* …

She was mocking my customary phrasing. I couldn't help but smile.

Maggie: How GOOD that made me feel.

Therapist: Well, was he rough in the sack, too?

Maggie: As gentle as a lamb, with great endurance. I know it just doesn't fit.

Therapist: Well, I guess Tim's shoes would be big ones to fill by another man or woman.

Maggie: I'm done with women. That was something I experimented with when I was younger. But to answer your question, yes, big shoes to fill.

Therapist: Maggie, do you like being hurt in general?

Maggie: Not emotionally, Doc. Hurt physically is okay, I don't mind it. But don't get me wrong, I don't want a black eye or anything.

Therapist: Maggie, I've had other clients, men and women both, who were in a stable and happy, dysfunctional relationship, and then, when one of them starts to make changes, well, the other one doesn't feel needed anymore. Usually, not even on a conscious level, it just unwittingly sneaks up on them and they drift apart. Relationships are hard for all of us.

Maggie: So, about yourself, you've been with your wife for a zillion years and you have daughters my age, or so I'm told by the guys in the waiting room.

Therapist: That's correct, Ms. Detective, except two sons, not daughters.

Maggie: I'm supposed to tell my darkest secrets but not you.

Therapist: I know, it doesn't seem fair, but that's the rules. If and when I feel a personal disclosure is relevant, I'll mention it.

Maggie: Listen to yourself, Doc, I mean, George, all of a sudden you get so cold and clinical.

I looked at her and didn't speak. I thought, "Here's another one commenting on process, criticizing me, my words, I'm sensitive about that ... I thought I had thicker skin than that."

Maggie: Oops, mea culpa, señor.

Therapist: Thanks for the insight, Doc, send me a bill tomorrow.

Maggie: That was so funny I forgot to laugh. Anyway, the drifting apart thing you mentioned before, you're probably right about that. I guess I'm learning here that there's a lot of stuff going on outside of awareness, which is really cool when you think of it.

Therapist: As has been said before, "like the big part of the iceberg, down there, hidden beneath the water ..."

Maggie: "Resourceful, watchful, waiting, deep inside."

She couldn't be too depressed, with the humor she had going today, finishing my sentences for me. At least she's picking up on some of my main points.

Maggie: No, you're not transparent or predictable, but you tend to repeat yourself.

As she talked, she showed a greater range of affect; however, I suddenly had the feeling that this session was getting away from me.

Therapist: Maggie, aside from how you're feeling today, tell me generally, are we on the right track with what we're doing here? We've met like eight or nine times so far.

Maggie: For sure, yeah, the constipation's improved but still there and I feel better about myself. My mom's even commented that I look better.

Her words were gratifying—and appeared sincere. It was time to move on.

Earlier life—and a detour

Therapist: You've said very little about earlier life. Were you a happy kid growing up?

She said she was happy early on, an only child, and got good grades in school. She felt like she grew up too fast, and her dad was a drinker and womanizer while her mother held the family together.

Maggie: My dad drank himself to death. I turned 16 the day of his funeral. My mom often had three jobs.

Therapist: When did you become, as you refer to yourself, a 'tomboy'?

Maggie: During my tour in Iraq.

Therapist: So, Graves Registration was your job, right?

Maggie: Yeah, tag 'em and bag 'em, all the bodies, with an occasional civilian thrown in the mix. It was hard to see dead kids.

Therapist: That's when your IBS started?

Maggie: Pretty much.

She fidgeted with the sunglasses on her lap. Her back became erect, shoulders back, and she shot me a steely-eyed stare. Maggie reached down for the lever on the recliner and yanked up the footrest. Her words were measured and even.

Maggie: Story time—my story—well, not really a story but something I want to tell you, not a lot of minutes left on your precious clock.

A night at PP's

Maggie: Did I ever tell you about that place in Phoenix I used to go to?

Therapist: Not that I can remember.

Maggie: It's kind of risqué, do you think you can handle it?

Therapist: We have some time left, go for it.

She proceeded to tell me about a bizarre sex place she went to a few years back. I had heard a transgender woman mention this place before but I'd never gotten any lurid details until now. Maggie slouched lower in the chair as she started in.

Maggie: The place is the Pleasure Principle, but people just call it PP's. It's in a big warehouse, open only on Saturday nights. You pay $50—cash only—to get in and once you're inside they have everything you could imagine: whips, chains, trapezes, men dressed up like little milk maids, women dressed up like Hell's Angels, you name it, they have it. Strobe lights, incense and the music is always the same: Enya.

This was indeed most interesting. I took a deep breath and closed my eyes.

Therapist: Go on, please.

Maggie: (in an exaggerated lower volume) … with your eyes closed you can appreciate what's going on in *the inside*.

Therapist: Get on with your story if you don't mind!

Speaking of inside, I was steaming on the inside, not from her mocking but because she had detoured me at an important time. Even at my age I remind myself at times like this, "It's about the client, it's about the client, George." She resumed and I generated an image of myself letting go of a balloon.

Maggie: The transgenders and transvestites were out in force that night. People would have all manner of sex with each other right out in the open, but if you wanted privacy, you could go behind some partitions. One time I recognized a doctor from here—he works over in Building 80. I don't think he saw me, boy, was he a drag queen that night. He was headed over to the area where you get urinated on from a high ladder. Are you holding up okay, George?

Therapist: Seems like it would be hard for a person to make up stuff like this.

Maggie: No making up, this was the real deal. Someone told me they closed it down, but I heard later that it re-opened in another part of Phoenix. There's no website, it's all by word of mouth. It was over a year ago that I was there. Anyway, they had women in fake Red Cross uniforms. They met you at the door. They probably screened out anybody too crazy or too loaded.

Therapist: Or underage.

Maggie: I didn't think of that. Other 'medical personnel' would do a 'mandatory exam' on you … and to answer your question before you ask it, yes, they used latex gloves.

Therapist: They sell drugs there?

Maggie: They did but not in the open. So, anyway, PP's is famous for the Jitterbug, a fake, vibrating fire hydrant designed to 'put out your fire'. It's—

Therapist: Spare the details. Say, we need to end soon.

Maggie: There's a bank of computer terminals where people look at porn and a video section where you and whoever could be taped doing whatever you want. The DVD costs extra, and food court. You should see how they adorned the hot dogs. People giggling and cheering, hundreds of 'em, all quite fun and festive, quite the place.

Therapist: And a good time was had by all.

Maggie: Oh, you're so serious. It was consenting adults, nobody got hurt, no laws were broken.

Therapist: Except for the drugs and probably not paying the sales tax.

I'd thought the place was an urban legend. I guess not. It was time to wrap this up.

Therapist: So, Maggie, this new information, thank you for sharing it, but beyond that, I'm thinking, why are you telling me all this, and as with all information, I wonder how it can be used to move therapy forward?

She answered quickly, as if she was anticipating those words

Maggie: Well, about direction, the forward stuff, all I know is that my old Nissan truck with standard transmission, hell, the second gear is broke and I'm lucky it moves forward at all, and for the other part, you're the first one to say that the WHY doesn't matter, that it's the WHAT that's important.

Therapist: Well, then the WHAT, what about it?

Maggie: You're not the only one who tells stories … but is it just a story?

She put the sunglasses back on and smiled. She slowly lowered the foot-rest. Maggie was weary and depressed again.

Notes for practice

She seemed genuine when describing that strange place. As she talked about it, my main thought—in addition to the detouring— was, "She's just trying to shock the old man." But that's looking at it through a narcissistic lens. The content of her account was indeed provocative but so was the dynamics. Was jumping into the one-up position via the sudden storyteller role a part of her coping style? I never would have guessed that after getting to know her for several sessions. The rest of that day I had a meeting with trainees, a marital session, and then a difficult family therapy session. During all of those I was preoccupied with PP's. I felt drained as I drove home that night. I exit off the freeway at a road called Miracle Mile and what I've done for years is use the turn lane at the light as my cue to leave everything at work until tomorrow. However, that evening I did one more thing: I ceased trying to problem solve the whole PP's issue and assigned resolution to my unconscious. Maybe that would help.

The next day, as I was seeing another woman—also with mirrored sunglasses on her lap—something occurred to me. It entered my mind as a jumble of fragments, fragments about stories and war, roadblocks and detours, orange cones at the scene of an accident, cul de sacs and one-way streets. Then it became crystal clear: All this was pointing to the need for exposure therapy. Yes, I needed to go after Maggie's wartime experience. That should be the obvious thing in the V.A., and I had let myself get distracted.

"Where is your mind today, George? Did you listen to *anything* I just said?!" asked the woman with the sunglasses on her lap. "Sorry, really sorry," I answered.

The case of Charles

I hadn't seen Charles for three weeks, as he had said on the telephone recording he'd be out of town with his wife for two weeks, and once returned "… I have to assist the missus at the gem show." The annual Tucson Gem and Mineral Show, the largest gem show in the world, is the most important commercial event in the city and attracts hundreds of thousands of visitors and vendors. I greeted him in the waiting room where he looked like he was holding court with other veterans, articulating something that had their rapt attention. He strode smoothly ahead of me to my office. He was carrying a boom box.

I regarded Charles as he sat across from me. He looked like he had come from his office, as he was neatly dressed with tan slacks, a short-sleeved, powder blue dress shirt and his customary bola tie, this one with an oversized turquoise clasp no doubt worth several hundred dollars. In his brown penny loafers the pennies were replaced by silver coins.

Therapist: No pennies in your shoes today.

Charles: Today my schedule was full of rich Mexicans from across the border, so the pennies became pesos.

Therapist: I forgot you speak Spanish.

His eyes began to circle. A look of delight, pursed lips, and …

Charles: Yeah, just like you but my Spanish is better.

Therapist: You've heard me speak it?

(Any therapy modality I do in English I also do in Spanish and I regard my facility as pretty good.)

Charles: I just assumed, looking at how you operate.

A nervous smile followed, then a quick bearing of teeth beneath bushy mustache.

Therapist: Well, you have many talents.

Charles: Aren't you going to comment on how good I look today … and why I brought this boom box?

Therapist: I guess you *do* look good, considering a full day of clients right after vacation. You had a lot of time with your wife. How did that go?

Charles shifted in his chair and crossed his legs. The smiled returned, quicker and more rote than before. His eyes closed.

Charles: Yeah, well, we'll have to get into that some time, but not now, please. I have a CD in here (pointing down to the boom box), maybe we can do some relaxation, hypnosis, whatever.

Therapist: Say, our first session, one of the first things you mentioned was insomnia. And anxiety. How've those things been?

Charles: Sleep's not bad. Anxiety is mostly better. In some ways it's different, morphed maybe.

Therapist: Morphed? Like into something … deeper?

Why, I still don't really know, but I was looking at Charles' hands spread out on his lap, and as he was answering my question, a sudden intuition suggested I try automatic writing or drawing at this juncture.

Charles: Yeah, I can't really put my finger on it. Like a song with sad music and happy lyrics.

I glanced over my shoulder to the oversized conventional clock on the wall.

Therapist: On a clock, fast second *hand*, slower minute hand, *seeding/ moving* of their own volition.

Charles: (eyes still closed). I didn't catch that.

Therapist: You mentioned sad music and happy lyrics.

Charles grimaced reflexively, then his whole demeanor darkened. His body became tense, arms rigid, and his breathing became shallow.

Therapist: Just resume those deep breaths, Charles, doing fine.

He reached back and flicked his ponytail, which settled awkwardly on his chest. He snorted and flicked it back over his shoulder. I thought, "This is good, maybe I can get some traction here."

Automatic writing

Therapist: You ever do any automatic writing or drawing, either personally or with clients? It might be good to do some unconscious exploration today.

Charles: Did some automatic writing a long time ago … in training … at the Erickson Foundation in Phoenix.

He opened his eyes and looked down at the boom box next to his chair.

Therapist: Some background music today?

Charles: Yeah, I have a CD in there, ocean waves and flute, but let's listen to something else, one of yours.

He pulled the recliner's handle and up went his feet. He closed his eyes and kicked off his shoes. I realized I'd told him previously to do anything he wanted to feel comfortable. Some clients will take you at your word when you give them such permission. Usually their preparing themselves for trance will be simple and innocuous, like taking off their glasses, readjusting their body in the chair, or taking a drink from their ubiquitous water bottles. One man, who was nearly deaf even with his two hearing aids, removed his hearing aids, causing me to think he wanted some quiet time rather than listening to my boring words! I've also had women who wipe off their make-up, or put on new make-up, and some who apply lip gloss. One man removed his tee shirt and I was distracted the remainder of the session by his hairy chest. Maybe there's more disinhibition in the V.A.; at any rate, be ready when you offer permissive suggestions.

I rummaged through a drawer and found one of my favorite relaxation CDs, Liquid Mind *(1995) I located an outlet, plugged it in, and started it up.*

Charles: That's nice.

Therapist: Let's see, you write with your right hand, correct?

Charles: I told you last time that I'm ambidextrous. But right hand will be fine.

Therapist: I'll be moving in real close, right next to you, is that okay?

Charles didn't answer. His eyes remained closed and he had started taking some deep breaths. He was already well into trance. I knew I wouldn't have to say a lot more for him to go deeper.

Charles: Sure, whatever.

His words were a mere whisper. I told him what I was doing and maneuvered his right hand on his lap and put a pencil in his hand. I placed a large, yellow notepad beneath the pencil.

Therapist: Don't write anything for now, because I'd like you to notice, just *notice independently how that hand* can operate, perhaps feeling like it's *separated* from your wrist *out there*, even across the room and as you *notice* that, you can begin to deeply *appreciate* how this process can be highly *int*eresting, even *int*riguing, and you *can't not* notice an *inc*reasing *focus*. *Who knows* what can be discovered today? Just letting it happen … (pause of 60 seconds)

Power word
Activate seed
Dissociation

Power words
Suggestions
Double negative
Direct question

And, Charles, I'm going to count swiftly down now from 10 to one, and as those numbers descend, backward, down, your experience can deepen … 10, 9, 8 … some people imagine themselves going down a *deep/steep* staircase 7, 6, 5, 4, 3, 2 and one.

Misspeak

Charles looked like he might be asleep. I needed to check on that.

Therapist: Charles, when you're sufficiently deep in order to do the work we need to do today, your unconscious mind can signal me by letting your left, yes your left index finger, twitch and develop a lightness all its own and float up in to the air. Take as much time as you need.

I closely watched his left hand, as I knew that in the low light of the office a mere twitch of the finger might be difficult to see. About 45 seconds later the index finger on his right *hand moved ever so slightly. The pencil lolled in his right hand so I reset it in his hand. I thought, "At least I know he's not asleep. Right hand, left hand, I'll take what I can get."*

Therapist: Beginning now, Charles, I would like your unconscious mind to generate anything at all that may be useful in understanding your problem. It can be anything at all, a word, part of a word, a mere fragment of a word … and your right hand will spell it out on that paper … involuntarily, independently, avolitionally, automatically.

About 40 seconds passed before the pencil began to move. From where I sat I couldn't make out what he wrote. The pencil stopped moving after two minutes, then he released it and it dropped to the floor. He looked exquisitely relaxed, maybe serene was a better word.

Therapist: Very good, Charles … you and the back part of your mind have done some potent work today, and I can imagine you feel quite drained … that's the way, doing fine, we're almost done … and in a moment, but not just yet, I'm going to count from one up to five and by the time my voice reaches five, you can re-alert as if waking up from a nice, pleasant, relaxing nap … 1, 2, (louder) 3, 4 (still louder) and *five*, okay, time to wake up!

When you've done this a while you realize that in general, the deeper into trance they go, the longer it takes for them to re-alert. After all, who wants to come back to the world from such a comfortable place? He required another minute or so of prodding and then he opened his eyes. We had run over and I had people waiting.

Charles: Boy, that's just what I needed. Thanks, George.

Therapist: Do you have any conscious recollection of what you wrote?

Charles: No, not at all.

I snatched the yellow pad from him and briefly examined what he wrote. It was all in capital letters: LYRE VANDEST. He grabbed the pad back from me, examined it, shook his head, and said he had no idea what it meant. I reminded him to practice relaxation. We hurriedly made a follow-up appointment, he left without his boom box, and I followed him out the door, ready to apologize to people in the waiting room for being late.

Notes for practice

When doing hypnotic work, it is vital that the practitioner maintain ongoing modes of communication. So, on a basic level, if I ask Maggie to drift back in time to when she last felt competence and mastery, I don't know when she's arrived there unless she tells me. I can ask for a verbal report, a head nod, or an ideomotor finger signal, e.g., "… when you're there, let me know by letting your right index finger move." Responding verbally in trance is thought to lighten trance, so after they speak, I ask them to "take one more deep, comfortable breath and sink back into your peaceful trance." Asking for a periodic response of some kind allows you to verify things and keep trance a two-way street of communication. If that's not done, I'm really disempowering them, as they get the idea that therapy means they're a passive vessel that's waiting to be filled up. But it also serves a more basic purpose in that I can tell whether or not they've fallen asleep, which happens a lot with all the medications people are on these days.

On a more advanced level, let's say that Charles and I are doing some unconscious exploration. I tell him ahead of time that, in trance, I'm going to ask him to designate three finger signals on his right hand (many opt to use the preferred or dominant hand, but I don't know that it matters). So, then, I ask for a finger that can mean "yes," one that can mean "no," and one for "I don't know or I'm not ready to answer yet." Having all three responses on one hand is important, as is having the hand visible (I prefer on the lap), so you can monitor responses. In trance, I ask Charles, "This problem (we've designated what the problem is), is your unconscious mind ready to let it go? Taking as much time as you need, you may answer with one of the responses on that right hand."

We have to be patient. Remember, we're consulting the person's *unconscious* mind here, and that covers a lot of territory. Sometimes a minute or more will pass before a finger moves. It is believed that a response is 1) available on the finger before it is on the tongue, and 2) that a mere twitch of the finger represents a true unconscious response, whereas a deliberate, big movement of the finger is the conscious mind responding. In this session with Charles, I asked for a response on one hand and he answered with the other hand, which happens now and then. I just go with it, no big deal, though this can mean reactance. You may be thinking, what about the *veracity* of finger signals? In other words, let's say I'm doing an age regression exercise with Charles, I ask him to drift back in time to when he did something he is really proud of, his "yes" finger signals, I ask him for a verbal report, and he says, "One day at work I cured ten children of stuttering in one session."

Now, obviously I can't verify that, nor would I want to. For good reason, Steve Lankton says, "We're not archeologists." What any of us experience or report during age regression could represent consensual reality as much as it could be fantasy, distortion, or even a blatant and conscious fabrication to impress the therapist. That's why the veracity is far less pertinent than *utility*. With Charles, I'm interested in exploring his experiential or psychic reality. His report of curing stuttering children is one more piece of data, nothing more, nothing less, something I accumulate, along with all other clinical data. Ideomotor finger signals needn't be taken at face value. What's more important to me is the process, specifically, *how* is the client participating in this mode of exploration and communication (Diamond, 1983). After doing this a time or two I will know if this is a good channel to watch. I try different things to see what works. If I'm wasting my time and theirs, I'd like to know that early on so I can just pull the plug.

Also, with several clients over the years, when I'm debriefing them I say, "Hmm, back there when I asked for a finger signal I didn't see any fingers move," and they say, "Oh, I *thought* my "yes" finger moved. You don't know unless you ask.

So you may say, "All this is just a fishing expedition." Of course it is! If you don't like fish, try something else, like crystal balls. Erickson had the person hallucinate (imagine) crystal balls in front of them, and the crystal balls were the bridge to the unconscious as he employed age regression, age progression, unconscious search, or other techniques. How about an imaginary TV or movie screen, or a person watching another who's watching a movie screen? There are innumerable bridges to the unconscious and all these bridges cross a river in which down there you see … yes, fish!

CHAPTER SIX

Perturbation and pattern interruption

Stirring the soup

Someone once asked me what I do and I answered, "I plant seeds and I perturb. That about sums it up." And they said, "Huh?"

Each session I offer suggestions that I don't expect people to agree with or act upon, and my hope and expectation is that some of the ideas will percolate in the unconscious and germinate down the road. With my garden, I don't just toss a handful of seeds on untilled soil because birds will eat them or they'll dry up and blow away. I amend the soil with compost and other things, which readies the soil for planting. With clients, I usually prepare the soil with things like ego-strengthening stories and anecdotes while I'm seeding suggestions, and hopefully the client's receptivity will grow. But sometimes that's not enough. That's when perturbation is called for. It doesn't take long to recognize a client who is so mired down and in sore need of the agitation benefit of perturbation. I recognize such a situation when I hear in my head the sound of a washing machine. That's right, I hear the AGITATOR, that cylindrical device you see when you open the door of a washing machine. Once the machine starts up, that gizmo rocks and rolls in there, *perturbing* big time. That is my image. It triggers my imagination and I immediately start pondering what I need to do next.

Perturbation in daily life

Perturb? Yes. You have soup on the stove and it's staying in a big glob, time to *stir* it. The fire in my fireplace this morning was barely alive. A few pushes with the poker and soon it roared back to life. When you brush your teeth you're performing a vital perturbation of the teeth and gums. Many corrective medical procedures have a perturbing function, like when the lithotripsy machine blasts your kidney stones. You cough and clear secretions, you unplug your drain. If you work in a dysfunctional organization and a new boss comes in, she's likely to shake things up a bit. In a tension-filled meeting someone clears the air. Perturbation is a common phenomenon in nature as well as in many facets of daily life.

Perturbation with new clients

Many times clients are *stuck,* stuck in patterns of behavior in which they unwittingly repeat dysfunctional behavior over and over again. They go to therapy, which will hopefully perturb the process so that receptivity to a new way of doing things can be generated, accepted and incorporated into everyday living. At least that's the way it's supposed to work. If you've been a therapist for more than a few weeks, you've learned that therapy isn't easy, and it's seldom a straightforward process where the client comes in, says,

> *"Here I am, here's my problem. Now tell me what to do and I'll leave here and do it."*

In fact, it's more like a darn chess game. The job is to help people *in spite of* themselves. You need to get in beneath the radar, and that means you're dealing with their unconscious. With Maggie and Charles, as perhaps with some of your clients, you recognize that perturbation needs to occur, but you can't perturb because you're not sure yet what the heck you're dealing with. I swear, with some of the clients I saw at the V.A., I could read *"The map is not the territory"* stenciled on their foreheads.

Say "uncle" in the ante room, write in the drawing room, or go far in the waiting room

Clients *coming in stuck* is one thing, and, to me, not really that challenging when compared to their being stuck *in* therapy. Over the past several years I've taken an informal poll among therapists in around the U.S. I ask them what they *do* when they're stuck. And you know how most of them answer? "I just wait" is how the vast majority respond. Now, their patience may be admirable, but I would have to give them low marks on imagination. Early on, I, too, "just waited," but not for long because I happened to read Erickson and speak to people who'd been trained by him, and soon I realized that there were much better things than waiting.

I talk to many therapists who've seen some of their clients for weeks or months and there is no real progress, or there's a step forward, then one back. The client is thinking, "Hmm, maybe I need a new therapist," and the therapist is thinking, "Maybe they *do* need a new therapist," or at the very least, they confide to me and others, "My best empathy and techniques are just bouncing off his armor and I feel helpless." I'm not thinking those thoughts *yet* with Maggie and Charles, but after some sessions I'm left scratching my head and wondering where all this is going.

However, one thing steels me, and that is archery. Archery? Yes, you know the big targets they shoot at, with the concentric circles. That's what I think of when working with any client, that big target, because that's just what the unconscious is, an immense target that's hard to miss. So, to continue the hackneyed metaphor, when you combine a big target with the vast array of techniques available in therapy, that's one gigantic quiver full of arrows waiting to be used.

Generating an evergreen epiphany

To nudge people from their old patterns, one of the techniques Erickson relied on was the ambiguous function assignment, where clients agree to do some new—and often extravagant—behavior assigned by the therapist. The idea was to perturb them, disrupt their unconscious, and generate new learning. Erickson's assignment often included climbing an urban mountain in Phoenix called Squaw Peak. He also would have people drive 10 miles out of town (Phoenix was mostly agricultural land in the 1950s and 1960s) and lie for 20 minutes in a drainage ditch near a cotton field. During this assignment an "Ah-HA" experience would result, a solution to their problem, or a new point of view. And like most of the cases Erickson described, the technique worked. The people were successfully perturbed. Erickson didn't assign an exotic behavior prescription right from the start. He evaluated their resistance and receptivity over several sessions, but mostly he built the relationship. They trusted him. And that's what you need to do before asking your clients to complete a between-session task that's out of the ordinary: Build the relationship. They'll do what you ask because you've built rapport, they know they're in good hands, and the assignment "fits." As Peggy Papp (1983) said, "A good doctor does not prescribe bad medicine." Steve Lankton, one of Erickson's students, learned his lessons well. His books show us some very imaginative ambiguous function assignments—a term and protocol he coined. This technique and other strategic ones are also explored in the works of Rubin Battino.

Now, as we'll see increasingly with Maggie and Charles, the emphasis will be on getting them to DO something. Not just talk about it. The emphasis is on their *behavior*. Usually it is set up with hypnotic language, story and anecdote, but my goal is always the target *behavior*. If there's no movement in therapy we shouldn't blame the client. It's up to *us* to make something happen.

Patterns in daily life

Daily life seems to be one interrupted pattern after another. We are involved in something, on our smart phones, on the computer, in a conversation, and then it happens: Someone sneezes, the phone rings, the dog barks, or a familiar song comes on the radio and we're carried back to a nostalgic time in the past. Our attention is diverted elsewhere and in seconds or minutes we're able to resume what we were doing. It is normal life. If we recorded all that we do between arising from bed and returning to it at night, definite patterns would emerge. No big deal, nothing new there, you may say. However, if it's *clients* we're talking about, then their daily patterns may be very meaningful.

Pathologic routines

All change in therapy involves pattern interruption. I'm depressed, experiencing sadness for months, and the introduction of talk therapy or medication disrupts, or interrupts, my routine of hopelessness. Negative thoughts diminish, my mood brightens, and new behavior is activated.

When I see a client, from the first minute of the initial session I'm listening for patterns, as I know that's where my interventions will be targeted. If the person is vague or not forthcoming, I ask and tell them why I'm asking. I'm unable to cite pattern interruption yet in Charles or Maggie, so I'll use Kathryn instead.

The case of Kathryn

Therapist: So Kathryn, let me get this right. In the morning, you get out of bed, go to the bathroom, get the coffee going and make enough for when your boyfriend gets up later; you grab the remote and turn on BBC World News; the dog is barking and needs to go out, AND right about then the thought hits you, "I'm a miserable failure, what an awful life I have;" and just then you start to feel nervous and you realize you better go outside for a cigarette. Is this anywhere close to describing it?

Kathryn: That pretty well nails it.

Now, if you practice some version of CBT, you're seeing where you might intervene. The same for a psychodynamic or NLP therapist, and the same for a strategic therapist—and we haven't even said if the problem is depression, smoking, relational problem, or something else. And, as I have Kathryn describe her average day at work, visiting her mother, ruminating in bed at night, arguing with her boyfriend, similar patterns emerge, just as they would for you and me. These patterns clients describe are gold nuggets, a gift-wrapped invitation for us to intervene and help them out of their problem.

Erickson showed us that if *one* aspect of the problematic pattern is interrupted, the underpinnings supporting the problem fall away, and improvement happens. Cade & O'Hanlon (1993), standing on Erickson's shoulders, have best elucidated how to do this. I call it O'Hanlon's List (Gafner & Benson, 2003), and here are a few examples from it:

1. Alter or change the rate or frequency of the symptom pattern.

2. Alter the duration, intensity, or location of the symptom pattern.

3. Alter the order of the symptom pattern.

So, with Kathryn, let's say my target is conflict with her mother. I've determined that the two typically argue heatedly in the late afternoon when Kathryn visits. When she arrives at mom's house, her mother is busy preparing dinner. It's then that Kathryn launches into a tirade, blaming her mother for mom's dearth of emotional and financial support. But I still need more information from her.

Therapist: How long until your mom is usually done preparing supper?

Kathryn: Thirty, forty-five minutes at the most.

Therapist: Then what?

Kathryn: We have coffee in the living room.

Therapist: It seems like *at certain times,* this arguing has a life of its own. Might you miss it if the situation improved?

Kathryn: Hell, no. I hate it. What's your point here anyway?

The Rationale

I secure her agreement to wait to argue until they get in the living room, thus altering both the *location* and the *timing.* But first Kathryn needs to know the rationale. You or I wouldn't try something new unless we're given a good reason. Often in therapy people will agree to a behavior prescription (task, assignment) when we remind them that nothing else so far has worked, "... so, Kathryn, why in the world NOT try something different?" However, with pattern interruption we want to use one of two rationales: To try and bring the symptom under *voluntary control*, or *"an experiment."* Voluntary control might work here.

Therapist: Kathryn, this painful arguing has really gotten out of hand. Maybe you or your mom has tried numerous things to make this better, but frankly it's out of control, don't you agree?

Kathryn: Yeah, I guess it is.

Therapist: That's why I'm asking you to do something for one week, to try and bring the arguing *under voluntary control*. Here's a card where you can track progress, just write down what happens each day. Are you willing to give this a whirl?

Kathryn: Sure.

None of us likes to think that our behavior isn't under our control. But don't take anything for granted. You want to set it up to succeed, not fail. So, anticipate roadblocks.

Kathryn: But she'll just bait me and argue anyway while she's cooking. Am I supposed to not defend myself?

Therapist: You can change the subject. You can do lots of things. You can deflect, maybe agreeing in part or principle, like, "Maybe you've got a point there, Mom." You're not agreeing with her, you're just deflecting, not letting her engage you in an argument. Here, we can role play this right now. I'll be you and you be your mother.

Were the target something else

If my target in therapy is Kathryn's self-punitive thoughts in the morning, I might ask her to alter the *order* of her behavior, maybe take her dog outside and have a cigarette before starting the negative monologue in her head. To employ the *experiment* option with her arguments with her mother, I'd say, "This nasty arguing, it's been going on so long, you guys have tried to make it better ... and let's try something here, a little *experiment* ..."

Why use the experiment rationale vs. the voluntary control rationale? I go with the one that first springs to mind as the better "fit." By the time you introduce this you've probably seen your client at least three or four times and have an inkling which one might work. It always amazes me how people can begin to feel better when seemingly innocuous changes are injected in the pattern. In most cases, when one change like this is injected into the pattern, the pattern falls apart. I'm reminded of those houses they have in tropical areas where it regularly floods. The houses are built up on poles and they're able to weather typhoons and torrents of rushing water; however, if you knock down just one pole it starts to wobble.

Sequencing

Another take on pattern alteration, *sequencing,* comes from Brent Geary (personal communications, 2002, 2013) at the Erickson Foundation in Phoenix, Arizona. This elegant technique involves feeding back to the client the specific *chain* of experiences (thoughts, emotions, sensations, images, or behaviors), or component steps, of a problematic behavior. Then, through deletion, disruption, distortion, or substitution of one or more of the steps, the *sequence is turned* in the desired directions.

For example, let's say anxiety is the target. The client, Natalia, typically experiences accelerated breathing, feelings of tension, diffuse perception, anxious ruminations, and an overall hyperactive presentation, which invariably leads to something undesirable, like having a cigarette, avoidance, or embarrassment. In intervening, the therapist feeds back these steps in the sequence, matching the client's experience. The direction of the sequence is altered, however, to something more productive.

"Natalia, focusing on *breathing* and how it can *slow down*, and noticing *feelings of tension* as they gradually *drift away*, and really *enjoying the changes* in perception that come with relaxation and trance, all this can allow you to *go inside* and *consider the resources* you are learning and using to help yourself."

The steps match, but the outcome (relaxing, exploring options, feeling calmer) is more desirable. Sequencing can be done in standard psychotherapy or within hypnosis. Clients readily learn that the problem is not global, such as "my nervousness," or "my bad habit," but is instead a series of discrete events that can be altered. The problem becomes a process rather than an amorphous thing. This technique offers you multiple ways to intervene in your clients' problems. Sequencing is a quintessential utilization approach. It is the client's own experiences that comprise the sequence, not something imposed from without. It affords both client and therapist closer "inspection" of the process of the problem, and multiple possibilities for modifying the problem.

So, you might be thinking here, "Gee, all these techniques he's throwing at us, how do we know which ones to use?" Well, just start out slow. You have a client coming in later in the week, and you get from her the component parts of the *sequence* of her problem. Then, the next time she comes back you're prepared to *match* her experience and *alter* the sequence in the right direction. Just like with stories. Tell an anecdote with one client, then read a story to the next. Try something new and see what works for **you**.

Other ways to perturb

The techniques presented above are pretty straightforward. However, the search for solutions, unconsciously speaking, can take many routes, and our tendency may be to first look deep. Sometimes that's a good place to look; however, you usually don't need a backhoe when a garden trowel will do. Oftentimes thinking and looking *laterally*— instead of down—may be more fruitful. Deep, sideways, these are all rather speculative constructs anyway, and maybe all unconsciously directed routes lead to Rome. Several years back, Brent Geary first opened my eyes to thinking laterally.

In the V.A., I saw many clients who figuratively shot themselves in the foot. In other words, in spite of their best efforts they would trip themselves up, over and over again. It could be in relationships, with addiction, employment, or in other areas. If they have the where-withal to admit that this is a problem, they may be open to some help interrupting the pattern. For shooting one's self in the foot, or for a vague presenting problem, e.g., "I don't know what's wrong ... I'm just not right ... I can't put it into words ..." I perturb in two major ways: Instigative story and instigative anecdote. I normally employ the anecdotes at the end of a story, say a story whose meta-message is equivocal, and the instigative story I use as a stand-alone story. I use both techniques within talk therapy and as part of formal trance. As part of a talk therapy session, I typically save a few minutes at the end of the session and say something like, "Okay, I'm going to read to you a little story (or tell you some anecdotes) that is directed at the back part of your mind, the part of your mind that has you hung up, and also the part of your mind where you will find a solution to your problem. You can just sit back and listen however you like." A favorite instigative story (in addition to Simple Rooms, used in Chapter 7) is Pills (Gafner & Benson, 2003).

Pills story

One day I saw Eloise, a client who was referred by her doctor for a rather interesting problem. The doctor had prescribed a particular medication—I forget which one—and for several weeks Eloise had taken the pills exactly as prescribed, one three times a day, with food. She religiously took one pill with milk and crackers at 8:00, 12:00, and 4:00. But the desired therapeutic effect had not been achieved, and the doctor indicated that Eloise would need to find a different way to make the pills work.

As you probably know, often when people are referred to a thera-pist they have already tried many things. Sometimes therapy is a last resort. They have attempted every possible solution, but they still have not gotten *from here to there*. In Eloise's case, she and the doctor had tried taking half a pill at 8:00, another half at 10:00, and another *half* at 12:00, 2:00, 4:00, 6:00, and 8:00. They had tried taking a half at 9:00, 11:00, 1:00, 3:00, 5:00 and 7:00, and they also tried taking a half pill on the half hour six times a day, and even one quarter of a pill 12 times a day on both the hour and the half hour. They even attempted an eighth of a pill every hour during the day and night, even though Eloise protested having to awaken every hour at night to take her medication. "Milk and crackers every hour is a bit much," complained Eloise. "With only one-eighth a tablet I have obvious concerns about therapeutic effect," said the doctor. He had never encountered such a vexing problem in all his years of practice. He was glad to wash his hands of her. "Maybe that therapist will figure this out," he mused.

After reading all the reports and discussing this with Eloise, we began to examine other ways of *getting from here to there*. As we discussed and noticed some new possibilities, both she and I came to appreciate the *infinite number of things* that could be tried. We agreed that the pills would still need to be cut into fractions, but that Eloise could use a different knife and a different cutting board. She had fifteen other knives at home and two alternate cutting boards, and she realized that a variety of other flat surfaces in her apartment might also serve the purpose. The pharmaceutical company had conveniently imprinted its name and the number 23 on the tablet. She could cut one pill on the 3 and another on the 2, and then a host of other cutting possibilities became evident.

She could also cut those pills during different times of the day, or she could have her mother cut every other pill. She could take one dose in the bathroom and one in the living room and another while driving to work. Instead of milk and crackers, she could take juice and half a cookie one time and soda and one-third can of tuna another time. She could have friends present while she cut or took her dose, or she could have the TV on, or if she played music she could have a classical music CD or a rock and roll tape, or maybe even one of her father's old vinyl records.

"I could even think different thoughts each time," Eloise joked. The whole thing seemed comical, but it was also serious, and because of the *infinite number of possibilities*, a solution was forthcoming.

Now, taken at face value, that's a very silly story. What numbskull would go to all that trouble? Well, that's the *conscious* take. The *unconscious* take, the metaphor, is that a person can be freed up to choose any number of routes to problem resolution. I have thus perturbed many stuck people with Pills and its cousin, Simple Rooms (adapted from a similar story in Rosen (1992). The same with instigative anecdotes like these (Gafner, 2004):

Instigative anecdotes

Robert Frost
One of the more famous poems of the English language, "Stopping by Woods on a Snowy Evening," surfaced in the mind of Robert Frost after he had been working all night on another poem. He got up from his desk and went outside to look at the rising sun, and as he gazed in the distance, "Stopping by Woods" *suddenly came to him*. "I always thought it was the product of auto-intoxication coming from tiredness," he explained.

Rings in a Dream
August Kekulé, the German chemist who solved the structural riddle of the benzene molecule, labored many days attempting to consciously solve the problem. Then, in a daydream, his unconscious mind generated a structure involving six snakes connected in the form of a hexagon. Upon arousing, his conscious mind recognized this metaphor as representing the elusive structure of the benzene ring.

The Shipworm
In the early nineteenth century in France, Marc Brunel had a lot of time on his hands in a debtor's prison. He found himself studying a common shipworm as it tunneled through a piece of wood. He noticed that as the shipworm gnawed its way into the wood, it secreted a liquid that hardened, and this firm base allowed it to keep pushing forward.

This inspired Brunel's invention, the cast iron tunneling shield, that enabled him to build twin tunnels under the Thames River in

London. The project was an instant success, as more than a million people used the tunnel in the first four months alone.

Painting Landscapes

Vincent Van Gogh journeyed to southern France so he could see nature under a brighter sky. "One feels that the colors of the prism are veiled in the mist of the North," he wrote in a letter. When he arrived, he threw himself into one of the most productive periods of his life, painting haystacks, landscapes, flowering trees, and anything that caught his eye. "I have a terrible lucidity at moments, when nature is so glorious that I am hardly conscious of myself and the picture comes to me as in a dream," he recounted.

Amplifying the metaphor technique

I can't remember whom I should credit with this technique, as I didn't think it up myself. Nevertheless, it is something I have used with success for many years. I employ it primarily within hypnosis, usually after I've seen the person several times; but I've also used it as part of talk therapy. It never ceases to amaze me how it can perturb longstanding problems. A procedure more than a technique, I would rank Amplifying the Metaphor right up at the top among hypnotic procedures. Basically, it involves asking the person to come up with a symbol that *represents the problem,* a symbol for the *absence of the problem,* and then amplifying both, but tying the symbol for not having the problem to an anchor. It is especially useful for anger.

We use this a lot in group hypnosis training. The technique is great for walking that line between therapy and training. Occasionally it can be diagnostic. Example: One Friday afternoon Amplifying was on the training agenda. My co-leader, Bob Hall, announced, "We know none of you guys have any problems, but for this we need someone who has a problem, big problem or little problem, doesn't matter, and you don't even have to reveal what your problem is." We had both zeroed in on a woman psychiatric resident, who looked very anguished that day. Bob subtly directed his question toward the corner where she was sitting, and she eagerly jumped at the chance to be today's subject. She looked quite relieved when it was over. We always ask the subject to at least reveal the symbols they selected. Besides her symbols, the young woman chose to reveal her problem, which was serious, and afterward we directed her to some help.

Let's see how Dr. Tracten gets traction with this technique

George: This darn anger, nothing works. I'm getting steamed up again just talking about it.

Tracten: Okay, George, here's what we'll do today. It's called Amplifying the Metaphor and I think you'll like it. Put your box cutter down for a moment and stop thinking about cutting, okay?

George: If you insist, Dr. Tracten, you always know what's best for me.

Tracten: Just sit back in that recliner, elevate your feet, close your eyes if you wish, and let yourself begin to breathe deeply, breathing in comfort and relaxation, and exhaling any doubt, or tension, negativity or nervousness, letting relaxation, yes, *deep relaxation* fill both your mind and your body. When you're sufficiently comfortable in order to begin this exercise, let me know by nodding your head … very good.

Amplifying *both* metaphors

Tracten: Okay, beginning now, I'd like the back part of your mind to drift and dream, dream and drift, because in a moment I'm going to ask your unconscious mind to generate a symbol or representation for your anger. It can be anything you like, a smell, a sound, a word, a concept, anything at all. For example, one man I was working with came up with the sound of dragging a shovel down the sidewalk, and we know what *that* sounds like. When you have that there, in your mind, a symbol *for the problem,* let me know by letting your "yes" finger rise … very good … holding up okay, George?

George: You didn't touch the box cutter, did you?

Tracten: I guess that means you're doing fine.

George: Let me tell you what symbol I selected.

Tracten: We'll do that later. Take another deep breath and resume your comfortable state … okay, here we go … next, I'd like the deepest part of you to generate a symbol or representation for the absence of the problem, for *not* having the problem. Again, it can be anything at all. If that's okay, you may nod your head one time … very good. Doing fine, George, that's the way … Now, returning to your symbol *for* the problem, that which represents this anger. In a moment I'm going to ask you to amplify it in your mind, exaggerate it, making it strong. So, let's say the symbol is a color, like red, I'll ask you to magnify it, seeing it in all its brilliance and intensity … and do that now, exaggerate-amplify that symbol NOW while I count to three … one, two, and three … and then *just let it go* … (pause for several seconds)

Okay, now, in a moment I'm going to ask you to do the same for your symbol for *not* having the problem, for the absence of the problem, while I count to three again … and while you do so, I'd like you to make your anchor, that familiar circle, by touching your thumb and forefinger together … and do so *now, amplify*, *make strong* that symbol for the absence of the problem while I count, one, two, and three … and now just relax the hand on your lap.

George: (after taking nearly two minutes to reorient) That was cool.

Tracten: So, mind sharing with me what symbols you chose?

George: For the problem, it was dragging my box cutter down the sidewalk. And the other one was waiting in line at the pharmacy for my Coumadin prescription, that and having a cigarette.

Tracten: Good job. The take-home message here is anchor, plain and simple, use your anchor. See you next time.

Notes for practice

Here's another situation where it all boils down to the anchor. No need for the client to remember symbols or anything else, just the anchor, as that connects up to all the unconsciously generated material in the session. What if, in the debriefing, they say, "I couldn't come up with anything." That probably means poor prognosis, for despite what you covered in preceding sessions and all the prompting in this session, their unconscious is putting up a formidable resistance to letting the problem go. I wouldn't waste more time on a person like that and would politely thank them for their effort. I've encountered such a person only once or twice in doing the technique probably a thousand or more times. Usually they really get into it and appreciate your effort at reaching them on a dearly personal level.

I usually reach for amplifying the metaphor before instigative story or anecdote unless intuitively—from knowing the person in preceding sessions—I have an inkling that story or anecdote might be a better fit, but there's no way to avoid it if you want to do meaningful work.

Fish again

Sorry, but the odor of fish is back. You may ask, "Is titillating one's unconscious in reaching for solutions just another fishing expedition?" Well, yes. But when you fish in real life you have to grasp that squirmy body with slippery scales and take the hook out of that poor fish's mouth, but not with this type of fishing. Here, when you weigh the catch it might be a pedestrian minnow or a pricey yellow-fin tuna, the true value known only to the client. For me, the joy is in the discovery, but also in the chase, all safe and on dry land.

Recovered memories

Searching unconsciously invites discussion on recovered memories. If that's your interest, make sure your malpractice insurance is up to date, and hike up your waders or hip boots because you're headed for frigid waters. It's essential to clarify the client's goal, and even then the client may *really* have something else in mind. I had a 40-year-old vet one time who said, "I want to know *what* in my past may be contributing to why I keep shooting myself in the foot." On its face, it's a decent goal. I first did some preparatory ego-strengthening sessions, to which he responded with moderate depth. I then did a search employing age regression, which went nowhere. The next session, I listened to the little alarm bell in my head, bit my tongue, stopped asking questions, just let the guy blab on for a long time, and I learned two important things. First, when this man *heard* age regression, he thought it was *past lives* regression (which I've never done), and second, he thought that this technique would aid in his recovery of forgotten or repressed memories of a supposed trauma in the Navy … "because if it's there, I need to file a claim." Ah, the color green again, the green poultice. I sent him to the grief and loss support group and wished him well.

I believe that if you engage in recovered memory work you are fishing, but fishing for barracuda. I don't like losing my arm to razor-sharp teeth, so I let braver people do that kind of fishing. I've had people whom I respect say that searching for past lives is interesting and valuable, but working in a government agency I never tried it. Yes, it does sound very far-fetched.

Earl the Pearl

Employing perturbation, pattern interruption and instigative stories or anecdotes requires thinking and planning, along with an active role of therapist. Each session, I have on hand stories (unless I can recite them from memory) or other things that I might need that day. Oh, sure, with plenty of my clients whom I saw supportively, I had a more passive stance. Like with Earl, a vet whom a colleague described as "of low gifts." He couldn't read or write and he had a very bad heart condition, but he was good with his hands and got by with odd jobs, cleaning swimming pools and repair jobs. Furthermore, he had a schizophrenic wife and schizophrenic daughter, and as a family, "they were dysfunctional family poster children," according to that same colleague. He said he got a lot of benefit out of "coming in once a month and getting everything off my chest," and I believed him, as he looked very relieved when he left. He would perk up and listen when I told him "how this other guy handled" a similar situation, and occasionally I specifically recommended how he might handle a problem, but mostly my therapeutic posture was quite passive.

And come to think of it, for our own self-care, we require a break now and then, and don't we need some clients like Earl?

CHAPTER SEVEN

Maggie and Charles are back

Case of Maggie

The last few times with Maggie I had gone back to asking if she felt suicidal, as she had some attempts—albeit not real serious ones—in her history. Seeing depressed people is so enervating that, frankly, sometimes I'm glad when they cancel. A month or so passed and then she was back.

On the street I would not have recognized her. She was wearing makeup, a fashionable print dress and heels, and she carried a bright handbag made from a Guatemalan mola. Her hair was in braids, shiny and obsidian. Overnight she had shed the tomboy look and could have passed for a model. She seated her mother in the corner. I greeted her mother, who nodded politely. She looked even more frail and gaunt than last time.

Maggie started speaking before sitting down.

Maggie: Job interview today at a high-end furniture store, commissions are high there.

Therapist: I see. Say, a Talavera pattern on a dress, I've only seen it on ceramic.

Maggie: It's from Guanajuato (a state in Mexico), just like on the trivets and plates.

Therapist: So, it's been a few weeks.

Maggie: Yes, I've been thinking about that—bodies, all those bodies.

Therapist: Huh?

Maggie: Yeah, I have also been thinking about why I mentioned PP's.

Therapist: Yeah, a few times back, I guess it was.

Maggie: Working with dead bodies and all.

Therapist: Really? I just thought you were distracting me, or you said it for the shock effect.

Maggie: Now, that's not narcissistic or anything.

Therapist: Better a narcissist than a sadist.

Maggie: I thought you'd say I was projecting.

Therapist: Boy, you know all the psych lingo. Anyway, PP's, working with bodies in the Persian Gulf, I'm never surprised how much these things connect up.

Maggie: "Like links in a chain," as you mention way too often.

Therapist: "All roads lead to Rome" may be more apt.

I thought, "Here we go, more word play and banter, back on the dance floor. I need to get down to business here. But she beat me to it.

Maggie: I'm no fool, you see it as your job to go after "the beef," remember that slogan, "Where's the beef?"

Therapist: Before your time and mine, a judge asked the notorious bank robber, Willie Sutton, "How come you rob banks, Willie?" You know everything, tell me how he answered.

Maggie: "Because dat's where da money is," I watch the History Channel.

Therapist: So, Maggie, let's cut to the chase here. You show every indication of having suffered traumatically from working with dead bodies over in the sandbox.

Maggie: If it walks like a duck and talks like a—"

Therapist: I'm not doing my job if I don't point that out. Others here in the clinic would tell you to leave and not come back until you're ready to talk about it.

Maggie: But you're not like that, according to the vets in the waiting room.

She was starting to simmer. Her mother's neatly folded hands had become nervous fingers in her lap. I was angry, too, caring too much, a narcissistic wound? Maggie was a darn interesting case; however, at that moment she was one more straw on the camel's back, one more vet who refused to get better, and frustration and anger boiled up in me. I moved my chair close to her mother.

Therapist: (speaking loud in Spanish) What about that, Señora? Your daughter has a problem and she's choosing to hang on to it when she could make it better.

Maggie: That's a low blow. Leave her out of this, damn you!

Just when I thought she might throw something at me, Maggie inhaled deeply, closed her eyes for a second, reached down for the handle and yanked it hard. Her feet rose quickly and she kicked off her shoes. I was already feeling bad about losing my cool. I had no business saying what I did. I'd never been in the service, much less worked with dead bodies.

Maggie: I was about to say that we've gotten away from the stories.

Therapist: Fine by me. But I *will* keep checking on this. No hard feelings?

Maggie: Just leave my mom out of this. She has enough to worry about. At this moment I need to go somewhere else, just do your thing, if you don't mind.

Therapist: Oh, the IBS, what number do you give it today?

Maggie: Around a five. I'm 'moving on'.

Therapist: Pass the fudge.

Maggie: Huh?

Therapist: Bad joke.

Maggie: Oh, now I get it. Yeah, bad joke.

I stole a glance at mom. Her hands had settled down and she now looked asleep, chin on chest. I collected myself and thought about a story. Alternating stories would be just right, I thought.

Therapist: How about some background music?

Maggie didn't answer. She had already drifted off but did not appear asleep. This woman had some capacity for going from aroused angry to calm. I already had a Liquid Mind CD in the boom box. I started it up. Just then I thought, "Was Charles the last one who listened to this? Had they crossed paths in the waiting room?"

Certainly they could be in the waiting room to see a prescriber, or for many other reasons. As I got the music ready I was thinking about how I needed to effect a pattern interruption. But interrupt what *pattern? The more I contemplated alternating stories, the more it seemed apt at this time. What pattern? The only one I could think of right then was the pattern of avoidance, the pattern of distracting me from the core issue. First, I needed to make sure she wasn't asleep.*

Therapist: Maggie, today I'll be telling you two stories, alternating one with the other. One's called The Good Spirit, and the other one is named Simple Rooms. You may nod your head two times if you understand this.

Two head nods came after about 20 seconds.

Alternating Stories: The Good Spirit and Simple Rooms

The Good Spirit
Taken from Gafner (2004); adapted from a story by L.W. Banks (1999)

Therapist: "A few years back, a friend of mine told me about a strange and wonderful place, Begashabito Canyon, on the western end of the Navajo Indian reservation. I was carried along on his journey as he told me about being there with Albert, a Navajo man. 'I couldn't tell his age,' he said. It may have been 50, or it may have been 75 years or more. I was walking with him in this canyon, and he mentioned looking for the Good Spirit, a rather intriguing concept, I thought at the time. 'Good Spirit?' I asked him. He never really answered my question. Instead, he looked away and began to talk about the light, chasing the ever-changing light of the canyon, and being consumed by the color and movement, the interplay of sunshine off the red stone mesas, the shimmering horizons, and the constantly changing wind, always the wind.

"During the course of the day he continued this banter, soft and absorbing, and only by listening very closely did I pick up his fleeting mention of the Good Spirit. I would have forgotten many of the details had I not hastily scribbled some notes before the sun went down. To be sure, some of the main points escaped my grasp as soon as he uttered them. Nevertheless, I continue to experience unconscious impressions from that day, gentle bursts from deep within, whenever I feel a taunting wind on my face, or when I dream about the red mesas.

"I accompanied Albert that day through the vast canyon, bouncing in his pickup truck on little-used roads. We got out and walked near the boarded up Cow Springs Trading Post. 'I follow the voices,' said Albert. His pace was deceptively quick, and I could hear our own voices reverberate off the walls of the dry riverbed. 'I feel like I'm walking in a dream,' I thought to myself. 'You are,' I thought I heard him whisper over his shoulder. Thunder cracked somewhere in the distance, and I realized that this was no place to be if a flash flood was on the way. At that moment he remarked, 'we can get out just up ahead.' 'When do we encounter the Good Spirit?' I asked. I really didn't expect an answer, but he did respond after several seconds. 'Years ago, a man was lost in here, and a violent storm was brewing. The man caught sight of something in the swirling dust up ahead. He urged his horse forward, and then he found safety.'

"'What was swirling out there? The Good Spirit?' I asked. He turned around and faced me. I was glad to stop and catch my breath. He then continued, 'One time, three Navajo children wandered away from their mother's sheep camp. A search party could not find them. As dawn broke, the children walked serenely into camp. "The man with the long coat came, and we followed him out," said the children.' 'No doubt it was the Good Spirit in another form,' I ventured. Just then Albert launched into another story. 'A woman was lost in the wash, the dry riverbed, one time during a storm. She was led to safety by an animal. Don't ask me if it was a deer or some other animal. The woman remarked that no sooner had she cleared the wash a great wall of water swept by.' The story brought me back to the present, the soft sand beneath my feet, and I thought of how a dry riverbed like this could transform into a raging torrent in mere seconds.

"I followed Albert out of the riverbed, and again we were moving specks in the vast red tundra. I saw a cornfield and heard voices, but there was no one in sight. In a few moments we passed some people talking to each other, but their voices were inaudible. 'Was that the Good Spirit?' I asked after we had passed by. If he answered, I did not hear him. My legs were heavy when we arrived back at the trading post. The howling wind was muffled once we were back in Albert's truck. He took his time starting the engine. I sat back, closed my eyes, and contemplated my experience in the canyon.

Back on State Route 98, we glided silently down the road. There was no other traffic. We drove over a pair of work gloves in the road. They were on fire."

(Story continued at the end of Simple Rooms *story)*

Simple Rooms

Therapist: One day, a person, let's call her Julie, came inside, from out in the cold, and she said her problem was that she was having trouble *getting from here to there*. So, I asked her, "Julie, in your house, how would you get from *one room to another*?" She then recounted all the possible ways she could think of for getting from *one room to another*. She could walk in, or crawl in on her knees; she could somersault in; she could walk in backwards; she could enter slowly or quickly; crawl in on her belly; scoot in on her back; enter brushing up against one door jamb, and then the other; or she could go in with big steps, medium steps, or on tiptoe; and she could even go around the house and climb in the back window, and then go from *one room to another*. I actually got out of breath just listening to her.

Finally, after several minutes, she thought she had exhausted all the possible ways to get from *here to there*. But then, as we discussed it further, it came to light that there were many other possible ways to get from *one room to another*. She could go in on the hour or half hour; she could go in after drinking a quarter glass of diet soda, or a half glass of whole milk; she could go in while listening to the radio; she could enter while thinking of something important one time, followed by having her mind blank another time; or she could have a friend present while she went into that other room. Or, if she crawled in wearing shorts one time, she could wear jeans another time.

She could even walk around the block one and one half times before going in, or she could take a taxi to the airport and fly from London to Paris and back again, and then she could go from *one room to another*. We were still coming up with a long, long list of possibilities when we ran out of time, and by then we both were very, very sleepy. At any rate, it was evident to me, and especially evident to Julie, that there was an *infinite number of ways* to get from *one room to another*.

(The Good Spirit concluded)

Therapist: "Back on the Indian reservation in Arizona, they saw the gloves on fire in the road. 'We turned around and headed back. We got out and looked down at the gloves. By then, one glove had turned to ash, and the other was still burning. We stood there for a long time and neither one of us commented. We then got back in the truck and continued down the road.'"

I waited for a couple of minutes. Maggie slowly came around, stretched, and looked at her mother, who had fallen asleep.

Maggie: Time to go, Mom.

Mother: Cuento interesante (interesting story), señor.

Maggie: I think it was at least two stories. I guess you could call them interesting. Now if that wasn't hypnosis, nothing is. When's my next appointment?

Therapist: Yes, Maggie, just reading a couple of stories can definitely hypnotize. Anyway, before you go, what do you remember about the stories?

Maggie: Gloves burning in the road and something about a house, a house, that's all I remember. Cow Springs trading post, I've been by there. That's really remote.

Notes for practice

Erickson was noted for fostering amnesia by doing such things as stopping in mid-sentence and making a phone call, or quickly re-alerting a person and launching into a shaggy dog story. Indeed, we commonly forget many things, especially in trance, but there are ways to hasten the process if your goal is amnesia and percolation. There are various techniques that employ confusion to accomplish this, but one very elegant way is with two stories, a technique I learned from Sonja Benson. How is this done?

Here, my target was Maggie's permission to talk about her trauma, and my means was perturbation—all on an unconscious level—in hopes that she could free herself up and let go. To do this, you prepare two stories. The first story is primarily a distraction, a device to absorb attention, while the second story contains key suggestions directed at your target. You begin the first story, leave it at a critical juncture, and immediately launch into the second story. You complete the second story, then return to the first story, and continue it to the end. I don't use a segue into the second story. The result is—if it works—amnesia for the second story. Again, in extrapolating from the research on paradoxical interventions, be patient while the suggestions percolate in the unconscious. The George in Dr. Tracten's office says, "Beware of fuzzy-headed notions," whereas George the author advises 10 to 14 days as the incubation period, while the researchers say one month (Shoham-Salomon & Rosenthal, 1987).

Now, from what I've seen from people who try this for the first time, therapists think, "Hmm, that first story, what an opportunity to exploit, I might as well stick a lot of suggestions in the first story, too." Nope, don't even go there. Keep it simple. You're assigning a major task to the person's unconscious mind and there's no need to obfuscate things. If ever in doubt, go with the law of parsimony: Less is more, and do only what is necessary to achieve the desired effect.

The case of Charles continues

Due to mutual scheduling conflicts, I didn't see Charles for nearly four weeks. In the interim, I spent some time online reading up on the circumstances of his being awarded a Purple Heart and the Army's Distinguished Service Cross, an award second only to the Congressional Medal of Honor. Briefly, the setting was in South Vietnam in 1968. Charles was a medic attached to an air cavalry unit. He was helping to evacuate wounded in helicopters when they came under fire from the enemy. Their two helicopters were destroyed and several soldiers were killed along with the other medic on the mission. As the lone survivor, Charles single-handedly rescued six of his fellow soldiers and began first aid for their wounds. Using other soldiers' M-16 rifles and explosives he protected the wounded and held off the enemy until help arrived. One source lauded his efforts in the loftiest of terms, citing Charles' "uncommon bravery, courage, ferocity and extraordinary disregard for his own safety in probably the single-most act of heroism in the war." In short, he was a highly decorated war hero. Like other war celebrities and prisoners of war I had known, his peace-time behavior was consistent in that he played down his part and praised the heroism of others.

In the interim I asked Charles to 1) write the words VANDEST LYRE with a bold marker on a 3 × 5 card and tape it to the dashboard of his Bentley, and 2) take some leisurely drives in the mountains and desert while listening to wind chimes music. Today, Charles looked rested, relaxed and confident. His smugness was back in full force.

Therapist: I read what you did in Vietnam, quite an accomplishment. I'm not a vet, as I told you, don't know what it's like to be shot at, but I've been able to glean a bit working here all these years.

Charles: You didn't miss anything … that was a long time ago, ancient history now. Anymore I don't even think about it unless someone brings it up. What were you doing in those years?

Therapist: I was a hippy with hair down the middle of my back, an antiwar protester, if you can believe it.

Charles: No doubt you loved Jane Fonda. You were one of many self-righteous hedonists, angry and unpatriotic; traitors, really. Yes, I can see you as that.

Interestingly, this time his eyes began circling after he had loosed his little barb, which I wasn't about to respond to.

Therapist: So, when you came in you said you felt "beaten to a pulp." Still feel black and blue, with some residual swelling, all healed up? If it was a 10 then, what might it be now?

Charles: A one or two, hardly there. A barely palpable tenderness is extant, if that aids your feeble metaphor. That last session helped me a lot. I'm sleeping well.

Therapist: How did it go—the words, driving and all?

Charles: I took five nice, long drives. Up the Catalina highway to the cool pines, out by the Desert Museum, out in Saguaro National Monument, all very pleasant. Nothing new on the words. I feel good, not much anxiety lately. It's been a few weeks.

Therapist: Maybe that's the answer: To stop coming here and take rides in your Bentley instead.

Charles: Disdain aside, you might have something there. I have done precisely that with some of my clients, especially when we were stuck.

Therapist: How stuck are we here, if at all?

Charles: Not at all. I think I'm making great progress. That automatic writing was highly potent.

Therapist: So,—

I never got to finish my sentence, as a woman had suddenly burst into the office, trailed by a harried-looking clerk.

Clerk: I couldn't stop her.

Charles: Oh, God, no, Bernadette! How could you!

Charles' wife bursts into the session

It was Charles' wife. With the violence of her entry I half-expected her to pull a gun out of her purse. Stranger things have happened here where people can legally carry concealed weapons. This is Arizona in the Wild West, after all.

Bernadette: Lies, lies, Mr. Gafner. You've been taken in by a first-class sociopath.

Therapist: Umm, I guess … well, why don't you sit down, if it's okay with Charles, it's his session.

Charles: I can't exactly say no. I cannot believe this!

There goes my plan for today, I thought. All of a sudden I have a marital session. I needed to remember that Charles was my client here, at least at this point. This was a highly-charged situation that could get out of control. I thought, "Great, she is sitting down, that's a good start. Ground rules, set some ground rules."

Therapist: Okay, we have about 45 minutes left. How about if I hear from both of you, say, Bernadette first for maybe 15 minutes or less, then Charles for the same. Then at the end we'll see where we stand.

They both grunted their approval. Bernadette launched right in.

Bernadette: I apologize for bursting in here, I know that's wrong, but this has been building up so long I can't take it any longer. I called him a socio-path, he's probably not that, but he can be so devious. Those words he has taped to his dashboard, he knows what they mean. He just doesn't want to admit it to you. Why can't he just take off the mask?

Then, the mutual fusillade commenced, back and forth, a litany of complaints, her excessive spending, his emotional distancing; she spends too much time at work and doesn't appreciate the stress of his job; she gives too much money to her kids; she can't trust him; he's secretive, he locks the door when he's on the computer and has magazines with nude women in the bathroom. I tried to keep order and set some ground rules but knew it would be futile. How many other first sessions with couples had I endured, the rancor and blame, attacking the other while defending themselves, each trying to convince the therapist who's right? All you can do is suck it up, try to impose some structure, and not let it get out of hand.

Therapist: Hold on for a minute. I need to ask my boss something.

I caught Alice, the director of the clinic, in a free moment and explained the situation. "What I'd like to do is continue to see him while I see them as a couple," I said. She reminded me that my main responsibility was family therapy. "Can't he see someone in town on his own?" she asked. I said, "He trusts the V.A., the V.A. knows where he's coming from, plus just about everybody in town knows him socially or from professional meetings. He'd have to go to Phoenix (a two-hour drive)." She said that ideally another in the clinic would see him individually but that with the increase in clients from the second Persian Gulf war he'd have to go on a waiting list for at least two months. "Doesn't sound like we can give him to a trainee," she said, "No way." So, I went back to my office with a plan.

Aside from a plan, getting up and leaving very briefly during a session has always helped clear my head and sometimes reframe the situation. He was shaking his fist at her when I went back in.

Therapist: Things ever get out of hand physically in your home? Last thing you need right now is the police hauling one or both of you to jail.

They assured me there was no domestic violence. They had several firearms at home but neither had ever threatened the life of the other. I asked them if now might be a good time to have someone hold the guns for them. Charles agreed to "store the ammunition in the garage—but only for a week or so." Fine, that's better than nothing.

Therapist: Let me run this by you: You guys badly need some marital therapy, and Charles, you seem like you could benefit from continued individual therapy. I can see you as a couple, if you want to do that, or you could go to someone in town. Charles, you may not want to see someone in town.

Charles: You got that right. We should both come here.

Therapist: So, let's do this. I can see you two together about every 10 days or so, say, for six sessions to start—then we'll see where we're at—and Charles, I'll continue with you about every couple of weeks, how's that sound? Oh, and before you go, let me mention pineapples.

Pineapple anecdote

Norma Barretta reminds us about the guy working at the end of the conveyor belt at the pineapple farm in Hawaii. His job was simple: Put the good ones here, put the rotten ones over there. Good ones here, rotten ones over there.

Bernadette: What's that supposed to mean? Charles, you know this stuff?

Charles: My mind is wasted right now.

Therapist: Norma uses that anecdote to remind us that *we always get what we're looking for*.

Bernadette: Oh.

Charles: Yeah, we expect the bad and that's all we see. I get the point. Maybe we'll talk about it, dear.

They concurred on the therapy arrangement. Bernadette mentioned that a few years back she went to a therapist for herself and didn't feel like she needed that now. I realized that with this plan some might fault me on ethical grounds, as I was biased having known Charles already. This was not the first time I'd done it this way, having had similar arrangements when there wasn't a Spanish-speaking therapist available for a wife, for example. In a busy clinic you usually end up doing what's expedient.

We were out of time. I still wanted to know what Bernadette meant about the words, so I asked.

Bernadette: Vandalism, that's what the one word means, and LYRE, connect the dots, George. L-I-A-R, get it? He lies and brags about it, and he gets his kicks making crank phone calls, scratching up my colleague's car with his key, spitting on his windshield; peeing on the floor in restaurants, stuff like that.

Charles: Am I supposed to plead guilty? So, I'm a bit passive-aggressive at times. Plenty of people like me. My clients *adore* me.

Therapist: That's some major hostility your wife is describing.

My head was spinning. I wish I hadn't asked. A week ago MY new pickup truck had been "keyed" in the V.A. parking lot. I asked him.

Charles: Don't be ridiculous, George. You are my ally in this war. And it is a war, make no mistake about it. We're on the same side here.

His words chilled me but what chilled me more was his expression when he said the words, that piercing gaze beneath those heavy lids while the eyebrows arched high in inquiry. A statement within a question; a truth within doubt. The incongruence was again slapping my face. Today, as Charles nervously moved his head back and forth, and as he ever so quickly flicked his ponytail from one side to the other, it came to me, what I had been dreaming about. A horse up ahead of me, its tail swishing back and forth. I'm behind, in an old-fashioned carriage, being pulled by that horse.

I got their agreement to take a time-out when things heated up, and to try and notice something they appreciated about the other person. Then they left. Thankfully, my last appointment of the day had canceled. I sat there with my head spinning again. I felt foolish for being duped by a master manipulator. The unconscious exploration—the non-verbals, the affect, everything—had seemed genuine, had fit the situation. I'd never known someone to fake all that, but now I wondered about the genuineness of even the automatic writing ... Now I had my work cut out for me. In taking on the challenge of them, I hoped I hadn't exaggerated my capacity for helping, and hoped I wouldn't regret today.

Notes for practice

Before they left, I asked them if they would listen at home to a CD I would make for them. I recorded it the next day and mailed it out. On it was the Slot Canyon story (Gafner, 2004), followed by instigative anecdotes at the end of the story. This story has many features of the ambiguous function assignment. I hoped to perturb Charles, but perturb in which way, I didn't know. Working in the V.A. all these years I knew that many times I need look no farther than war and guilt.

Slot Canyon story

The following account, dated September 10, 1955, was discovered among the papers of Arthur Sliceman, a psychiatrist who moved to Arizona from Iowa in the 1930s. Dr. Sliceman is long deceased, and the client's name in this account is omitted for reasons of privacy.

"I have been in therapy for my problem for the past seven and a half months. I am writing this report for my therapist, Dr. Sliceman. I undertook an assignment for him, and thinking back on it now, I believe that the objective of this assignment was accomplished.

"I was bogged down in life, in therapy, in all ways, and Dr. Sliceman convinced me to take a journey, an arduous journey, to a place of my choosing, where I would discover an answer to my problem. I chose to try and find the Secret Pass in the Black Mountains in northwest Arizona. I had read various accounts of this area, which has seen lost Spanish missionaries, vengeful Indians, and Union soldiers from the Civil War turned miners defending their veins of gold.

"I drove my '54 Oldsmobile as far as I could and got out to walk. I walked for several minutes in the bone-dry dust and suddenly felt as if in a dream. I found myself in a steep gully choked with loose rock and thick brush. I slid down the flinty shale, hoping to find another ledge. I can still hear the cries of cactus wrens way up above. The collared lizards moved, but I could not hear them. There were large boulders all around as I continued my descent. Soon, I was in a winding sandy wash, with 100-foot red granite walls, and there were caves way up in the walls. I could barely see high desert greenery way above.

"I continued walking and soon I encountered a massive sandstone cliff face split by a curious dark, narrow slit. Undaunted, I squeezed my body into the aperture. It was both dusty and moist in there. I had only a canteen, no flashlight, and I was not prepared for total darkness on a blazing bright day. I inched along, first on hands and knees, and then on foot. I tripped on something. My hands fumbled blindly down there. I could tell it was shredded canvas and bone. I continued on, not certain if I should turn back or forge ahead. Could a precipice await me?

"I lost my sense of time as the path wound deeper into the cliff. Thinking back, I had suddenly lost my fear, and during that time I contemplated my problem and the reason for undertaking this venture. A tremendous fatigue came over me. I crouched down and squeezed my knees to my chest. Then, I lay down and my eyes closed all by themselves. Some time later I awoke to a loud thumping of my heart and a rushing sound in my ears. My mind swam in disorientation. I realized where I was, but from which way did I come? I rose to my feet and moved, holding my hands out in front of me, feeling my way, but there was nothing to feel, as I moved on.

"After what may have been seconds or many minutes, the darkness gave way to a veiled physicality, then a filtered light, and soon marvelous tapestry walls surrounded me. I blinked my eyes and looked all around me. Where did the light come from? I could see no sky. I had wandered into a slot canyon, a wind-and-water-fashioned sanctum of dancing shapes and swirling colors. Jagged edges of rock blended with soft curves. This was a visual symphony. No, it was a sandstone symphony! I remember the quiet, the silence. Deep purple changed to red and tan, and soon my feet were kicking small rocks and dried tumbleweeds in a dry riverbed. I shaded my eyes from the intense glare of the sun. I had lost both my canteen and sunglasses along the way.

"Dr. Sliceman had given me instructions that were both explicit and general. I was to go alone to a natural place of my choosing, and some time during the journey I would discover something important about my problem. Well, if only I possessed words to describe what I experienced in that slot canyon. How could my problem *not* have changed as a result?" (Adapted from Taylor, 1992; Fatali, 1991.)

Instigative anecdotes (Gafner, 2004)

Helen Keller
Helen Keller looked forward to passing through what she called the "portals of sleep," where her dreaming mind let her experience "clear seeing all night long."

Labyrinth
Our English language is very flexible, but it also may promote confusion. Consider the five ways we have of making *labyrinth* into an adjective: labyrinthian, labyrinthean, labyrinthal, labyrinthine, and labyrinthic.

After the Pond
Edwin Way Teale was editing an edition of Thoreau's *Walden*. As he checked the writer's journals he discovered that a large proportion of the entries were made *after* Walden left the pond.

Post-It Notes
Post-it sticky notepaper happened when a 3-M Company researcher, Spence Silver, needed to make bookmarks for the hymnals for his church choir.

Mark Twain
Mark Twain once remarked that the greatest of all inventions is accident.

CHAPTER EIGHT

PTSD and war

Persian Gulf War (383 U.S. Dead)

In August 1990, Iraqi leader Saddam Hussein invaded and occupied neighboring Kuwait. January 1991 began 42 days of relentless air and ground attack by an allied coalition with participation from 15 countries. This brief war ended February 28, 1991, when most Iraqi forces in Kuwait either fled or surrendered. With the terrorist attacks on 9/11/2001, U.S. and allied forces invaded Afghanistan. In 2003 U.S. and allied forces invaded Iraq. At this writing in April 2013 both wars continue. Among allied forces, some 9,000 have been killed, the majority from the U.S. and U.K.

Exposure to trauma and stress in the Persian Gulf War (PGW)

The majority of authors studying the PGW concluded that PTSD rates among U.S. military personnel are generally lower than those from prior wars, with the exception of heavily exposed units, such as Graves Registration. In 1991, Graves Registration was renamed Mortuary Service. Among numerous studies, PTSD rates in PGW personnel range from 3–50 percent, with most studies on the lower end. One study evaluated 3,000 Army personnel deployed to the PGW and found that PTSD rates within five days of return were modest, 4–9 percent, a finding substantiated by other studies. Female soldiers reported higher rates of PTSD symptoms than men, along with depression, anxiety and health problems. Several other studies found higher rates of PTSD overall in women and ethnic minorities. Sutker, et al. (1995), among others, found a strong positive correlation between stressor intensity and adverse psychological outcomes.

Southwick, et al. (1995) studied longitudinal consequences of PGW service and found moderate levels of PTSD symptomatology in two National Guard (civilian soldiers in the U.S.) units at one and six months. Among the major symptom categories in PTSD, re-experiencing (intrusive recollecting), avoidance/numbing, and hyper-arousal, generally hyper-arousal was the most severe. The authors conducted a two-year follow-up of the original cohort which revealed further increases in symptom levels, with hyper-arousal still the most elevated.

SCUD missiles

I remember speaking to several returnees who described frightening SCUD missile attacks. Especially worrisome was the fear that the missiles could bring chemical warfare, and soldiers were required to hastily don gas masks and protective equipment, day or night. Bleich, et al. (1992), in their study of psychiatric sequelae of SCUD missile attacks on Israeli civilians during the PGW, also concluded that the threat of chemical warfare affected the number and nature of stress reactions.

As you may recall, Maggie dates the beginning of her constipation-predominant IBS to "when a SCUD missile flew over and scared the shit out of me." However, later in therapy she reveals details of her mortuary duties which were more significant stressors than SCUD missile attacks.

PTSD among mortuary workers in the PGW

McCarroll, et al. (1995) found high levels of distress among U.S. military mortuary workers *prior* to the arrival of human remains. The authors concluded that fear and discomfort with mutilation and the grotesque, and defensiveness or denial, were significant predictors of intrusion and avoidance, with the results having implications for staff selection, training and interventions. Prior distress aside, various studies confirmed high rates of PTSD among people who had performed mortuary duties in this war. Sutker, et al. (1994) studied

24 Army reservists who endorsed anxiety, anger and depression as well as multiple health and somatic complaints. Fifty percent of this group met criteria for PTSD, a diagnosis strongly associated with depressive and substance use disorders. The authors cited the gruesome aspects of body recovery and identification in a war zone as stressors of significant negative impact. In another study of PGW mortuary workers, Sutker, et al. (1995) found current and lifetime PTSD rates of 48 percent and 65 percent respectively.

McCarroll, et al. (1993) found that handling human remains was associated with increased intrusion and avoidance symptoms, and those who were inexperienced at handling remains had elevated PTSD symptoms relative to controls. Pre-war sexual abuse in women is associated with wartime psychiatric morbidity, especially PTSD (Engel, et al., 1993). Interestingly, this is one factor not related to Maggie. Excluding combat-related duties, among the factors associated with the development of PTSD in the PGW—mortuary duty, inexperience in mortuary duty, female, ethnic minority—abuse is the lone absent factor in her case. Associated with a PTSD diagnosis were health problems, depression and substance abuse, all of which were endorsed by Maggie.

In my work at the V.A., around 2001, I worked with a 39-year-old man with florid PTSD who had not been in a war zone but whose duties were similar to mortuary workers. He was in the Coast Guard on the Great Lakes and he recounted finding and handling numerous bloated bodies ("We called them 'floaters'," he recalled) among the drowned, along with mangled and disfigured bodies from accidents and fires. He declined EMDR treatment and therapy consisted of supportive hypnosis, but only *after* each incident was thoroughly verbally processed and reframed. This helped him considerably, but what helped him more was that all this was now a part of his record, which was used in determining his 100% service-connected status (full disability, some 2,800 tax-free dollars a month at that time).

Barriers to treatment

Fortunately, military personnel today have access to an array of mental health treatment modalities, many more than were available to returnees of the PGW. The stigma attached to seeking help has eased, though many returnees from the current wars in Iraq and Afghanistan (chiefly Air Force and Army returnees) told me that their mental health records were not confidential, and that seeking care could hinder promotion. Nevertheless, both psychiatric assistance and psychotherapy are available today during active duty. Once personnel leave active duty there is a range of help available from the V.A., which has literally pumped billions of dollars into their system to meet current needs, especially assessment and treatment of PTSD and traumatic brain injury.

However, as was the case after the Vietnam war, personnel are slow to seek help. Even though current returnees have the highest priority and are fast-tracked for substance abuse and mental health treatment, many eschew it, as they yearn to resume family and career, not desiring reminders of the war. Maggie was typical for the PGW, seeking treatment many years afterward. I asked her and others why they waited so long to seek treatment. Their answers varied but generally fit into three categories: 1) family or law enforcement propelled them, 2) the stigma diminished as they saw their friends seek help, or 3) years of failed adaptation eroded denial of their problems.

PTSD treatment in the V.A.

World War I (116,000 U.S. Dead)
Very little help for mental health issues was available to these veterans when they returned to the States at war's end in 1918. The most organized help of any kind was for tuberculosis, and many spent years in TB sanitariums. The forerunner of the modern V.A., the Veterans Bureau, came into being in 1930, 12 years after the end of the war. Up until the 1990s I saw veterans of WW I ("the war to end all wars"), and heard stories about trench warfare and mustard gas attacks. By then these men were very aged, and mental health

144

needs were typically identified as part of geriatric medical care. Had these veterans been heavy drinkers or smokers, they would not have survived until then, and any PTSD had been successfully contained for decades. Earl T., who was a prisoner of war of the Germans for several weeks, described "nightmares during the day," but such re-experiencing didn't prevent him from success in business and family life. He patiently endured people like me who were curious about his successful adaptation.

World War II (405,000 U.S. Dead), Korea (92,000) and Vietnam (58,000)

U.S. involvement in World War II from 1941–45 saw some 16 million U.S. men and women in uniform, and in 1945 when they came back from Europe and the Pacific many citizens feared these "shell-shocked" returnees. Veterans' hospitals could not cope with the influx of head injuries, amputations and other problems. However, Congress soon revamped the system, with one major improvement being the V.A.'s affiliation with universities to train residents in medicine, surgery, and psychiatry, along with interns in psychology, social work, nursing and other allied health professions.

In 1970, I worked in a state psychiatric hospital in Illinois which housed chronic schizophrenics and the brain-injured, many of them veterans. One, Annie, had had two lobotomies to try to control psychosis. One day she bit the watch off the doctor's wrist and swallowed it down. An employee was assigned to monitor her bowel movements and a day or so later the watch was retrieved and washed. The grateful doctor held it aloft for all to see and exclaimed, "This Timex didn't lose a second." In those days, insulin shock therapy, wrapping people in cold sheets, and lobotomies had fallen out of fashion. Thorazine was the main agent to treat psychosis. I remember one man for whom Thorazine was used *diagnostically*. No one could tell for sure if he was psychotic, so he was given massive doses of the agent to see if it would affect him. Sure enough, he adequately tolerated it, so he received a psychotic diagnosis. In those days we used the latest edition of the *Diagnostic and Statistical Manual* (DSM-II), which was about one-half inch thick.

After the war, PTSD was not in the nomenclature, but people with that disorder were labeled traumatic neurosis, a common diagnosis in the V.A. Also at that time, many with what we now call PTSD were mistakenly diagnosed as schizophrenic. I knew several veterans whose diagnosis was switched to PTSD after the diagnosis first appeared in 1978 in the DSM-III. In the 1950s and 1960s, stays in the hospital were often a year or more. Individual psychotherapy was solidly psychodynamic and there was little opportunity to discuss trauma, as a "good therapist" successfully dissuaded veterans from talking about their wartime experience. An exception to the psychodynamic approach after the war was the work of John and Helen Watkins, who were psychologists way ahead of their time. They pioneered exposure techniques within hypnosis and heralded what is now known as age regression, abreaction and reframing (Hammond, 1990), possibly the most effective of several exposure techniques within formal hypnosis.

Sam Atterbury (personal communication, 2013), a V.A. social worker who retired in 2003, described standard assessment and treatment of WW II veterans in V.A. hospitals after the war. He was an intern in the Kansas City, Missouri V.A. in the late 1950s. Each WW II vet received a mental health work-up that included a detailed psychosocial history, full battery of psychological testing including projective tests like the ink blot test; psychiatric evaluation, review of functioning and response to past treatment. All this was done *before* beginning treatment. The completeness of the work-up, especially evaluation by a clinical psychologist, is much different from today's V.A. where by comparison very little assessment is done, as clients typically begin therapy shortly after their first interview in the mental health clinic.

Many veterans of the Korean War (1950–1953) avoided veterans' hospitals. In fact, many avoided even identifying themselves as Korean War veterans. Korea was not only a war "we didn't win," but a notion prevailed that these men had been "brainwashed by the Red Chinese" (as in the *Manchurian Candidate* movie), and therefore could not be trusted. "They were like shadows, we seldom saw them," one V.A. physician from that era told me. So there was much heavy drinking and suffering in silence by these veterans and their families. Not until after the Vietnam War did many venture into the V.A.

Vietnam War

Some nine million served in the Vietnam War (1963–1975). The time period heralded the next major upgrade of the V.A. system. A friend of mine, Carlo, age 65, spent two years in military and veterans hospitals, paralyzed from the waist down after being shot in the back in Vietnam. He recalls being one of 50 paraplegics housed in a large room in a Boston veterans' hospital. "We talked some to the nurses who were taking care of us, but there was no psychologist or anyone else around," he recalls (personal communication, 2010). According to many Vietnam veterans, not only was Vietnam "a war we lost because we had one hand tied behind our backs," (meaning that the U.S. could have won the war if they had bombed North Vietnam and not suffered under an overall policy of restraint), a vigorous anti-war sentiment in the country blamed returning military as "baby killers." Unlike previous wars whose volunteers and draftees were comprised primarily of the psychologically fit, some of these veterans were premorbidly dysfunctional or problematic. I knew many whom the local judge had given a choice between jail or military service; and most chose the latter.

Early in the war there was a program dubbed "McNamara's 100,000," in which military service was marketed to poor and uneducated young men as a path to social and career advancement. Entry requirements were eased for even more than 100,000 of these men, who came from primarily rural areas and city ghettos. Most ended up in combat in Vietnam. I saw several of these veterans. All were illiterate or mentally retarded. One man from Mississippi had an IQ of 65 and somehow he had been responsible for directing an artillery strike. His error resulted in nearly 100 "friendly fire" deaths. He had PTSD from before the war and now he was plagued by guilt and re-experiencing from Vietnam. He coped poorly, drank excessively, and had a succession of wives who enjoyed his generous V.A. disability benefits. Psychotherapy was no help to him.

Help from medication

However, this man with the low IQ *was* helped by psychotropic agents. Little attention is given to medication issues in this book, but we should not overlook their immense contribution. Without them people would be unable to manage intense affect, work, sleep, or hold a family together, much less participate in psychotherapy. In family therapy I had many wives of veterans complain of the veteran's over-sedation. For sure, in hypnosis I could expect some to start snoring before two minutes had passed. Medication doses can be adjusted, easier than tweaking the equivalent in psychotherapy.

Substance abuse

Many heroin addictions began in Vietnam. I knew several Vietnam veterans who, early in the war, were able to ship home in their duffel bags large quantities of marijuana and other drugs. Accordingly, flourishing substance abuse was part of adjustment issues. Some of the angry and hostile veterans continued to wear camouflage clothing and lived isolated lives long after the war. Few of these alienated veterans wished to deal with the cumbersome bureaucracy of veterans' hospitals, so the V.A. opened hundreds of Vet Centers, small neighborhood counseling centers that advertised "help without hassles." Vet Centers still operate today and now see veterans of current wars along with those of past wars. Among the current, large homeless population in the U.S., many are Vietnam veterans.

Psychotherapy and PTSD

Intrusive images

Many times they are re-experiencing symptoms of PTSD for which clients seek psychological or psychiatric help. Flashbacks ("It's happening again!") and intrusive recollections may cause significant distress. These are predominantly visual in nature and can take the form of "film clips" of part of the trauma, single images, sounds, smell, sensations, or thoughts. Eliciting these experiences from the client readily guides the therapist to the parts of the trauma that are most disturbing (Holmes, et al., 2005). Ehlers & Clark (2000) argue that intrusions are the sensations that occurred in the moments just before the main trauma and function as a warning signal, thus explaining why intrusions induce a sense of serious current threat. According to one cognitive model of PTSD, intrusions reflect points in the trauma memory that have received inadequate processing. This is because memory at moments of extreme arousal is encoded primarily in a sensory-perceptual manner, rather than as a verbal narrative. This form of memory encoding is more likely to be triggered as involuntary intrusions. Conversely, memories about which people have created a verbal narrative, e.g., actively processed in therapy or elsewhere, are less likely to be retrieved involuntarily (Holmes, et al., 2005).

The elements of this discussion need to be conveyed in understandable terms to clients, as they badly need help in understanding why they behave like they do. Maggie, like some veterans, was interested in explanations, and also similar to other clients with PTSD, she was interested but only up to a point. It seems that too much explanation and detail may overwhelm them.

EMDR and cognitive-behavioral therapy (CBT)

In a randomized, controlled trial involving civilian trauma survivors in the Netherlands, Nijdam, et al. (2012) compared eye movement desensitization and reprocessing (EMDR) to brief eclectic therapy, which consisted of imaginal exposure, cognitive restructuring and other components. The researchers found both treatments effective but EMDR resulted in a faster recovery compared with gradual improvement with brief eclectic therapy. Now, these results mirror the current state of research on therapy and PTSD where both EMDR and any number of versions of CBT totally dominate the literature as effective treatments. As such, these evidence-based, manualized approaches predominate inside and outside the V.A., but this was not always so.

During the Vietnam War a new school of therapy, behavior therapy, burst on to the scene. Among techniques such as reinforcement, extinction, and desensitization, was flooding, which meant that in a highly structured, 20-minute-or-more session, the client was inundated repeatedly with a negative stimulus (the stressor), thus activating the fear response over and over again so the client becomes habituated to it. Nowadays in many circles, flooding, which was renamed prolonged exposure, or PE, may be less intense, consisting of talking about, say, the killing of people in a village in Vietnam, over and over again in individual or group therapy. One technique commonly used is having the client make an audio recording of the stressor and having them listen to their own voice describe the stressor over and over again. I use that technique with Maggie in this book. Thanks to Albert Ellis and others, starting in the 1970s a cognitive component was added to the behavioral in what we now call CBT. What in the nomenclature was flooding became PE, which is now encompassed by the term *trauma-focused therapy*.

Trauma-focused psychotherapy is practiced world-wide

Edna Foa and colleagues (Powers, et al., 2010) conducted a meta-analysis of two decades of world-wide research of treatments for chronic PTSD. In studies involving medication only, more clients responded to medication (59%) compared to placebo (38%). However, the best evidence and treatment guidelines suggest trauma-focused therapy is more effective than medication and should be considered a first line treatment for PTSD. Their analysis demonstrated that trauma-focused CBT, EMDR, stress management and group trauma-focused CBT were more effective than non-trauma-focused treatments at reducing PTSD symptoms. As such, they note that trauma-focused therapy is a highly effective treatment for the disorder, resulting in substantial treatment gains that are maintained over time.

Watching part of a movie over and over again

At the V.A., I saw a man who had been disfigured from a helicopter crash in Vietnam. Thirty years after the war, he cowered with anxiety and fear whenever a helicopter flew over in Tucson. He had been helped some by individual and group therapy, and his sleep and nightmares improved with medication. He was referred to me for hypnosis, but before any hypnosis was done he and I agreed on a plan of brief exposure therapy. In the movie, *Apocalypse Now,* there is a scene where air cavalry helicopters invade a Vietcong village. Not only are the helicopters very loud, but so is Wagner's *Ride of the Valkyries* music blasting from speakers on the attacking helicopters. With the volume up high I had him watch this, over and over again, and at the end of each viewing he rehearsed deep breathing and an anchor. No actual hypnosis was ever done and he hated me for putting him through this; however, he had to admit that he could now tolerate helicopters flying over him.

EMDR

Thanks to Francine Shapiro, the inventor of EMDR, therapists finally had a true brief therapy modality, invented in a moment of serendipity, that in many cases worked wonders. In fact, just a few years back, a plethora of studies showed that EMDR had more research support for treating PTSD than any other modality. For years, academics loved to bad mouth EMDR as a "quick fix" that couldn't be explained theoretically. How many other therapy techniques, not to mention inventions in everyday life, have originated from a sudden burst of inspiration, rather than flowing rationally from theory? Shapiro happened on EMDR quite by accident and it may be the most compelling therapeutic development of the last century. At the Tucson V.A., I was one of a group of therapists who received EMDR training when it became available in the early 1990s. I went on to employ it with some 200 clients, some at the V.A. but more at the university refugee clinic where I volunteered to treat victims of torture. I estimate that more than 60 percent benefited significantly from its application, most after only a few sessions.

I remember Maria, a woman from El Salvador, who in the early 1980s woke up covered in blood on her living room floor, her family slain around her. She fled north and ended up in Tucson. Fast forward, to the mid-1990s and the refugee clinic, where she told her story to doctors who immediately referred her to me. She made it to the waiting room of the clinic several times, but always fled before she could be seen. A few months later she finally entered my office.

I explained EMDR, she agreed to begin, and I had done less than 10 passes (moving my finger back and forth in her field of vision while she held the image of her living room in her mind), when she dissociated, staring off in the distance. I told her, "That's fine, Maria, take as long as you need out there," and I read a newspaper for ten minutes until she reoriented. She then said she had to go and when she left she looked somewhat less distressed. When she returned in two weeks she looked radically different, calm and happy. "The other maids at the hotel say I'm not nervous anymore," she said, adding that her husband couldn't believe the change in her. Other responses to EMDR were less dramatic; however, they were convincing enough so that for PTSD the first thing I would reach for was EMDR, which has finally been accepted as an evidence-based, trauma-focused therapy.

Culture and EMDR

The cultural perspective was always intriguing. One woman from Guatemala described government gunships blasting an elementary school in which all her children were killed. She didn't view this as a catastrophic stressor, but as something normal "because it happened to everybody." Accordingly, her level of distress was low. After one session of EMDR it stayed low. The doctor who referred her insisted "she must be more symptomatic secondary to what she experienced," but I held out for no further treatment. "She sleeps well, she's not anxious or depressed. Are we trying to create a problem here?" I asked. Back to Maria from El Salvador, who was helped by one session of EMDR. "Why do you think you were nervous and sad?" I asked her. "Oh, from some pill I took in my country," she answered. Such was a common explanation of refugees and who was I to argue with them? With the technique, abreaction can come swiftly, like gasoline on the fire, and you better have the box of tissues nearby. It is used with Maggie in this book (but not described), but as the results were equivocal I had to move on to other techniques.

Current V.A. treatment

Nine million veterans are enrolled in the V.A. nationwide. Those who receive outpatient mental health treatment may visit mental health clinics at 152 medical centers, 817 freestanding outpatient clinics and 300 Vet Centers. As such, the V.A. is the biggest employer of psychiatrists, psychologists, social workers, nurses and other mental health professionals in the country. EMDR is used along with other trauma-focused treatments, such as CBT, which predominates in a group therapy format. Veterans attend focused, structured group therapy with like populations, e.g., a PTSD group for returnees from Afghanistan, PTSD group for Vietnam veterans, a group with a depression focus for older veterans, a group with a PTSD focus for women raped in the military, etc. Individual therapy is available and with time-limited sessions.

Up until 2009, the V.A.'s group and individual therapy offerings were more general and permissive, where, for example, Vietnam vet support groups went on for years, or a therapist would see an individual client for a long time. Hypnotic treatment continues to be offered at the Tucson V.A., but generally for problems other than PTSD. In the immediate vicinity of Tucson, population one million, there are some 97,000 veterans, with 52,000 enrolled in the V.A. system. The mental health workforce for these veterans is 13 psychiatrists, two psychiatric nurse practitioners, 15 social workers and six psychologists. PE as part of CBT is done on a regular basis along with cognitive processing therapy (CPT), acceptance and commitment therapy (ACT). Indeed, throughout the nation the V.A. is the foremost expert in treating those "nervous from the service."

Complicity in Compresses?

However, trauma-focused therapy is not practiced in all quarters. Some therapists shy away from exposure techniques in general because of its aversiveness. "I don't like inflicting pain on my clients," one PTSD therapist told me. Also, from the client's standpoint, many don't like constantly opening up an old wound, even if they're told that the technique will likely make them better. Accordingly, nowadays, I believe, some therapists concentrate on the cognitive at the expense of the behavioral and sometimes exposure simply does not get done. It seems to be less thorny and more palatable for some therapists to practice an avoidant approach, like mindfulness-based therapy, or acceptance and commitment therapy (ACT). Certainly these and similar approaches have demonstrated results. Fortunately for me, over the years my primary responsibility was family therapy, though in individual therapy I saw a wide range of clinical problems, of which PTSD was one. If my job had been to see *only* PTSD clients and conduct exposure sessions all day long I'm sure I would have soon escaped it for something easier.

I don't downplay the value of kindness and listening in supportive therapy, as I've done it for many years. However, with PTSD, we currently are compelled at some point to actively address the trauma. Some are not ready, just as we may not be ready to "lance that boil," even years following the trauma. Warm compresses are better tolerated, but if we keep applying compresses for months or years, can we become part of the problem?

I strongly support going first with evidence-based approaches. However, in the case of PTSD, exposure within a trauma focus may not be for everybody. Pitman, et al. (1996) found that exposure techniques may exacerbate depression, panic, and alcohol consumption, whereas Allen and Bloom (1994) noted that exposure therapy was contraindicated in clients with marked psychological dysfunction, personality disorder, suicidality, impulsivity, substance abuse, or resistance ("My God, that describes just about everybody I see," commented one V.A. psychologist when reading that). Furthermore, Litz & Blake (1990), in their survey of prominent behavior therapists, found that exposure techniques were used in *only half* their PTSD cases. Why? Again, it's too aversive.

Edna Foa, perhaps the foremost U.S. researcher on PTSD treatment, is a rare exception to others in that she acknowledges that standard treatment isn't for everybody. In her 2009 compendium on the subject she recommends that we remain open to novel approaches. To this end, I try to make the case in this book for building a founda-tion of ego-strengthening before attempting corrective measures in PTSD cases, like Maggie's.

One issue I have with some current therapists, and especially new therapists recently out of grad school, is that they don't know what to do if 1) CBT does not work, or 2) if the client asks for something else. In the tradition of the macho medical attitude, "Well, if it doesn't work, we'll try it again, and then again, even stronger if necessary." More of the same should not be the only option.

Therapy as we know it may not be for everyone

In Sam Atterbury's ongoing group therapy with ex-prisoners of war from WW II, therapy was more than just supportive warm com-presses. The clients in the group were their own experts and the ther-apist was but a guide, gently prodding here, refocusing or redirecting there, if discussion got off track. People were gently drawn out and the group, an organic entity all its own, knew who was hurting that night and that person was encouraged to abreact while the rest lis-tened, with endless patience, without judgment, and with very little feedback afterward.

I remember quite vividly one group session. The men came from all over southern Arizona, usually 15–20 of them. They assembled an hour early in the lobby, chatted and had coffee. Then, at the appointed hour they moved to the group room. As the therapist, I greeted them: "So, how's everybody doing tonight?" Some small talk followed for a few seconds, and then they looked at Charlie. I didn't notice but they did; Charlie was in a bad way and without saying a word Charlie was encouraged by the group to begin. They knew Charlie and they'd heard his story before, but that didn't matter. Charlie began to speak in a low voice about the POW compound in the jungle, and how the Japanese had quickly zeroed in on Billy, who sounded psychotic. "They put him in that bamboo cage in the sun right in the middle of the compound, and we heard his screams day and night as they prodded him with bayonets," said Charlie. Charlie's voice rose as he went on for more than 30 minutes. Billy mercifully died after three days of torment and agony, and then Charlie finished, breaking down and sobbing, great, inconsolable, heaving sobs. One man put an arm around him, and no one said a thing. They didn't have to.

In some ways it was like an Alcoholics Anonymous meeting. If someone didn't feel like talking that night, fine, they still received benefit in terms of modeling and support. This seemingly structureless format looked nothing like a current PTSD group, but it worked. Can it be replicated today? Not with the session limits and content directives (evidence-based) imposed by insurance companies and the agencies themselves.

Once I was referred a WW II vet, Juan, who needed help for insomnia. Trazodone helped some, but he wanted to "relax my mind." In his PTSD group for WW II vets he had revealed something highly interesting, but nothing I've ever been able to verify. Three days after the Allies landed at Normandy there was a tremendous urgency to land vehicles and supplies on the beach and move them inland. Juan was a paratrooper on the beach and his orders were simple: "If any of those colored truck drivers turn yellow and run away, shoot 'em." Well, he said he shot and killed some 30 Black truck drivers—fellow American soldiers—who abandoned their trucks. "Every night for 30 years I see their faces when I try to go to sleep," he said. Two sessions of hypnosis did not help him. I asked Sam Atterbury, who also conducted this therapy group, if he believed Juan's story. "An unqualified yes," he said, "plus I have my own confirmation." His confirmation? "The group, they can always tell who's genuine. They readily sniff out the fakers, and this guy's for real," he said.

In the 1970s in Argentina the government killed many "subversives," and their bodies were never found. The mothers of these disappeared persons began to hold public demonstrations on the square and the resultant Madres de la Plaza de Mayo became an instrument for both political change and sorely needed emotional support for the families. This involved no therapy as we know it.

In the 1970s several people died during an air show at the Ramstein Air Force Base in Germany. A woman Air Force vet, whom I was seeing in family therapy, said she was there that day. "I found the Italian pilot's helmet," she moaned as she recalled the event. "You found a helmet, so what's the big deal about that?" I asked. "The pilot's head was still *in the helmet*," she gasped. She was also raped in the service and attained full disability from the V.A. This woman benefited from family therapy and group therapy for PTSD, but psychotropic medications may have helped her even more.

In the Balkans in the early 1990s, "ethnic cleansing" resulted in the torture and deaths of hundreds of thousands. I saw one young veteran as part of family therapy. He had served in Bosnia and he sobbed as he described having to bulldoze hundreds of bodies into a pit. "Some were still alive, I could hear their screams," he said. Did that really happen? His affect was congruent. He dropped out of therapy and I never saw him again. War is odious, many things happen and some things are covered up. In the late 1990s I knew a man, I'll call him Marwan, who had probably the worst PTSD rage I've ever seen. His torture in two different prison camps was documented in the reports of the UN and other agencies. He was forty years old but looked like eighty. Nearly every bone in his body was broken and some of his other stressors included mock firing squads, having to sleep with cadavers, and having to watch as the Serbs slit the throats of some 200 children. If anybody needed therapy and medication, Marwan certainly did.

However, he could tolerate no meds save aspirin. He didn't want to be touched, so our treatment of Zero Balancing (Edmunds & Gafner, 2003), where the physiotherapist employs gentle lifting and tugging while the psychotherapist tells him stories, was not an option. A counseling intern there spoke Italian as did the client, so I supervised the case. Psychotherapy per se wasn't done. Case management was done, which included basics about paying his bills, shopping, and vital information, like "... here you can't beat your wife or kids." This helped him immensely. But what helped him even more was learning English, telling his story in the public schools, and getting on the internet where he met other survivors. Marwan had always been a good cook and he parlayed his skills into business, where for the past 10 years he has had three successful restaurants.

Finding help in affinity

Do you have any clients whose identity *is* their disorder? Oh, more than one? It's difficult to get them outside themselves, isn't it? I saw a couple once—this was his tenth marriage—and the topic of discussion was chores in the house. The wife did everything and was exhausted and resentful. When I gently inquired whether the husband might occasionally wipe the kitchen counter, he responded, "I'm not going to *co-depend* on her and besides, I can't do anything in the kitchen because of my *PSTD*." Right, his *PSTD*. He took extreme umbrage at my audacity and they never returned. Oh, darn.

Michael B. is a good example of a polar opposite to the above gentleman. A former U.S. Marine and Vietnam vet with chronic PTSD, he develops community programs for children as well as vets, and employs interpersonal effectiveness and creativity in nudging vets with chronic PTSD to *get outside themselves*. Of course, for Mike, a major means of doing this is helping others, which he notably models for vets. An avid student of history, Mike noted that after WW II there was a successful program in the U.S. whose purpose was teaching ballroom dancing to vets to help them move beyond themselves.

Mike uses the word *affinity* to describe the primary principle operating in assemblages of vets, be it a therapy or support group, or a social and benevolent organization like the Marine Corps League, or Veterans of Foreign Wars. He cited understanding of idiosyncratic non-verbal behavior as a feature of such affinity. For example, the group or meeting concludes, people stand and prepare to leave, and one participant reaches in his pocket for his car keys. His hand becomes stuck and he fumbles in grasping the keys. This occurs over the course of only a few seconds, but it arrests the attention of others, as this very thing happened to them in Vietnam. As the man finally produces his keys, another man sums it up verbally: "Just like in a firefight, I needed to reload and my hand got stuck reaching for a clip (of ammunition)." Certainly similar interactions take place among former teachers, policemen or others with a shared history; however, the quality and intensity of affinity may be greater among combat veterans. Mike's wife has also made a major contribution, founding one of the first websites in the U.S. that is a resource to families of PTSD clients.

The "Performative"

Psychoanalysts emphasize the role of "the performative" in treating PTSD, so that people can begin to break out of stuck grief in order for mourning to be transformed. (I have to admit, "performative" sounds a lot more elegant than *doing something*.) To underscore the importance of behavioral activation, one analyst, film-maker Donna Bassim (personal communication, 2013) has successfully broken through the grief of 9/11 survivors in New York City by escorting them to the 9/11 site and having them *sign the guest book*. A therapeutic program in Tucson takes Vietnam veterans *back* to Vietnam. Led by a clinical psychologist, the group of eight or so vets returns to sites of battles and other places dear to them. One of those vets was a client of mine and I remember his account of a profound reframe effected by the visit to where he was wounded: "There's a school there now ... and telephone lines ... and you should see how they've turned the bomb craters into duck ponds!" This group and others like them bring medicines and other needed items to their destinations.

People in Arizona who conduct therapeutic riding (equine therapy) claim they have seen improvement in PTSD. Dance therapy, art therapy? With all of them, clients are *doing something*. The Patriot Riders, mostly veterans and many with PTSD, in addition to serving at funerals of the dead from the current wars, accompany the "traveling wall," (the portable version of the Vietnam Memorial in Washington, D.C. on which are etched the names of U.S. dead in the war). Millions have visited the original wall and traced on paper the names of loved ones. Rolling Thunder, another veterans motorcycle organization, repaired houses in New Orleans after Hurricane Katrina. There are myriad other examples of the performative and helping others, both of which may help repair the moral injury of PTSD better than any psychotherapy.

In conclusion

As I write this in 2013, I think back on the early 2000s when I saw Maggie and Charles. Certainly the V.A. was a different place in those days, probably more open to non-PTSD program staff's seeing PTSD clients, as there were many clients to be seen and not as many staff dedicated to treating them as currently. If nowadays someone like Maggie or Charles requested "story therapy" or hypnosis, they might be told they need to try evidence-based treatment first, which is understandable. However, if they said, "I don't want that," or "I already tried that and it didn't work," they may or may not be referred on to the person in the hypnosis training program who took over my job when I left. It would all depend on the clinician they saw and that person's biases.

Theoretically, with all PTSD clients, exposure and abreaction need to happen for improvement to occur. Whether that happens through therapy, journaling, religion, meditation, or, "telling my story" like Marwan, maybe it doesn't matter. Our orientation and bias is toward therapy, but thinking internationally, most people in our sad and violent world have no access to therapy, and they muddle on as best they can. Even in our prosperous Western world many don't or can't partake of any kind of therapy, and we can only speculate on how they abreact silently in dreams, or as part of a religious or cultural tradition, or abreact openly to a trusted friend or family member. Some do nothing and remain scarred and dysfunctional forever, and some eventually get better, just as they do with therapy.

CHAPTER NINE
Using story techniques

Alternating stories with Maggie

Over the next month I saw Maggie twice. She looked less depressed, said she enjoyed her job, was making good money, and got along well with people at work. When mom attended, she looked thin and weak. Each time I used alternating stories, which allowed me to slip in an instigative story and capitalize on her propensity for amnesia. During non-trance portions of the session I gently urged her to say more about her mortuary duties in the war, but always redirected discussion to something else. My plan now was to monitor her and continue to try to erode her defenses with suggestions embedded in the stories. I didn't know how long I would go with that approach. One constant was her appreciation of—and good response to—the stories. Yes, indeed, I was getting frustrated with this case. As with Charles, I was growing weary and I was concerned that my preoccupation with these two cases was hurting my other clients, my trainees, and everything else that demanded my attention at work. Fortunately, I was feeling less debilitated by then from past radiation treatment, and I was not allowing work to bleed into my life at home.

Charles and Bernadette

Marital therapy is slow going with Charles and his wife. Like many struggling couples, all they know is the unhappiness of bitter conflictual behavior. Like a broken record, the dynamic is attack—defend, defend—attack, while avoiding each other the rest of the time, painful but familiar. I reminded them again about using a time-out, but they offered lame excuses. When they're ready, they'll embrace that and other measures, I thought. But for right now it's always the other person's fault, and each sees little good in the other person. I spend most of this session seeing them separately, which is my practice with most couples, as it allows me to deliver complimentary directives. In doing so, I ask them to suspend judgment for the time being. "You may not believe this will make things better, but be patient here, do it for the sake of the marriage." As each completes step-wise tasks, they should start to trust both therapy and each other, and before too long they'll feel good about each other again. That's the hope and the plan.

Active role of the therapist

Now, this not only requires a very active role by the therapist but it also sends the message that we're building on positive things rather than focusing on correcting negative things, which is what most people expect in the first couples session. There were some highly positive things going on here. First, the goal for both parties was to make the marriage better. Neither one was threatening separation or divorce, "... *that's another good thing, rare around here,*" I mused. I asked them to do at least one thing each day, however small or insignificant, that the other person would appreciate, and they agreed. Wonderful! However, both quickly tried to redirect the discussion to the negative, which is the stance of virtually all unhappy couples mired in bitterness and blame, as they are waiting for the other person to change. Charles reiterated his wife's emotional distance and lack of warmth and intimacy, while Bernadette focused on Charles' penchant for petty vandalism and his disappearance for a couple hours each week. In couples therapy, the task of the therapist is to get each person to take a step toward the other, even though they really don't want to, for therein lies the solution. If couples don't see anything good happening after three or four sessions they may bolt from therapy, and I couldn't blame them.

What needs to happen with couples early on

I asked each to remember what it was like when they first met, trying to help them recall when they were actively pleasing each other. "What are your partner's favorable qualities?" I asked. "He's a good provider," answered Bernadette, while Charles pointed out that she is masterful with gems and beads, which is the business she operates. Neither response is an affective diadem, but I'll take it, as these are things they badly need to hear from each other. But it's not always that easy. Then, you have to prompt them.

Patrick's relationship

Around the same time, I saw another couple. When the partner, Patrick, was unable to come up with any good qualities of his partner, I reached for metaphor to prompt him: "Patrick, it was another gay couple I had in here last week, he thought and thought, and finally admitted his partner had a nice smile." Water off a duck's back, no penetration, so I asked about the partner in the kitchen, the bedroom, at church, with the children, with his own parents "*... anywhere in there you can think of anything good about him, Patrick?*"

I don my cheerleader hat here and put a full-court press on getting Patrick to say *something* good about his partner, even if it's something from years ago. If I still come up empty, I'll dismiss his partner for a moment and then lay into Patrick about how he needs to come up with something here, and how the partner needs to hear it, or else we can't move forward. That usually gets his attention, but if it doesn't, I might send him home with the task of generating some things, "*... and when you have two things, call and tell me and we'll make another appointment.*" I then tell his partner that Patrick has a little task and that hopefully we'll be resuming soon.

So, all along here I'm thinking that Patrick may not want this relationship to get better and he's too passive to say so. I've had many couples who became hung up like this when the unforthcoming one is going through the motions so he can say he tried and so his conscience is clear because he's hooked his spouse up with help before he bails out. Now, some of you may be thinking, "Why in the world does George turn something simple into a big high-risk power struggle?" Because I want to know early on if they're going to be customers or just window shoppers, as I don't care to waste their time or mine. I know many therapists who wouldn't be this direct and would spend several sessions on genograms and extended family history before ever engaging the nitty-gritty. If that works for them, I respect that, but it doesn't work for me.

Plenty of times I've had a family therapy referral and the identified client (or even the one "who really needs to be here") doesn't attend. So, I have to work with the warm body in the room. Sometimes by working through one you can motivate the non-attending spouse to show up, but usually it doesn't work out. I take my hat off to you if you work with couples and families, as client behavior in individual therapy often has an obvious social context that is hard to address without the others present.

Couple dynamics and marital therapy

Couples usually demonstrate unique ways of behaving, which becomes evident as they describe the relationship. Early on, Charles and Bernadette appeared to be in an attack-defend mode. Let's say a man with depression shows passivity in relationships. His relationship dynamic may be _approach-avoid_. Other common dynamics in relationships are _control-resist, demand-refuse, discuss-avoid, criticize-defend, and accuse-deny_. In the case of approach-avoid in another case where the direct approach wasn't penetrating the husband's thick skull, I took out the background sound machine that I sometimes use in hypnosis, turned it to the "ocean waves" mode, and asked the husband if the sound of the waves washing up on the shore and then receding reminded him of anything. After a minute or so, he said, "Maybe your point is that I approach my wife up to a point, and then I retreat." Bingo! And as I didn't want to embarrass him, I did this with his wife out of the room. You never want to do anything that will cause one to lose face, as conflicted couples are often so sensitive and looking for any excuse to quit therapy "... _because that damn therapist is on your side._" Over the years I bent over backwards to try to be fair in marital therapy but inevitably someone would angrily blame me for taking sides. Therapists are only human, and when you get these couples where one is tyrannical and defensive (usually the man in heterosexual relationships) our sympathies may be transparent, especially non-verbally. One of the reasons hypnosis appealed to me years ago was because it gave me a break from seeing warring couples (and families) all day long. It is most gratifying when you can help save a marriage; however, in doing marital therapy you put on hip boots, wade out into the cold water, and suddenly realize, "This is my life."

Couples and themes

Besides dynamics, another thing I keep in mind is what Peggy Papp (1983) calls *themes*. In my work at the V.A., a common theme was *illness versus health*: A woman hooks up with a disabled veteran and soon the novelty wears off. Other themes are *teacher versus student, closeness versus distance, and rescue versus escape. Responsibility versus irresponsibility* is also common: One person resentfully takes care of everything and complains about it, the other person tries to help out but doesn't do it well enough, and the responsible person says, "There we go again, if I don't do it, it just doesn't get done!" I liked to intervene in that theme. Typically, while seeing them separately within the session I would gain the passive person's agreement to name one small thing he could do every day, e.g., clean the cat box, or hold his wife's hand (after he washes *his* hands) while they watch TV. Then, I would prompt the other one to notice the partner's new behavior and give them a kiss on the cheek, or some other reinforcement when they see the behavior. Thinking about how Charles can be professorial and sanctimonious, I would have expected their theme to be teacher versus student, but it was clearly attack-defend with closeness versus distance creeping in there as a close second.

Ideally, then, I could keep up this noticing new behavior as they see that taking risks pays off. The reciprocity continues to build and pretty soon therapy concludes. However, they can throw a monkey wrench into this step-wise approach, and then I need to wax strategic. So, if after the fourth session the wife says something like, *"He's only being helpful because you told him to,"* or *"He's being nice but I can tell his heart isn't in it,"* anticipate that, it's probably coming. That's the time when metaphor can be real helpful, so maybe I'll tell her a little story about another wife who also had reservations at this point in therapy, and how suspending judgment, being patient and "looking on the bright side for now" can get her past this juncture. I might add, "His heart may not be in it now, but it will be once you guys are happy and trust this change." Admittedly, my words may strike her as trite and very unconvincing, so if that's not good enough for her, I might need to say, *"Look, he's making a much better effort than a lot of husbands I see and you need to appreciate it."* She may really want the relationship to end, but I don't feel like I'm on solid enough ground with her yet to ask her that, so instead I'll query, *"Another wife I had in here last month, she was at the point you are, and she was so accustomed to this for all these years, and I wondered, maybe she wasn't ready for this to get better."*

Saying that to her is one step away from wondering if SHE isn't ready yet, and she could be insulted by both ways, even though I deliver it gently with extreme kindness. So, in addition to not sitting between her and the door, right then I'm going to watch her non-verbals. If she balls up her fists and explodes, it may just mean she *is* insulted and that she's trying her best under darn stressful circumstances. If her reaction is mild and passive, it may mean yes, indeed, she's not ready for this to get better. Interpreting non-verbals is tricky. That's why I just keep sending out probes, trying to gauge what's going on here. Just like in individual therapy, I need to identify the roadblocks and clear them out of the way so that therapy can proceed. Once they're pleasing each other on a regular basis and they feel secure, communication, intimacy and everything else will fall into place, and then I can cease this risky high wire act. So many things that go on in therapy with couples and families, I can't blame therapists for liking only one person in the room at a time.

Unfortunately, the literature on marital therapy shows us that more than half of the couples who make such gains will backslide within a year. I saw several couples who came back for a tune-up after a couple of years, and I wonder about all the others who made some gains and then faded away after a few sessions. Life is tough on relationships even under good circumstances. Think of your own situation: It's seldom easy, is it?

Back with Charles and Bernadette

I asked Charles to come in for the second time in today's session.

Therapist: So, what's going on with this disappearing act every week? I can see where your wife is suspicious. No affair or anything?

Charles: I knew push would come to shove. Okay, I'll tell you. There's a community of Montagnards in town. I go there once a week and give them pro bono therapy. We owe a lot to them. I'm paying back, if you will.

This development took me aback. These ethnic minority tribesmen in Vietnam were strong U.S. allies in the war. Those not killed afterward were placed in "re-education" camps and some were not released until nearly 20 years after the war. Some emigrated to the U.S., where they were highly regarded by U.S. veterans. Charles' "paying back" was intriguing.

Therapist: Well, why not tell your wife this? Why keep it secret?

Charles: She doesn't give a shit about me or anything I've done.

Therapist: Well, think about it, she may care about some things, you never know.

I didn't care to delve into his acts of vandalism, at least not now, when there were more important relational things to address. I just figured that when he was feeling angry and hostile, or maybe sexually frustrated, he got some relief from passive-aggressive actions. Not unlike cutters who feel relief after slicing up their arms. I left to invite Bernadette back in. It was time for the Cactus story.

Therapist: You guys heard of the Cactus story?

Charles' eyes began their circling. He was between the twinkling expression and pursing of lips when I acted, not in the mood for one of his barbed insults.

Therapist: Pattern interruption.

Bernadette: What?

Charles just glared.

Bernadette: So, it's about a prickly pear cactus, a cholla cactus?

Charles: Most of his vapid stories have to do with the saguaro, George's favorite cactus.

Therapist: Yes, the saguaro, you are so omniscient, Charlie.

Charles: I hate Charlie, you know that.

Cactus story

Therapist: This has to do with a couple unlike you two, as they moved to Arizona from one of the north-eastern states, possibly up by Canada, I don't recall, and it really doesn't matter. Anyway, these people carefully observed a three-foot-tall saguaro right outside their front door. It was way too young to start growing any arms yet, and they were eager to see it grow into a mighty green titan like the ones in the surrounding desert. Christmas arrived and they forgot about the cactus for a while. But in early January they were concerned once again.

The cactus hadn't grown at all since they moved to their house six months ago. "It must need fertilizer," said the woman, so they gave it a dose of Miracle Gro. But the weeks passed and it remained the same size, exactly 36 inches. "It must be thirsty, let's water it," said the man, so they threw a bucket of water around the base. Another month passed and it still hadn't grown, so they watered it some more, a bucket of water every other day for a week. The saguaro became pale and started to lose its needles. "It's sick," said the woman, "it must need more water." So, they watered it even more, and soon it looked worse. They both agreed it must be really thirsty and need more water. Now, what do you think happened to that cactus?

Bernadette: It must've died. Even I know that you don't water cactus, especially in the winter.

Charles' timing was perfect, as he pursed his lips just as she finished.

Charles: Embedded suggestion for children, Doctor. Oh, I forgot, you don't have a Ph.D.

Therapist: You need a bigger piece of turquoise in that bola tie.

I didn't intend discussion of the metaphor and I moved on to other matters. Either the metaphor took root in fertile soil, or they became tired of fighting and decided to trust again, because when they came back next time both reported on successful use of the time-out. We could now move on.

The Cactus story cuts through the resistance of any problem where the person is unreceptive to the notion of doing things differently. With any of us, something doesn't work and we repeat what we know, what's familiar. That doesn't work, so we try harder, doing more of the same on and on. The Cactus story is something that often short-circuits the process for individuals, couples and families.

Two days later Charles is back

Today, he wears a new bola tie with an oversized turquoise clasp. He has fifty-cent pieces in his penny loafers. He looks relaxed, peaceful. I wonder how he could have jammed those big coins into a slot in the leather made for pennies.

Charles: Okay, I told her.

Therapist: Told her what?

Charles: About my volunteer work. She thought it curious, didn't have much else to say. She seems to have lightened up a bit.

Therapist: Not so critical, more affectionate, or what?

Charles: Both, in some ways. I like that Cactus story. I used it on somebody yesterday.

Therapist: Oh, really, for what kind of problem?

Charles: A couple with problems, just like us.

Therapist: Oh, good for you. So, I don't really have much planned for today. You feel like doing anything special?

Charles: I guess another story, you name it.

I regarded Charles. He had that smirk on his face again, like he's in charge and he's doing me a favor just being here. On that day I didn't know that the marital situation was starting to improve, and as I regarded Charles at the start of the session, I anticipated a fusillade of invective about Bernadette. I didn't want to discuss marital issues. But there was no invective, I was wrong. What's going on here, I wondered.

I also thought that even if he requested a story today so he can in turn use it with his clients, that's fine, I have no problem with that, as suggestions in the story can still get through to him. I wondered if I was losing my grip on this case. What was I seeing Charles alone for, anxiety? There was something fishy about his volunteer work. There was still something deeper going on here that had not been revealed. If so, how long can I go on trolling for that? At least with Maggie the goal was clear. If his anxiety is better, why should I keep seeing him like this? With so many people it's guilt.

Therapist: Charles, when you first got here, one of the things you said right away was "I feel beaten to a pulp." How's that feeling now?

Charles: I feel pretty good now, I guess. You're right to inquire about the body's role in psychopathology, I always do that. "The body knows," as they say.

Therapist: So, Charles, you feel guilty about anything?

Charles: Well, I feel guilty about having an attraction to some of my women clients, that's all.

Therapist: Nothing that you dream about, that penetrates your consciousness when you least expect it. Nothing about Vietnam?

Charles: Nah, why should there be?

He had betrayed a slight stiffening at the mention of Vietnam, and all of a sudden his eyes were doing that circling thing again. Then came the twinkling expression and the pursing of his lips. I waited. No sarcasm, no insult, nothing, simply a bland expression and minor fidgeting. He reached inside his shirt for some reason.

Charles: Say, let's get on with the story, if you don't mind. I need to be back to the office.

Road 302 story

Therapist: Connie Inskeep lived in Tusayan, the small village that lies outside the main entrance to Arizona's Grand Canyon. Today was her day off from her job as a guide for river raft expeditions through the 200-mile-long Canyon. For months a solution to her problem had escaped her. She thought, "Why in the world didn't I do this earlier?" And just then she did what had always worked for her in the past, assigned the problem to her unconscious mind. "I'll just let it percolate there, deep inside," she thought as she turned the key to start her truck. "Who knows when I'll discover the answer?"

It was a sunny autumn day when she set out in her truck on Forest Service road number 302. The deeply rutted road made for very slow travel. After a mile, she stopped when she glimpsed a family of elk in a grove of pine trees. She turned off the key and ever so slowly stepped from the truck. The animals appeared oblivious to her as she focused her binoculars and zeroed them in. Her breathing slowed, her body was motionless, frozen in time, and her mind drifted to the elk and back to her body as she thought, "How can my heart be thumping in my chest when my breathing is so slow?" Just then another incongruence penetrated her consciousness—it was a roll of thunder on this cloudless day.

Her mind meandered far away from Arizona and back to the elk, present time and past time pleasantly blurred, as mental absorption hastened and bodily relaxation cascaded to even greater depths. She breathed very deeply, once, then twice, and was carried away on a current of reverie. She didn't remember getting back in the truck, but soon she found herself going down that bumpy road again. After a mile or so, she stopped when a flutter of wings caught her attention off to the left. It was a flock of wild turkeys. Once again she got out and raised the binoculars to her eyes. She watched the birds for what seemed like many minutes before they moved on into the woods.

Her body remained in the same position, wooden and unmoving. The realization of her parched mouth and throat coincided with the thought that the lens on a binoculars does not blink. Right then she thought, "There's really nothing at all that I need to do right now, nowhere I need to be, nothing to know, nothing to think about; all I have to do is just be here right now and breathe," and with that she drank some water and peered again through the binoculars. She moved them a few degrees to the left and saw a person beneath the trees. He or she was looking directly at her. She lowered the binoculars, took a deep breath, and looked again, but the person was gone … and now a single elk filled the lenses.

Something beckoned down by her feet. She knelt, grasped a stick, closed her eyes, and in the sand her hand began to draw. The hand moved of its own accord, as if it belonged to another. When she opened her eyes she glimpsed the figure in the sand. "Is that an elk?" she asked herself. Connie sat on the ground, in cross-legged fashion, just like on the playground in elementary school in Ohio. She remembered sitting there, legs tingling with electricity when Billy approached and asked her if she was all right. She couldn't remember how she answered, but she did remember with vivid clarity when Billy blew up a balloon, a shiny red one, tied it off, and then gently poked his finger into the side of the balloon. It bulged under the pressure of his finger, which he wiggled ever so slightly, and then he asked, "Connie, is my finger *inside* or *outside* this balloon?" At that moment she blinked her eyes and when she opened them the balloon was gone, as was Billy. "Why, I'd forgotten all about that? Well, right now I'd better continue down this road," she thought.

Soon—it seemed like many minutes but probably only several seconds had transpired—Connie was back in her truck, enjoying the slow, gentle jostling of the rugged road. From out of nowhere her problem—yes, that vexing problem—surfaced and danced across her conscious mind. Not only danced but did cartwheels, rapid and whirring, jeering and mocking, and then it dissipated and all was placid again. Her eyes focused on a stand of hardwood trees. Maple or walnut, it didn't matter. "All I need to do is breathe, nothing else," she thought, and one very satisfying, deep breath followed, and she was once again immersed in the lulling movement of the truck, its engine the rhythmic purr of her kitty cat.

She knew that a fire watch tower lay just up ahead but she could not see it. She approached a haze up ahead, was it a fog? No, she could smell it, it was smoke, and then visibility became very limited. She glimpsed numerous small fires, backfires set by foresters, and then she saw one of them, a ghost materializing off to the right. He waved as she continued into the smoke. There it was, the metal watchtower. "Made from a giant erector set," she thought. Connie pulled off the road and parked a few feet away from the tower.

She climbed the steps and soon was up on top, where she looked out over the haze to the vast red stone chasm and the north rim beyond. She gazed upon it for several seconds and then something bright appeared out there, a brief flash of light. Just then something stirred within her, and all of a sudden Connie had her answer.

When Charles had pulled up the footrest on the recliner he'd kicked off his shoes. When they landed, the large coin in one had dislodged and now he was groping on the floor in the darkened room for it. I turned off the music. Charles looked like he had drifted off pretty good.

Charles: That was a good one. I'll have to remember it.

Therapist: The idea is to *not* remember it—consciously anyway.

Charles: Yeah, I don't agree with that. I always talk to them about it right after.

Therapist: So, the part where the guy rides his motorcycle off the cliff wasn't too jarring?

Charles: Really? I guess I missed that. Well, no matter, I have the rest locked in right up here (pointing to his head). I can take a poor story like that and craft it into a good one.

Therapist: You're a man of endless talents. So, Charles, what are you doing outside of here to stay well?

Charles: Well, she and I went to a movie the other night. I go for rides in one of my Bentleys. I take deep breaths and clear my head between clients.

I turned the music back on and moved my chair close to Charles.

Therapist: We still have ten minutes left. Here, watch my hand.

I did a quick eye roll induction by placing my hand in front of his eyes, moved the hand up and instructed him to follow the hand, letting his eyes roll up.

Therapist: And as they roll up they can gently close and you can sit back in the recliner and prepare for a quick little story called Tyranny of Ten (Gafner, 2004).

Tyranny of Ten story

When she was younger, Betsy Tierney went to the gym five days a week, always arriving at the same time, week in and week out, tote bag over her shoulder, broad smile on her face.

"We could set our watches by you, Betsy," called out the personal trainers behind the counter. "Only if it makes you feel better," she answered, "something that may best be forgotten," she added. They just smiled as she strode away. Now that she was older she visited the gym just three times a week, and at home she occupied her mind with less strenuous pursuits, like boiling water for her tea. "I put it in the microwave for exactly two minutes, and I watch the clock tick down, 9, 8, 7, …, and when it's done, I put in the tea bag, and I watch it for a precise amount of time."

Frank often saw Tierney at the gym. He said to her once, and only once, "Well, watching you, and how methodical you are, many things can happen, like becoming transfixed by the details, or having my attention arrested by the overall precision of the operation." "Yes," answered Tierney, "my mind does indeed become immersed in the process; however, Frank, you can simply ignore me and turn your attention back on yourself." Her words gave pause to Frank, who then watched her walk briskly to the back of the gym. He watched her at the leg press machine, 10 repetitions precisely, followed by a brief rest period, and then exactly 10 more, up, down, up, down … and at the dumbbells she flexed her grip 10 times on each bar, and then hoisted them, up and down, up and down, 10 times, and then waited precisely five seconds, and then another five seconds, and repeated the procedure. She hollered out to Frank: "Ten seconds in between, you catch that, Frank?"

Frank just stood there, fixated by her precise routine and she continued, hoisting each 15-pound weight 10 times, waiting five seconds and then another five seconds, and beginning all over again until she had completed 10 sets of 10 on each side. "My arms never get tired," she whispered to Frank. "But what about your mind?" asked Frank. "My mind's only getting warmed up, and whether my mind's warm or cold, I see the number 10, a big one and a big zero—quite distinct imagery," she responded, wiping the sweat from her brow 10 times with each hand before slinging the towel over her shoulder and striding off to a large barbell.

She lay down on the bench, scratching the back of her head one time with her right hand, and then reached back there with her left hand for nine more deliberate scratches. She was catching her breath now, and then, inhaling and exhaling but two times, she followed with eight more quick inspirations before reaching up and grasping the bar, flexing her hands five times on the left, five times on the right, and then five again with each hand.

"Hey, don't you think you should slow down?" asked Frank. "After all, you're not 25 anymore." "No, my years total twice 25, and that's 10 times five if your calculation is slow," she told Frank. She was back at the dumbbells, and snatched 25-pounders this time. "How about 20 repetitions with one arm and none with the other, or six on one side and seven on the other?" asked Frank. "That's an interesting proposition, Mr. Frank, maybe even curious," she answered, as she began the same routine, flexing, then releasing 10 times, right and left, and lifting 10 times on each side.

Quite exasperated by now, Frank asked, "Tierney, when you're a hundred years old, will you still have the same routine?" Tierney responded before he had finished his sentence. "I did this when I was 10, probably will when I'm a hundred." "But by then you'll be underground, six feet under," noted Frank quite smugly. "No, 10 feet under, not a mere six, it's prearranged, and all paid for," answered Tierney.

She once again was immersed in her routine, and Frank's mind drifted off to something else, tent worms and sand flies. He ignored the itch behind his left shoulder and soon he became absorbed in his own routine.

Charles: Whew, that one was kind of a mind fuck.

Therapist: All in the service of helping those who sacrificed so nobly for our country.

Charles: Sarcasm doesn't become you. So, you think I had a dishonorable discharge?

Therapist: No, where did that come from?

Charles: I dunno, I gotta go.

Notes for practice

As he went out the door he reached inside his shirt again and then it hit me: He was wearing a recording device! An honest client would have simply asked and I'd have gladly consented, or said, "Well, let's just start the video camera here and do it right." Frankly, I don't know how many times my sessions have been covertly recorded, six or eight times *that I know of.*

The first time I found out was when an irate wife called and said something like, "My husband keeps playing over and over again where you said I need to be more affectionate." Yes, the individual therapy client was recording the sessions and using them on his wife. Other times it came out in marital sessions where, for example, one of them said, "I played it for him, and he didn't believe he had such a grating voice." When I looked into the few cases where I knew it was going on, the vet often had worked in military intelligence. I told one, "Good for you, gathering this vital intelligence, I hope you send it to the Pentagon." I would always tell trainees, "Watch what you write in the record, they usually get a copy of it, plus you never know when it will end up in court. But also watch what you *say* because more times than we know it might be recorded", yet another mystery of the V.A.

As far as Charles goes, I decided on the spot to surprise him with the unexpected, a rapid, directive induction followed by a perturbing story. I was feeling that my initial fear had been confirmed, that I should not have embarked on both individual and couples therapy. As a couple there were modest gains, but I didn't know where it was going with Charles alone. After the last session I met with my psychologist friend, Bob, and he told me about one of his challenging cases, and I discussed this one. One for metaphor himself, he said, "Remember that Willie Nelson song about gambling where he says, 'know when to hold 'em and know when to fold 'em'?" "So, I'm throwing good money after bad?" I asked him. "I'd give that guy a farewell gift, some silver dollars for his penny loafers," he said, and I thought of a retort to the old American caveat, "Don't take any wooden nickels."

Story techniques

A story for a 64-year old man with heart failure

In the mid-1980s, we had a 64-year-old man who gave the staff fits in the geriatric clinic. Herman had terrible congestive heart failure and was on a strict, low-sodium diet. Every day he ate two meals at his favorite delicatessen and had potato chips and pizza at home. Once a week he'd be in the emergency room with swollen ankles and life-threatening heart failure. Usually he was sick enough to be admitted to the hospital and then he'd order out for pizza to eat in his hospital bed. Out of frustration, the doctor even ordered him to weigh himself at home *every hour* so Herman could see how much weight (fluid) he was putting on. Nothing worked. The cycle continued. Herman, a short man, was irrepressible, always cracking jokes, and would light up a room when he entered. As such, it was difficult for staff to be angry at him.

I was called in to help with this case, and I had no idea what to do. Then, I realized all I needed to do was follow the basic dictates of strategic therapy, first *joining with* the client. I sat down with Herman and reviewed with him what he was doing and he admitted to eating even *more* salty and greasy things than we'd known about. I joined with him by saying, *"Yes, I understand you like this good food, Herman, it's so enjoyable ... you've eaten it all your life ... I appreciate your telling me this."* Talking to him like this was a potent neutralizer, as all he'd known was people scolding him for two years. Then, I added on with a reframe: *"This is all you know, you're doing the best you can to please the doctors, life is short,"* that kind of thing. "Fine and dandy, thanks for talking to me," he noted before adding, "My ride will be here in 20 minutes." I asked, "Time for a quick story?" "You bet, tell it." I asked Herm' to sit back and listen. Like a lot of elderly people, he cocked the ear with better hearing toward the speaker. I moved my chair closer to his right ear and began with moderate volume.

Storm Clouds story
Taken from Gafner & Benson (2003)

Although I hadn't been born yet when people were preparing for World War II, I've read some history and knew that Germany was angry about the way they were treated after World War I. I realize you know all this, Herm', but in the mid-1930s Hitler was getting stronger and stronger. Under the noses of everybody, he was building a war machine, but outside of Germany *few were aware of it*, and most of them couldn't have cared less. They still remembered the First War and tried to block from their minds any reminder.

Hitler got stronger and stronger, and pretty soon he began to flex his muscles. First, he took over the Rhineland, offering up some lame excuse for military action. He grew stronger and stronger, but still *nobody believed it*. They just *hoped for the best* while they caved in to the dictator. He occupied the Sudetenland, and next Czechoslovakia was sold out. And Hitler got stronger and stronger. Then he invaded Poland in 1939 and made short work of them. Still, people *refused to believe* what was happening, and then Holland, Norway, Belgium, and Denmark fell. Much of the world continued to *hope for the best*, standing by and watching as he made quick work of France. The U.S. began to aid England, which by this time was getting bombed pretty badly, and in 1941 Pearl Harbor happened. Finally the allies wised up and *did something* before it was too late.

Herman smacked his lips and reached for his cane. "You know I'm Jewish, right?" he asked. "Well, I could've figured by your name," I answered. "Well, I'm not religious, but that was the main reason I joined the Army—even before Pearl Harbor—because of what Hitler was doing to the Jews. I had lots of relatives in Poland. They all went to the gas chambers." "A very nasty business over there," I said. Then he left. That was the first session.

Adding on with a behavior prescription
The next time I saw him I added on to the joining and reframe with a paradoxical prescription. I told him, "Herm', this heart failure

business is out of your control … you don't look depressed but just the same, you're killing yourself, we both know that, so let's prepare for the inevitable … I'm here to help you however I can." I then took him over to the Details office of the hospital. This is where they handle death benefits. I'd called the lady ahead of time, so she was ready, explained to him what his survivors would receive, and then she took out an American flag and announced, "… this will go over the coffin, won't you be so proud to have this beautiful Stars and Stripes over your coffin?" This lady was good!

Herman answered, "I don't know how proud I'll be when I'm dead." Okay, this was starting to sink in on old Herman. You know it hits home when they show a recoiling, and his response was a blank expression and stark silence, not his usual garrulous banter. We walked back to my office and on the way I said, "We have one more very important task," and soon we were sitting down and writing his obituary. "Don't you agree, Herm', that we need to get this done now, while we can, and get it all spelled out clear, as this is what they'll be reading once you're pushing up daisies." We got a few lines done and then he said he had to go. I had no more sessions with him, but whenever I saw him in passing, I reiterated the Wildermuth principle: Don't forget to breathe.

Unethical treatment?

His next visit to the clinic in two weeks showed a physical exam that was unremarkable for the first time in ages. In the ensuing years he had no visits to the emergency room and only one hospitalization. Progress notes during that time described him as "quiet, not garrulous like he used to be", and "adhering to meds and diet." He passed away nearly three years later. One of the last notes in his record stated that he felt "accepting of things but depressed." Now, in discussing this case with others, most were supportive of the intervention, especially since Herman's medical team endorsed it. However, some have told me things like, "It's *his* business what he does, maybe he should have died happy", and "You manipulated him into doing what the doctors wanted, do you feel good about that?" That stung a bit. I've spoken with several doctors and nurses who staunchly defend "patient education"—instructing people what to do and informing them of possible consequences if they don't comply—as the only ethical approach to problems like this. I've also been told by nurses and doctors that this approach with Herman was dangerous and highly unethical, and I responded that his former course was plenty dangerous and "I think it's unethical to NOT try something else." A few questioned intervening like this "in a case like this involving 'passive suicide'." Well, when the doctor told me I had cancer the first thing I did was buy some Lawry's salt—the heck with sodium restriction and hypertension—and I'm still living my new life of passive suicide. I've prescribed the symptom with many problem behaviors but never when the person was actively suicidal. Just what is passive suicide? My aunt quit taking her blood pressure pills "so I'll have a stroke," which is what happened. Now, that sounds like passive suicide.

Other story techniques

It's important for you to employ techniques that you like and that you're comfortable with, and that is especially true for stories. I have used all of the following both within formal hypnosis and without. With something like amnesia, though, it helps to have at least a moderate depth of trance. If not aiming for amnesia, I might go back and forth several times between two stories, rather than alternating but once. Some have asked me, "Why not *three* stories?" If the extravagant and overly complex is your cup of tea, go for it. I embrace the "law" of parsimony: Do only what is necessary to achieve the desired result. So I usually keep it simple, and I think two stories is more than enough.

Because alternating stories just one time was effective with Maggie, I repeated it over several sessions not described in the text. When I happen on a technique that produces a highly desirable response, I'll usually stick with it until it 1) it no longer elicits the desired response, or 2) it becomes so distracting that it draws the person's conscious mind into it. Remember, this is an *unconsciously-directed* approach, so I want my thrust to be outside of conscious awareness.

But with Maggie, this is only a means to an end, as my target is a very conscious, here-and-now exposure of traumatic events.

Anecdote within a story

Therapy addict George is back to see Dr. Tracten, this time for his cigarette habit. With the doctor today is his intern, who insists on being called by his last name, Buster. Buster has read George's record before the session, so he's somewhat familiar with the client. Tracten asks Buster if the client is ready to give up cigarettes. "Well, depends on his stage of readiness, you've read Prochaska (Prochaska, et al., 1992), right?" "I guess I have, can't remember. I go by intuition, Buster, and one day you will, too," he said before asking him how he would attack this smoking problem. "Go right after him with the Eating Dirt story (Gafner & Benson, 2003), says Buster. But Tracten has a better idea. "George smokes five packs of cigarettes a day. He's been to a stop-smoking group, tried the medication patch three times and ripped it off each time, and failed oral medication. So, let's go for just an intermediate goal: *Acceptance*. I want him to simply *accept*—not fight against—his smoking.

Just last week George, in anguish from a nicotine fit, asked the doctor, "Is it possible for us to meet outside under that big mesquite tree so I can smoke?" Of course, the answer was no. Dr. Tracten handed his trainee a page of paper and said, "Buster, in the session read these anecdotes when I nod to you. In the past this client has had brief dissociative episodes which were pleasant. In fact, when I saw him just last week I delivered some interspersal suggestion within my hypnotic patter, like, 'Very good, George, drifting off like that—*acceptance of anything is good*—and you can deeply appreciate ...', uh, I forget what else I told him." "So, you did seeding, sir," said Buster. "Very good, son, you're catching on," answered Dr. Tracten.

George is seated in the office between Buster and the doctor. Right now, Tracten is thinking about the basketball game he saw on TV last night. In basketball, an extreme measure is the full-court press, and the good doctor is pondering the therapeutic equivalent. He says, "Buster, step outside the office with me for a moment." In the hallway, he explains. "Buster, this is a chronic and severe problem for George, this darn smoking, and today we want to reinforce the acceptance suggestion, you with me so far?" "Yes, indeed," answers the eager student. Tracten then adds, "Today, we want to throw everything up against the wall and see what sticks." "Just like spaghetti," says Buster. "Or basketball. Let's go back in," says Tracten.

Once seated, Tracten snatches a photo off the bookcase. It is the doctor in his youth, catching a football. He hands it to George. "Here, look at this," he says, and by *accepting* it the suggestion has been non-verbally seeded, this seed as well as the previous one, that is outside of George's awareness. This goes on like this until the client has seen all eight photos. George is thinking, "Looking at all these boring photos really makes me want to have a smoke."

Tracten now picks up a book. "I'm going to read you part of a little story called The Playing Field." "Knock yourself out," says George. He had been wondering how Tracten was going to amuse himself today. Little does he know that the seed will soon be activated.

Tracten: Just settle in George. You can keep your eyes open, or just let them gently close. Breathing in comfort and relaxation and you may begin to *wonder*, possibly *imagine*, or otherwise *contemplate* if you can pay attention with your *third ear*, or the *deepest* part of you, or if it means you will *amuse* yourself inwardly*, involuntarily, avolitionally*, or with *no conscious effort* on your part, as there's absolutely *nothing at all* that you need to know, or think about, or change; in fact, you don't even have to pay attention to the words.	Binds of comparable Alternatives Alternatives Alternatives Alternatives Alternatives Alternatives Alternatives Alternatives Not knowing/not doing

The Playing Field story
Taken from Gafner and Benson (2003)

Tracten: This is a story about a man named Nestor Nalga, who was seated on a big rock in the Mojave Desert. The rock overlooked what is commonly known as Racetrack Playa, or the Playing Field, the place where stones as heavy as 300 pounds have been known to move mysteriously along the perfectly flat surface, leaving long, shiny tracks in the cobblestone silt.

Buster: *AX*el *SCEPT*ter hired a moving van, as he needed to go from here to there, not an easy undertaking, everything considered. Once the truck was loaded, he set out. It was a hot, sunny day and after a few hours he decided to give in to fatigue. He pulled into a rest area along the highway, turned off the key, sat back, closed his eyes and let himself *drift and dream*.

Embedded suggestion

Tracten continued the story about how these big stones mysteriously move in Death Valley National Park in California. At intervals, Buster inserts further anecdotes about how Axel Scepter stops at a friend's house and accepts parcels which he will mail at the post office. George has drifted off nicely, glad he has stuck around for the session. Tracten is pleased that he saved his notes from three weeks ago, the notes he used with a client who was struggling to accept his daughter's disability.

"Thanks for the help," George says to Buster at the end of the session, totally ignoring that pompous Tracten. He doubts whether all this gibberish will help him with his smoking, but he'll be back because his wife insists. He returns in two weeks and they have a frank discussion about George's apparent new-found acceptance of his smoking. Tracten isn't sure, so he asks. "So, that means you're not struggling against it anymore, huh, George?" The client nods affirmatively. "Well, there has to be a beauty in that, maybe something serene in such acceptance, don't you think?" George says yes. He concurs he has a new perspective but has no idea how he got there, but it really doesn't matter.

His wife could care less about this acceptance business, as George's cigarette consumption has increased to nearly six packs a day. She wonders if this "story therapy" is a waste of time. Tracten says to Buster, "Now it's time for the Eating Dirt story, you read it today." "Eating dirt?" queries

George. "Yeah, you'll see," says Tracten. George sits calmly with his eyes open as Buster conducts the session.

More stories follow in subsequent sessions, along with suggestions for pattern interruption and slowing down in sequencing. This is difficult because the client smokes all day long. How he holds his cigarette and cigarette brand are altered. Soon George is rolling his own cigarettes and he is down to only 10 cigarettes a day. "Your Eating Dirt story worked wonders," Tracten says to Buster who beams proudly. Tracten believes the number of cigarettes will diminish no further, and after eight total sessions therapy concludes. George has his anchor, a circle with thumb and forefinger, to aid with urges. George's wife is already bored by the CD he listens to every day. "It's cheaper than Tracten," George says. "Or cigarettes," she answers. She complains, "I don't think I'll ever eat molasses again," referring, of course, to the Molasses Reef story. She thinks the Eating Dirt story on there is just fine. George doesn't smoke in the car or the house, only out on the screened-in "Arizona room," or sun porch. After a year, George has a daily consumption of three cigarettes, sometime one. His wife wonders if that rumbling cough will ever go away.

It can be continuous, mutual, without an ending, or within a story

When a story touches a client, I'll often repeat it. But just repeating it can be boring, so I'll convert it to a continuing story. I'll sketch, say, six continuations to be employed for six sessions. I keep in mind my target and build the continuations around that. Remember, a story is a means to deliver suggestions. It is mostly fluff, or meaningless filler, and the therapeutic part is usually metaphor, embedded suggestion or interspersal taking place within the story. It's not necessary to repeat the original story each session but you can allude to it. The easiest metaphor is always "somebody else," and the easiest content is ego-strengthening.

So, if one session I tell Maggie The Greenhouse story, I can return to the same people in the greenhouse who now turn the discussion to some other plant, person, or thing that healed itself, the bark on a tree struck by lightening, or a lesion on somebody's arm, for example. Or one person tells the other another story about how a damaged coral reef began to heal (borrowing from the Molasses Reef story), or how the seed from a maple tree overcame all odds and grew to maturity (borrowing from the Maple Tree story). Perhaps the two people begin an alternating story, or another person shows up and she has a story to tell. I like the surname Inskeep, and he (or she) is in many of my stories. The possibilities are endless. Just don't make it too elaborate. Remember what your target is.

So, let's say you're thinking of trying out a continuous story. You've jotted down a few ideas, borrowed a story from a book or two, but you don't have enough to even complete an outline. What do you do? This is what I do: I assign the task to my unconscious and then just forget about it, go on to other things. You watch, within a week or so an idea will surface. We employ the client's unconscious in problem resolution, and it's just as important to employ ours.

A device I've used progressively less over the years is a story within a story. Now, I know this looks like alternating stories, but there are some key differences. With alternating stories, we go back and forth from one story to the other, sometimes several times, a technique that's indicated for the analytical engineer type; but if the goal is *amnesia* for the second story, the first story is stopped at a key juncture, the second story (which contains the target suggestions) is told to its conclusion, and *then* the first story is completed. A story within a story is simply that: A second story is sandwiched in the first story. Start the first and stop it some place; then, tell the next story to its end, and then finish the first one. The rationale for that? Well, frankly, I did that when I was tired and bored, when it was late in the day and I was maxed out on caffeine; or, when I had a busy day and— quite selfishly—I needed some variety to keep me sharp, that's when I most often used story within a story.

Mutual storytelling technique cocReating

Richard Gardner (1971) first described this technique in his work with children. I have used it mostly with children, but some with creative or interested adults. I tried to get Charles interested in this, but he wouldn't cooperate with it. Also not described in the transcripts, I used this with moderate success with Maggie. This technique requires a creative or playful person who's willing to risk embarrassing herself, and most clients don't fit in that category. Not so with children! With children, I often use the Family of the Three Bears. For example, I introduce what we're doing and then I start, "It was early in the morning at the home of the three bears, Momma Bear, Papa Bear, and little girl Bear. At their home in the forest they were sitting down for breakfast." Then, I nod to the child who continues the story, "… and the breakfast was an Egg McMuffin® from McDonald's, my favorite restaurant." I then gradually steer things toward the target, whether it's enuresis, poor grades in school, or (with the parents present), the adults' parenting the kid or blaming her for their marital problem.

Of course, mutual storytelling can also be this: Therapist tells a story, preferably a short one, and then the client tells a story, possibly related to the therapist's story, depending on how you structure the session. Whenever I've tried it this way, the client chatted on in a free-association monologue, I had to cut them off after 30 or so minutes, and there were hard feelings and a wasted session.

Story without an ending

Usually it's the more creative or introspective client whom I can engage with this technique. I used it with both Charles and Maggie, though it's not described in the text. Therapists use this most often for unconscious problem solving or when stuck. If the goal is unconscious problem solving, formal hypnosis better lends itself to depth of exploration, but not all the time. By unconscious problem solving I don't mean recovered memory work. At the V.A. I saw a guy who said, "I can't remember anything before age ten." That was his goal.

He was hoping to find out, through hypnosis, about his early years. I told him we didn't do recovered memory work and that maybe his mind was protecting him for a good reason.

Now, if the person says, "I have something nagging in my mind, *focusing* something important that can help me in life, but I just can't put my finger on it," that is a good problem for unconscious exploration or unconscious problem solving. So, too, with the person whose goal is, "I really want to find out what's holding me back from succeeding in life." However, not so with one guy who said, "I can't decide whether to divorce my wife." He and I worked out a plan where he would take a survey of every other home in his trailer park, asking the neighbors whether or not he should stay married. When he returned in a couple weeks, he said, "I got to the fifth one and stopped 'cause right then I decided to stay married." He didn't need a story without an ending or hypnosis, he needed a behavior prescription that would perturb him into deciding.

CHAPTER TEN

A curse and the Greek chorus amidst continued therapy

Maggie returns and her mother reveals the curse

The mirrored sunglasses were back, along with the black Arizona Diamondbacks baseball cap, with the ponytail falling through the hole in the back of the cap. No crucifix on a chain like other times. No makeup either, and the odor of marijuana. This was the third session in the last eight weeks. In other sessions she looked similarly disheveled, said she didn't feel like talking, and asked for a story instead. Two times during the story she'd fallen asleep. I noticed in the record that she'd seen a psychiatry resident, who had given her trazodone for sleep. When asked about it, she said she took it only occasionally "when I can remember to."

I was feeling hopeless again about this case. I thought back on the other sessions and how as I was reading stories to her I had in mind an image of an 1800s British clipper ship bobbing anchorless on the high seas. The fact that lately I'd been listening to an audiobook about Commander Hornblower may have explained the image, but that's how I felt. I regarded Maggie. She looked sullen and hostile like when she first came in and I could see why someone had labeled her as a borderline. Her mother gestured to me from her seat in the corner of the office. I moved my chair close to her. She looked weak and resigned, desperate? In a croaky voice she spoke.

Mother: In Spanish we don't have a good word for it. How do you say it in English, a word I heard once, is it wildness?

After a bit I figured out she meant wilderness.

Mother: That's it. She's been walking in the wilderness.

Therapist: What are you talking about?

Mother: She was cursed before she left for over there.

I didn't know if I'd heard her right.

Therapist: She was cursed?

Mother: Sí, sí, exacto.

Sure enough, I'd heard her right: cursed.

Maggie: Don't listen to her.

Therapist: Humor me here, Maggie. Remember, I'm trying to help. Change chairs with your mom. Just do it.

Her mother rose slowly, walked with her cane to the recliner and plopped down into it. Maggie took her mom's chair and put her head in her hands. I pulled the handle for her mom and up went her feet.

Mother: Oh, this is nice like this.

Maggie: I know what she's going to say.

Maggie covered her ears.

Therapist: Okay, Señora, what can you tell me to help your daughter.

Mother's smile was replaced with a look of dread. She looked straight ahead, lips tight. We were now treading in forbidden territory. Should I restrain mom here?

Therapist: I know this is hard. Tell me only a little bit, if you can.

Stony silence. I waited. Then the damn broke.

Mother: Someone put a curse on my Margarita!

Therapist: Really? When? How terrible!

Mother: I can't.

Maggie: I'll tell you! It started two months before I shipped out for training. First it was some white powder on the morning newspaper. We didn't think much of it, but then it happened again. Then, in the middle of the night we heard stones on the roof. Bang, big thuds. I went up there on a ladder and found them the next day. It was awful.

Therapist: Who would do such a thing?

Maggie: We don't know. Everybody knew I was shipping out. Maybe somebody thought a Mexican girl shouldn't be a soldier, I don't know.

Mother: Mexicans can be very mean.

Maggie: Then the phone calls started, after midnight when we were asleep. Hang-ups, breathing into the phone, stuff like that.

Mother: Yes, stuff like that. Then the worst, the chicken.

Maggie: Yeah, the bastards smeared a dead chicken on the front porch, the guts and everything. They smeared it in the shape of an M.

Therapist: M for Maggie?

Maggie: Go figure.

Mother: With a crucifix placed in the middle of it.

Maggie: That was a week before I left. Then it stopped. It hasn't happened since.

Therapist: What else?

Mother: Tell the doctor.

Maggie: Then, in Kuwait it happened again, the crucifix and the mutilated body, human body.

Therapist: The mutilated body in the Persian Gulf. Tell me about it. Take a deep breath, reach inside, and tell me everything.

Maggie broke down and sobbed. Mother sobbed. I felt myself trembling. I breathed in deeply and tried to clear my head. I needed to push on.

Therapist: (in a much lower volume) Come on, you can do it.

Maggie: No, no, no, I can't!

I waited and observed her. She was distraught, exhausted. We were done for today.

Therapist: Maggie, you've taken a giant step here today. This takes courage to face. I'm proud of you and I'm sure your mom is, too.

Her body was suddenly wracked with greater sobs, like giant waves they came. Her mother left the recliner and went to her daughter. As best she could manage she balanced with her cane and put her arm around Maggie. Nothing was said for several minutes. I had to break out another box of Kleenex.

Therapist: Would you do something for me at home?

I thought I heard a yes through the tears.

Therapist: I need you to write down everything about the body and the cross so I can see this in black and white. I have a plan. Believe me, this is a break-through. Soon, very soon, you can start to feel better.

Maggie: Sure, whatever.

A plan was now forming in my mind. After she wrote this down I would have her record her words so she could listen to it over and over. I would have her record it here with me, then for a session or two she would listen to it here. Then listen at home. The time for prolonged exposure had arrived. But first, she had to write it. If she didn't, my plan was no good. If she didn't, I could have her tell me about it here during succeeding sessions, that was plan B.

As far as addressing the original curse, I had some ideas, as I'd dealt with this before. We made a follow-up appointment. Afterward, I cornered my friend Bob, the psychologist, who was familiar with this case. He concurred that I was on the right track; however he was very direct about something: Boundaries. "George, you're too involved in this case," he said. "and I know you know this, but you can't do it for her, she has to do it herself." I rather took the last part as an insult but didn't say anything. I would take his words to heart and let them percolate. Then he added, "Be prepared to lose her. She could drop out of therapy now, or kill herself. Does she have access to a gun?" I knew she had at least two pistols, but she hadn't made any threats. But she'd had psychiatric hospitalizations triggered by suicidal thoughts. I'd call her and ask her to have someone hold her guns for the time being.

Notes for practice

This was the fourth or fifth time I'd encountered a curse as a presenting problem (Gafner & Duckett, 1992). One time, I was referred Ray, an elderly Mexican-American WW II vet, who was observed yelling at the devil beside his bed in his nursing home on the V.A. grounds. I immediately thought delirium, but it was nothing like that, as he was cleared medically. After a couple meetings, I had his interesting story. He was cursed ten years before at the onset of Parkinson's disease "… when my body became as rigid as stone." Furthermore, he had been cursed much earlier. While growing up in a small copper mining town north of Tucson, "… two Anglo boys put something in my soda pop that put me to sleep, and then they hit me on the head with a baseball bat." That was at age ten.

In both of Ray's curses familiar trappings (dead animal on the front step, stones on the roof, etc.) were absent. Concrete evidence like that are strong convincers, especially to an outsider like me. Nevertheless, in Ray's mind he had been cursed and had kept it bottled up inside for many years. My treatment for him involved reading him humorous stories in Spanish about Mexican witchcraft. Very soon, he was laughing at the whole deal and no more devils were observed at bedside. I continued to see him every few weeks for a couple of years until he died, reading him books like Hemingway's *Old Man and the Sea* in Spanish.

During that time he asked me if I knew any curanderos (healers). I located an elderly Mexican woman curandera and took Ray to her home. She had an altar set up in her house and said she healed with prayer and herbs. Ray asked for help for the pain in his feet. It was intriguing to me how this woman evaluated him, especially his belief system, in mere seconds, and then began her work with prayer and holy water. She gave Ray some bee ointment for his feet and then we left, total time there about 20 minutes. Other people were waiting to see her. Some months later I asked Ray about the foot pain and he said it was better, as "... she helped me a lot."

Dora and Antonio

In another case, I was seeing a Mexican-American couple in their sixties, Dora and Antonio. He was paralyzed from the waist down from 20 years earlier when he was shot during a robbery of their bar in California. Their presenting problem was, you guessed it, a curse. For months, at least once a week, someone threw a stone on their roof, or they found dead Colorado River toads (large poisonous toads in the desert here), or human feces on their front porch. After the first session they were having a picnic in their back yard when Antonio choked on a piece of meat and ended up in the intensive care unit with a collapsed lung and on a ventilator—a consequence of the curse, they believed. I saw Dora alone for a session and by the second session with her the vet died in the hospital.

All of a sudden the harassment stopped: No stones, no turds on the porch, nothing. Dora knew that her husband's family did not like her, so she surmised that they hired an elderly bruja (female witch) in the neighborhood, and that the bruja paid kids to do the dirty deeds. "Some people can be very mean," she said. She also revealed that every two months for years she had been driving back and forth to California for her affair with a man there, "The Jew." I figured that the couple's focusing on the harassment united them and diverted their attention from their unhappiness, that is, the curse served a definite purpose. Why did it suddenly stop with the husband's death? Who knows? Again, in this case, I had no doubt that the harassment did in fact happen. The last time I talked to Dora she was moving to California to be with her paramour.

Fausto and Carmen

In still another case, I was seeing a Mexican-American couple in their late eighties, Fausto and Carmen. The wife picked up and examined a prop I kept in my office, a container of "anti-jinx powder." "Do you believe in this?" she asked. "I've seen a few things over the years," I answered. "We don't believe in that stuff, that's ridiculous!" she said. Her reaction was way too strong, I thought. About ten minutes later, she picked up the can of powder again and said plaintively, "Maybe you can help us."

They then told me how they had faced similar harassment (stones, toads, feces, dead chickens) over the years and figured that his family had hired a bruja because they didn't like his marrying a woman from "across the line" (the border to Mexico). A professor at Arizona State University was known to be a curandero. I called him and he went to their house. I asked them the next session what happened. She said, "He did a limpia (a cleansing) with burning sage ... he spent two hours there ... he was sweating like a bull ... his Mexican wedding shirt was soaked." Shortly after he left they felt a palpable levity, or easing of tension in the home, and they found a family Bible that had been lost for 20 years. And the harassment stopped.

I've asked several Mexican-American friends what they think about brujería and curanderismo. A few believed in it, but most said something like, "This is *not* something we talk about, much less joke about." Most of them not only don't talk about it; they also don't like it and don't believe in it. "It's all witchcraft," more than one said, meaning that even the curandero or healing part is also brujería, or witchcraft. Being devout Catholics, they resented that curanderismo is linked to their religious faith.

Charles and Bernadette are back

They looked relaxed and happy when they entered the office, holding hands and absorbed in a light banter. There had been very little conflict, they noted.

Therapist: So, has trust returned?

Bernadette: So it seems. This is the best we've been in a long time.

Charles: What can I say? Oh, we've listened to that CD a few times.

Therapist: Good for you. Say, what about Charles' "disappearing act?"

Bernadette: I understand it's something he has to do. We've talked about it at length.

We talked for a while more and it seemed like they had definitely turned the corner. This was going to be a short session, an easy one for me.

Therapist: Let's make an appointment for a month. If you're doing fine, just cancel it. I *do* want to see you guys in no longer than six weeks. Of course, I'll be seeing Charles. How's that sound?

They were fine with that plan and had no other questions. I told them I had a story with which we could end the session.

The Pond
Taken from Pollan (1994) and Gafner & Benson (2003)

A man told me a story once that began with his forty acres back in Indiana. As he started to tell his story, I wondered about its relevance and how long a story it would be, but finally I just sat back and listened to the words without trying to read any meaning into their content. It turns out that this man had always wanted a tranquil pond at the back of his house, a nice pond with plant life and fish, something he could enjoy for a long, long time.

Not caring to do the work himself, he hired a crew of workers and soon trees were cut down and a place was cleared far back from his house. Next, they brought in a large bulldozer and excavator. In several hours the man gazed upon a ten-foot reddish brown gash in the earth's crust. He wondered if the 50 by 125-foot hole would ever fill with water, but he knew that eventually the clay-lined hole would fill right to the top.

With the melting snows of winter and the heavy showers of spring, the pond filled up in no time. One day he noticed algae floating in the water, and soon the sound of frogs filled the air at night. In June, various insects buzzed over the water and aquatic plants appeared along the pond's edge. He knew that all this life had not materialized miraculously, but that it had been borne on the wind or carried unwittingly by the feet of waterfowl.

Eventually the pond looked like a part of the natural landscape. One morning he even spotted the tracks of deer, raccoons, and other animals along the rim. He thought about something he had read once by Henry David Thoreau, something to the effect of "no sooner will you dig your pond and nature will begin to stock it." But nature didn't just stock his pond. Nature had seemed to strike a natural balance between predator and prey, parasite and host, each with its proper place in the larger scheme of things. As the man observed it all from his back porch one evening, he proudly contemplated what he had accomplished. "This is the way it's supposed to be," he thought. "This is something I can enjoy until the end of my days."

One month followed another and pretty soon two years had passed. The man paid less attention to his pond, just assuming that its natural balance would always remain in effect, that the pond would always take care of itself. He traveled to Europe and was gone for a couple of months. When he returned in late summer the pond appeared to be clogged with weeds. However, he thought this was only a temporary condition, and he took another trip, this time for six months. While away, he read a book about ponds. The book mentioned that as algae and weeds grow, die and sink to the bottom, the water becomes shallower, and as more light reaches the bottom, the weeds grow more and more. Rushes and willows on the shore encroach upon the water, which steadily diminishes until the pond becomes a swamp, then just a wet spot. Finally, what was once a pond turns into woodland, which is exactly what it was at the beginning.

He hurried home from his trip and feverishly began raking out the algae and weeds. He stocked the pond with a special kind of carp that eat weeds, and planted cattails to filter out new sediment. Pretty soon his pond was again pulsating with life. He even noticed some things that he had not seen previously, an aquatic spider, and tracks left by a fox. Any trips he took from then on lasted only a month or less and he subscribed to a magazine called *Perpetual Pond*, though he had problems with the title.

Bernadette had listened with her head on Charles' shoulder, her eyes closed. Charles had also closed his eyes. Both took several seconds to reorient.

Bernadette: A good lesson in there.

Charles: Not too bad a story. I've improved on it and composed a companion story, The Lake.

Therapist: A man of endless talents is you, Charles.

Bernadette: Was that hypnosis, George?

Charles: Just a story.

Therapist: Just a story.

Charles returns by himself

Three weeks later Charles was back. In the meantime he had developed a vocal tic, a periodic clearing of his throat in mid-sentence. He appeared more anxious today than other times. Today, he had on shorts and running shoes. I had some material prepared for him today.

Therapist: No work today, huh?

Charles: Nah, took the day off. I drove out by Picacho Peak to see the wild poppies in bloom. They are actually so gorgeous that I was inspired to write a story about them. When I'm done, I'll get you a copy.

Therapist: I wrote a story once about flowers, columbines. Right when I was going to use it the shooting happened at the high school in Columbine, Colorado. That story went in the shredder.

Charles: Well, you probably still have it in the word processor. Give it to me and I'll use it, change it to some other flower, maybe even give you a reference if I publish it.

Therapist: Nah, let that one stay buried. So, how are you and the missus doing?

Charles: A-okay, peachy keen, couldn't be better.

Therapist: So, does that interfere with your fantasies about women clients?

Charles: Nah, fantasies are harmless, I still have 'em. I keep my one-eyed snake zippered up.

Therapist: You look a little nervous today. Are you doing alright?

Charles: Top o' the mornin', life couldn't be better.

Therapist: Hmm, you look a bit out of sorts, like anxious.

Charles: Well, looks can be deceiving. Map is not the territory and all that good stuff.

Therapist: So, Charles, let me get into something here. First, I wanted to mention, well, if I seem tired today, my mind is *shock/shot*, seeing too many clients, you know how that is. My truck has *shock* absorbers, but I don't by any stretch of the imagination. I may be *way off base* here, I'm sure *wrong* plenty of times ... and I was thinking, I've seen you now *ten or fifteen* times, most often late in the *afternoon* to go with your work schedule, and I've seen you and Bernadette maybe *four* or five times, seeing you and her *together*, as well as separately within the session, working with you guys on implementing some things, and there've been a few *stories* along the way.

Misspeak and activate seed
Repeat seed

One-down position
One-down position

Truisms
Truisms
Truisms
Truisms

Truisms

Charles: Yeah, man, now you're rambling, what are you getting at?

Therapist: Just bear with me here, I'm getting there. I worked with *another guy* one time, a professional man like you, though he was a major in the Army and a pencil pusher, not a hero like you, and he had a problem, I forget just what it was, but I told him some stuff similar to what I'm about to convey to you, and that was also after some case consultation.

Metaphor

Charles: Yeah?

Therapist: I've been rather stumped by your case and I took it upon myself to get with some of the staff here for consultation.

Charles: Where's my confidentiality here?

Therapist: I'm free to consult with others. This is all for your benefit, Charles.

Charles: Yeah, go on.

Therapist: So, I ran everything by them and I hate to admit it but I was *shocked*, yes, *shocked*, appalled and aghast by some of the responses. They gave me their considered opinion and advice, which was this:

Activate seed
Activate seed

Greek Chorus

1. *One person said you're doing the best you can and that I should cut you some slack.*

2. *Another said you could crash your Bentley if you listen to a relaxation tape that I made you, and that I might need legal advice.*

3. *One said you're holding back on something vital, possibly a deep, dark secret that is "festering like an abscess deep within," her exact words.*

4. *Another said that your situation will definitely get worse before it gets better.*

5. *And the last person, who often is wrong, feels that a significant revelation may be forthcoming within a couple of weeks.*

Charles: And what about you, what do *you* think, George?

Therapist: Hell, I don't know what to think, that's why I asked for help!

Charles: God, man, I don't know what to think. This is really weird.

Therapist: Here, I wrote the five opinions down for you.

Charles: For my edification?

Therapist: I guess.

He snatched the paper from my hand and beat a quick exit. No good-bye, no "thanks," no "Let's make another appointment," nothing, definitely a good recoil.

Notes for practice

I had written out the Greek Chorus last night, and even this morning I was feeling pretty ambivalent about springing this on Charles. First, I wondered if he was familiar with the Greek Chorus technique. Even if he knew it, it probably didn't matter, for in working with therapists who are clients, I've found that when I put my finger on something dear, with a technique like this, or even with a simple metaphor, distress takes over and conscious reasoning is cast aside. Some years back I was attending a workshop where the speakers were from the Mental Research Institute in Palo Alto, California, and John Weakland said that paradoxical behavior prescriptions used with therapists who are clients in therapy, people who themselves practice paradoxically, are as effective as when used with clients.

Greek Chorus is like the ambiguous function assignment in that it is indicated when we're stuck and need a bolt of lightning to spark movement. During those years, how often did I use it? Oh, I did it myself or helped a trainee design one maybe five or six times a year, not that often. By the time we get to that point in therapy we know the client well and know how to slant the list, usually with one or two target suggestions, while the others—however ridiculous or provocative—serve to distract. In keeping with the response time for paradox in the literature, I'd expect a response usually within two weeks to a month if I've hit home.

To date, I've been rather flying by the seat of my pants with Charles, and decided to employ this on a hunch alone. Clearly, there was a strong recoil from him—and not just a narcissistic injury—so I felt that this just might perturb. If I don't hear from him within a week or two, I'll call him.

For weeks I've had a hunch that something about Vietnam had fueled the initial referral and was now maintaining guilt. Why guilt? Again, just a hunch. Two things have worked for me over the years when something inexplicable seemed to be operating beneath the surface, something I couldn't put my finger on. Number one, if the diagnosis is unclear and things just don't add up, I suspect substance abuse, perhaps an addiction not yet revealed by the client. And number two—which applies in the case of Charles—when I suspect something not yet revealed is operating below the surface, the G word immediately springs to mind. That's right, *guilt*.

CHAPTER ELEVEN

Therapy nears its conclusion

Maggie is back

Therapist: Where's your mom today?

Maggie: She's with my cousin this morning.

Maggie was calm and controlled, her mood was serious. She didn't look stoned.

Therapist: I hope you aren't too angry with your mom, you know, for busting you.

Maggie: I guess she had to do it. She's my mom, she's old. She's been through a lot with me and my problems. She doesn't care for this dialysis routine.

Therapist: Now the cat's out of the bag.

Maggie: I don't like that expression. I love my kitty cats. Most days they're the only thing that keeps me going. You talk about managing stress. Well, petting them takes away my stress.

Therapist: How's the IBS going?

Maggie: You know, it's kind of up and down but mostly up. Overall, I'm not that constipated anymore.

Three weeks had passed and I was able to squeeze her in today when she called to report she had written her statement. I saw from my chair that she had typed it in a very large font.

Maggie: Here you go, that about sums it up.

Therapist: I've got bad eyes but I'm not that blind.

Maggie: You're ancient, aren't you? Didn't you meet Freud once?

I laughed inside, her humor was back!

Therapist: Thanks for doing it. I'll look at it in a minute.

Maggie: All this is damn shameful, the curse and all. With Mexicans that's something always lurking in the background, but it's nothing you talk about.

Therapist: I realize that. The subject is not new to me. Now we need to do something about it. There are two things to do here: number one, we'll work with your statement—that will help a lot, and number two, the curse. Any ideas you have?

Maggie: Nope.

Therapist: You know any curanderos?

Maggie: Nope again.

I regarded the cross she wore around her neck. This was bigger than any crucifix she'd worn previously. A central construct of curanderismo is that God works through curanderos, or folk healers.

Therapist: The ones I knew are dead or moved back to Mexico. Others I've heard about I wouldn't recommend.

Maggie: Why not?

Therapist: Well, if you really want to know. There used to be a guy down by the rodeo grounds. Supposedly he was into santería, I don't know. I heard about a young woman who went to him because her 2-year-old daughter was in a coma from a swimming pool accident. He told the mother, "Bring me three thousand dollars," which she scraped together from relatives and a high-interest loan. Then, he said, "Kill a chicken, take out its heart" and do such-and-such "and your daughter will wake up." The mother did exactly as she was told and the next day her daughter died.

Maggie: There's as much evil out there as good, they prey on people. I've heard shit like that.

Therapist: Not long ago I was seeing a couple, both in their forties, neither the vet nor the wife knew much English, the wife was a real nervous Nellie, anxious as all get-out. The next session, she shows up and she's totally calm and happy. I asked her if she started pills, or what, and the vet said he took her to a curandero off 22nd street, and he cured her. When I saw the wife separately, she revealed that the "healer" told her he'd make her well if she followed his instructions precisely. So, she took off her clothes and he had intercourse with her, among other things. She was cured in one session.

Maggie: She probably wasn't getting any at home.

Therapist: Exactly. The thing is she thought there was nothing wrong with it, like the doctor tells you what to do and you do it. There's no professional board to report that guy to.

Maggie: But the curandero made your job easier.

Therapist: So true. It's just weird, all that stuff. So, back to you here. Are you on good terms with any priest in town?

Maggie: Father Sean over at Santa Inéz, he's cool, been around the block.

Therapist: Okay if I talk to him?

Maggie: Sure.

Therapist: You'll have to go to Release of Information and sign a release. He doesn't need to know any details about your case, just the general curse stuff.

Maggie: Go for it.

I turned to her statement. How long had this been in coming? Many months and how many sessions? I couldn't remember for sure.

Maggie's statement

"Those coming back from Iraq now call it the sandbox, we didn't say that exactly, but we called the locals sand flies, stuff like that. So, I'm writing about my job in the Army there, mostly in Kuwait, and

I don't remember the exact dates of things, but it was early 1991. It was mostly boring, to tell the truth. Wasn't like the wars heating up now in Iraq and Afghanistan, where we're getting a lot of people killed, all the IEDs along the road and stuff. We waited around for some unit to bring in body bags, or we'd get a call on the radio to go out to a collection point and pick them up. People think we did autopsies and cleaned the bodies and all that, but no, we had orders to just try to determine identity and especially collect stuff their families would want, shit like credit cards, wedding rings, etc.

"We'd see a lot of flea collars, the ones for cats, around their ankles. The bugs were so bad they wore these things which they said later was really toxic to the person. Bug bites, rashes, on the skin. Like I said, we'd do our thing and then they'd get sent to Dover Air Force Base in Maryland, I think it was. So, anyway, in the building—sometimes it was a big tent set up—you've got these large metal tables. We'd typically have incense burning and Black Sabbath—way too loud—on the sound system. Sometimes we'd get interrupted from work or sleep when a SCUD was coming in, have to quickly put on the protective suit and all and cower by a berm outside. During one attack I puked in my gas mask, and the Sergeant called me a "chicken shit Mexican girl," and he was right about that, but I didn't like being teased by the others.

"Sometimes in a bag you'd get parts of two people, even a civilian or Iraqi, part of one of them, and maybe a kid's leg, the kids were tough to see. So, one night I had to report over to another table to help out, it was one of ours, just a torso, no head, no arms, just one leg with a flea collar around the ankle, no way to identify him but you could tell it was "a him" because he had a ragged piece of penis and no balls. This guy had clearly been mutilated. Something was eerie, strange about this body. The nipple stud the guy had. He was darker skinned, like maybe a Mexican. Body piercings weren't allowed, but a lot of them had them anyway. When we rolled him over he had a chain sticking out of his ass. I pulled it out, a big gold chain came out and on the end of it was a cross, a crucifix, and something was familiar about it, and then it hit me, this was Jimmy X from Tucson, I went to high school with him, in fact I dated him for a few months. My mother sent me cochitos every week (Mexican molasses cookies in the shape of a pig) and right then I puked cochitos all over the table. I thought right then that I'd been cursed. What else could it be? Here I was, holding that chain and dead Jimmy right there on the table, it was too much. Later they confirmed it really was him. I run into his parents and his sister at church and I think, "If only they knew." They sent me to the doctor. He gave me some pills and I tried to sleep but I couldn't. It was awful. All I could think about was that chain and cross and the embarrassment of puking. I couldn't get it out of my mind and I still can't. After that whenever I got cochitos I gave them away. I don't know what else to say. That was the worst thing that happened to me. Now it's out."

I re-read it. Someone had brought cochitos into the break room just this morning.

Therapist: Maggie, you mentioned the Sergeant. Was there any sexual abuse from him or anybody else?

Maggie: Not to me, I heard about some stuff like that, but not to me.

Therapist: How does it feel now that you've got this out?

Maggie: I don't know. It was hard to write.

Therapist: To give me something to go on, on a scale of zero to ten, with ten being the worst, how bad do you feel about this right now?

Maggie: Maybe an eight or nine.

Therapist: This is a big step. Let's say you buy something shrink-wrapped, like a six-pack of water bottles. They're real hard to get out, but once you release the first one, the rest come out quite easily. Now you can start to put this behind you. You won't ever forget this. Your duty in the sandbox, but now you can start to see it in a different light and put it in the rear-view mirror.

Maggie: If you say so.

I checked again for any thoughts of suicide, reiterated the plan and rationale for having her record the statement and then listen to it here. I reminded her to listen to her original CD on a regular basis and went over other measures for stress management. For the first time I was starting to feel good about this case.

Charles' surprise visit

Eight days after Charles' quick exit, I was eating lunch outside my office. I was sitting on the ground, my back up against an ancient mesquite tree. It felt wonderful to escape from the frigid air conditioner and I didn't at all mind the 110-degree heat and 2 percent humidity. I had gotten take-away from a nearby Mexican restaurant: two cheese enchiladas, two carne seca enchiladas, and a bowl of albóndigas, a spicy meatball soup. All of a sudden I sensed the presence of another. I looked up from my food and saw a pair of penny loafers at the end of tan Dockers slacks.

Charles: You're hard to track down.

Therapist: Well, you caught me.

Charles: I need to see you as soon as possible.

Therapist: How about in 20 minutes when I'm done here?

Charles: Why not right now?

Therapist: Charles, I realize it might be important, but so is my lunch. I can skip a meeting at 1:00, come back then.

Charles: If I must.

Once inside
Therapist: So, what's going on?

Charles thrust some handwritten pages from a yellow legal pad.

Charles: Read this. I wrote something up.

Charles' statement

"It was August 15, 1968. I was 18 years old and I had been in Vietnam for six months and hadn't seen any action, though we were on high alert from some sapper attacks. That day I was with a unit working in a support capacity somewhere outside of Saigon. The medivac landed in a clearing near where a platoon had taken casualties. I think a Huey with several soldiers also showed up for support, I forget exactly. Typically, the enemy engaged you fiercely for a short time and then melted into the jungle. I was one of two medics attending to our wounded. I had mostly been a medic at hospitals, and this was the first time I had seen any real action in the Air Cavalry.

"Two guys with sucking chest wounds—we stuck them with morphine and left them, and soon they were gone. Some others were wounded and unconscious, I think one head shot who died instantly. We put the KIAs in body bags and loaded them up. I was shaking all over. This war was real all of a sudden. I had just opened a new pack of Camels and was working my Zippo lighter when all hell broke loose. Somebody radioed for help and we took cover. Mortars came in, a blizzard of AK-47 fire, it seemed like a whole battalion was pasting us. Guys were dying all around. I took some shrapnel in the shoulder. Then I burrowed myself in under some bodies in the tall grass. In there, I took a round in the buttock. I closed my eyes and peeked out every so often. There were screams and smoke and explosions and blood, it was really awful. This thing went on for maybe 15 minutes, I don't know.

"The other medic, the only guy standing now, picked up an M-16 and started firing. It looked like he was firing off many clips, I think throwing grenades or something, too, he kept changing positions, and during all this he attended the wounded the best he could. I mean, that guy, he was super-human, a real hero, holding off the enemy, and how he didn't get killed I'll never know. Finally, help came, I think the Air Force dropped some bombs on them and a Cobra blasted them, they came in force. And right before they landed the hero medic takes a round in the forehead and is dead instantly.

"As they landed I emerged from hiding, holding an M-16, and before I could say anything, this lieutenant shouts something like, "Look what this guy did!" He screamed, "He held off the fucking dinks!" I can still hear his words there in the smoke and noise. I didn't say anything. I didn't know what to say or do, I just stood there. They were searching the bodies of the enemy, and this one, a girl no more than 16, something fell out, I picked it up, it was a picture of her parents smiling. I can still see their smile. I think some of our wounded survived, I don't know how many, the ones that lived, most were unconscious, and they didn't see anything. They talk about "the fog of war," that was one dense fog there that day.

"They kept me out of the action after that. Not too much later there was a big ceremony with photographers there and they pinned the Distinguished Service Cross on me. I was told that headquarters badly needed a hero right then and I was it. I just smiled and said some crap like I was proud to do my duty for my country. Back home I was a big hero and I got to kind of like it, almost like I believed it really happened. My parents went to their grave believing I was a big war hero. That's fine.

"Over the years I've told myself that I served a purpose, they needed a hero and I was it. I never told anybody this before, not even my wife, so now I'll have to have a talk with her."

I read it once. I couldn't believe what I was reading. I read it a second time and started thinking about the implications of this. My mind was spinning and I tried to collect my thoughts.

Charles: You finally got what you were after. You feel better now?

Therapist: This is about you, not me.

Charles: I wonder about that.

Therapist: This whole deal, coming clean and all, getting it off your chest, zero to ten scale with ten being the worst, what number you give it at this moment?

Charles: An easy nine.

Therapist: That number should go down in time. What about anxiety, feeling "beaten to a pulp," how're those things?

Charles: Don't you ever give the numbers a rest? I'm fine. Rest of my life is going great, we're getting along at home, my practice is booming, and when I find myself fantasizing about women clients I think about something else. I go for a ride in the desert when I need to. I got another Bentley, did I tell you?

Therapist: Good for you. Say, the drinking. Are you drinking heavy?

Charles: Never did. Two fingers of Chivas at bedtime, that's my limit.

Therapist: Good.

Charles: So, what's the next step here?

Therapist: Up to you, you know that.

Charles: You think I should go public with this and return my medal.

Therapist: I never said that.

Charles: But you *think* it, I can tell.

Therapist: So, you're a mind-reader now, a man of limitless talents.

Charles: The real hero, the medic who was killed, I checked into this. He left no wife or kids and there's only a few cousins left, all in Vermont.

Therapist: So, going public would really serve no purpose, would it? I mean, how anti-climactic, who in the hell would care 40-some years after the fact?

Charles: My thoughts exactly. But I need to tell my wife.

Therapist: You bet. What do you say we get together in about a month, you come in with Bernadette.

Charles: Sounds like a winner.

Therapist: Oh, one thing. You've been doing your volunteer work with the 'Yards. I'm glad you're doing that. That has to be good for the soul. After this confession today, if you think you need to do anything else, as a penance kind of thing, well, that could help bring the number down from a nine. You might want to watch a movie called *The Mission*.

Charles: I'll rush out and rent it tonight. Anyway, the zero to ten thing, you're too obsessed with those stupid measures.

Therapist: That's the first time I've heard any sarcasm out of you. The measures, some famous psychologist once said, "If you can't measure it, it's just poetry."

Charles: Poetry works fine for me. Maybe I'll even write a story about you.

Therapist: Spare me! That would be one boring story that would put people to sleep.

Charles: You've got boredom down to a science.

Therapist: On that note, let's reschedule. Remember what I told you way back, to regard the Wildermuth principle.

Charles: What's that again?

Therapist: Don't forget to breathe.

Notes for practice

Charles got me thinking about how his confession was more about me than him. Certainly I'll own the impetus of it, going on a hunch that something important was operating beneath the surface. Jeffrey Zeig (personal communication, 2003) reminds us that our guide should always be the client's response, as opposed to being guided by our techniques. To that end, I'll feel better about this case if Charles' SUDS level goes down.

Charles caused me to recall a movie, *The Mission*, which takes place in seventeenth-century South America. A Spaniard kills his brother and he goes to a priest and asks how he can pay a penance for his terrible sin. The priest assigns an arduous physical ordeal, dragging a heavy load up a steep jungle mountainside, up to the top and back down, up and down every day. After doing this for weeks the exhausted murderer asks the priest when he will know he has paid sufficient penance, and he is told, *"Only you will know when you have suffered enough."* It may be a long stretch to compare murder to deception or fraud; however, as Charles has apparently assuaged his guilt to some extent, further penance may not be in order. If it is, only he will know.

I've assigned that movie several times over the years. People come to us burdened by guilt from past deeds. Oftentimes they want us to tell them both what to do to free themselves and for how long they should do it. That's usually a fool's errand for us; however, we can meet them halfway by assigning something like *The Mission*, along with the assurance that they can generate the means and duration of the penance. In this business we can be grateful for anything that doesn't have to come from us.

CHAPTER TWELVE

Farewell to Maggie and Charles

Maggie's priest

Mexican Catholics talk about "padres gordos y padres flacos," fat priests and lean priests. On this day I found myself in the office of the latter at a modest little church in Tucson's barrio. I waited for Father Sean while he finished confession. Not much bigger than a closet, his office had a small desk piled high with books and magazines. Open on the desk was the Tucson Weekly, *the free arts and entertainment paper. The floor was cluttered with boxes from the local food bank. Social activist posters covered the walls along with a photo of the priest standing with Pope John. He soon arrived.*

Father Sean: Nice to meet you. I've known Maggie and her mother for several years. What do I need to know to help this young lassie? I understand that a crisis is occurring.

The priest had a strong handshake and a piercing but warm gaze. He looked to be in his fifties and he had a ruddy complexion. He spoke with an Irish accent. He was clearly very busy and got right down to business.

Therapist: Father, are you familiar with curses?

Father Sean: Oh, so that's what this concerns? Unfortunately, I am all too familiar with this phenomenon. There are some very mean people out there.

Therapist: The devil operating?

Father Sean: If you will.

I filled him in on what I knew. He listened patiently. His gaze never wavered, which caused me to glance at his posters more than once. I then asked him what he would recommend.

Father Sean: Most shameful, a very nasty business. In your work you see the evil of war. Here, I see a similar evil, though from a different kind of war. To answer your question, we must counter the work of the devil with God, specifically with God's working *through* people who have the *don*, or gift.

Common in many cultures in the developing world, especially in rural areas, is the folk healer. Traditionally in Mexico a future curandera was identified as a young girl, one of the rare few who possessed this don, *or gift. One elderly curandera told me that at age five in rural Mexico she could predict the weather, or look down a long row of corn and determine the precise location of an aberrant corn stalk. She was then apprenticed to a curandera from whom she learned to diagnose conditions such as susto (fright), empacho (constipation), or curse, all of which are treated with herbs, massage, and similar means. Common to all curanderas is that they employ prayer and receive their powers from God.*

Therapist: You have a curandera in your parish?

Father Sean: No, but I know one. With or without money, Lola will help. She will "do her thing," as they say, and may also recommend further measures.

Therapist: I know this sounds dumb, but what do you estimate her rate of success is with curses?

Father Sean: Probably better than yours, 60 percent or higher.

Therapist: Wrong. Didn't anybody tell you that the V.A. cure rate nationally is 99 percent?

Father Sean: I don't mean suicide rate.

Therapist: We don't joke about suicides at the V.A.

During the current wars in Afghanistan and Iraq, the military, especially the Army, is perplexed about the high suicide rate. The V.A. (which treats personnel once they leave the military) estimates that 22 veterans a day commit suicide.

Father Sean: Okay, okay, that was out of bounds. You develop a gallows humor in my work and it's not often I can let it loose.

Therapist: So, logistically, how does this work?

Father Sean: I have a car leased by the Diocese. I'll pick her up and bring her back.

Father Sean visits the V.A. a week later

Father Sean: Not easy to park out here.

Therapist: A lot better than it used to be.

Father Sean: Well, I'm sure you want to hear about our visit to Lola's.

Therapist: Indeed!

Father Sean: Okay, so I drive her to this little house out off Old Nogales Highway. We had to wait while she saw some farm worker with a bad cough. She listened with a stethoscope, saw him for only a minute, I'd guess, and said she'd pray for him. She told him to get to an emergency room right away because his symptoms screamed pneumonia.

Therapist: Did he pay her?

Father Sean: I think he gave her some food stamps and coins. Once I saw someone pay her with a live chicken. From what I understand, she likes it if you can give her something, but if you're real poor you're excused. So, she took Maggie in. I sat on a chair not far away. She told us to turn off any cell phones and asked if we were recording it, and of course we weren't. I think my being a priest made her a bit uneasy, though she's seen me before. One thing about Lola is she sizes up the person really fast, all in a few seconds, especially sizes up the person's level of belief. With Maggie, she eyeballed her, then just nodded and smiled, like Maggie had passed the test or something.

Therapist: Did she have an altar?

Father Sean: Yeah, an elaborate altar with saint candles, a lot of candles burning in general, had some incense going, smelled like Nag Champa. It was semi-dark and glowed in that room. She asked Maggie about the curse. Maggie was pretty nervous going in but while there she was very calm. Lola mumbled prayers over her, shook out some liquid she said was Seven Seas water, and then she had Maggie lie on the floor, on her back, and she began a *limpia*, a cleansing, you know what that is, with burning sage, she passed it up and down Maggie's body. She paused a long time in the area of her stomach, asked her if she had a problem there, and Maggie nodded. Then she had her sit in the chair again, she said some more prayers, and then she told her she was healed—except that Maggie needs to do one more thing: Burn 10 candles at El Tiradito (Little Castaway) shrine, one each night for 10 nights, and pray for 10 minutes there each time. That was it.

Therapist: How did Maggie seem afterward?

Father Sean: Very serene, at peace. When we stopped in front of her house she asked me to pray with her for a minute. We did that, then she walked briskly into the house and I drove off.

Therapist: How do you think she'll do now?

Father Sean: I'd guess she might do okay. There's just something *troubling* about that young woman.

Therapist: She has a moral injury. We see that a lot at the V.A.

Father Sean: Now, that diagnosis I know about.

Therapist: Her mother said a different person came back from the sandbox. A mother would know.

Father Sean: War is our business and business is good.

I thanked the priest for his help, knowing that his involvement was critical if Maggie were to get better. I admired his versatility, how he could comfortably navigate in different worlds. Father Sean arose from his chair, we shook hands, and he started for the door. Then, he stopped and turned around.

Father Sean: Do you ever think about when you're done working, when you'll have to leave the Maggies of the world behind?

Therapist: You mean, when we're no longer needed?

Father Sean: You've got a family, I assume.

Therapist: Yes, wife, kids, grandkids. They mean the world to me, don't know what I'd do without them, but I know what you're getting at.

Father Sean: The Maggies, the Church, that's the only family I have, a few cousins in Ireland.

Therapist: The *being needed* part, that's a tough one. We delude ourselves into thinking we're so good at helping people that we become indispensable. There's a pride there.

Father Sean: I know what you mean. The pride part, rein that in, bad for your soul.

Therapist: You've still got a lot of years ahead of you. Good luck. Let me know if I can ever help with anything. I sincerely hope you stay being needed for a long, long time.

Father Sean: Adios.

Finishing up with Maggie

Over the next two months, with stops and starts and cancellations, we were able to make the recording and listen to it five times, all in the office, as she declined to also listen at home. Maggie's nightmares, which had returned when we began exposure, were now infrequent. Her distress while listening to the recording steadily diminished and after the fifth time her SUDS was "about a two." Some therapists might have pushed her farther, but I was satisfied with a two, plus I was tired, and she had to move on.

The diagnostic emotions for PTSD in the DSM-IV are fear, helplessness or horror. A mistake I used to make was to stick to these at the expense of other, often more compelling emotions, like shame, guilt and disgust. With Maggie, certainly the three standard emotions applied, but I would have been very remiss had I not thoroughly processed shame and guilt, and especially disgust. Also, something not in the criteria, but something I saw often at the V.A., as well as in Maggie, was distress at witnessing injustice or unfairness done to others. The following summarizes both her intrusive recollections and the material processed, in addition to listening to her statement:

Typical distressing situation	Cognition	Emotion
1. seeing injustice	"I could be next."	helplessness
2. seeing amputees	"I could have done a better job over there."	sadness
3. cochito cookies	"I can't control anything."	disgust, shame, guilt

Maggie asked for a different story to listen to, so I recorded one for her, Seeing Things Differently (Gafner and Benson, 2003).

Seeing Things Differently

Someone was telling me once about how he learned to see things differently with the passage of both time and distance.

It was the Fourth of July holiday and he found himself on a boat that was slowly going farther and farther out into the water. It was 3:00 in the afternoon, and he watched various activities on the beach, things that he could see quite clearly, in fairly vivid detail.

There was a lifeguard perched way up on the lifeguard chair. He had one of those floppy hats on his head, and mirrored sunglasses, and that white stuff on his nose shone brightly in the sun. A volleyball game was going on, off to the right of the lifeguard chair. All around, people lay on blankets, and the sunscreen on their bodies glistened in the heat of the day. An oversized red umbrella stood out like a crimson flower blossom. Children splashed in the water, and he could hear their gleeful cries above the crash of the waves.

Everything became a bit blurry as the boat got farther from the shore; however, as a telescope was mounted on the back of the boat, he began to watch everything through the telescope, which all of a sudden brought the beach back into sharp focus. The boat continued its journey, out from the shore.

As time passed, the details of the beach through the telescope kept changing, ever so gradually. He could see that the volleyball players were still in motion, but he could no longer see the ball. People continued to splash in the water, but he could no longer hear their voices. They may have been children, but they could have just as easily been adults. The lifeguard was still perched on high, but there was no white on his nose. The oversized umbrella was now orange, or was it brown? He stepped back from the telescope, closed his eyes, and contemplated what he had seen.

Several minutes later—or maybe it was longer than several minutes—the sun had descended, and it was not quite as warm on his back as before. He put his eye to the telescope once again, and everything before him took on a most curious aspect. The lifeguard chair remained prominent, but he could not tell for sure if a person was still sitting on it. The volleyball game appeared to have stopped, just as people may have ceased lying on the sand. He saw only flickers of movement in the water where the children had been playing, and was it the umbrella that was buffeted by a gust of wind? The only sound was the boat's motor. He closed his eyes again and let his imagination drift and dream.

A while later, the sun had sunk farther down in the sky, and as he put his eye to the telescope once again, the sight before him had become only sea and shore in the distance, water and coastline, as the boat continued out.

Later on in life, he continued to experience many things, with time and distance in between, seeing them one way, and then another, and often he reflected on that journey out from the shore.

Maggie's therapy is concluded

She had a new boyfriend and had begun a bachelor's program in computer science at the university. Three months after her last visit, she called to say her mother was dying and wanted to see me. Mom had voluntarily removed herself from dialysis and with only a few days to live had developed uremic frost, an eerie-looking green fuzz, that covered the skin. "Thank you for helping my Maggie," she said in a weak voice. I smiled, but words did not come to me. Her eyes closed. I sat there another 10 minutes while she slept. Finally, I gently grasped her hand on top of the sheets. Her eyes opened briefly as I stood up to leave. Then they closed and I left. I didn't see Maggie as I exited the house.

Three years later I ran into Maggie at the Fourth Avenue Street Fair, an event that draws a half-million people on the weekend. As if running into an old friend, I greeted her enthusiastically. She was polite but cold. I was just someone else from her past, as well I should be. She had moved on in life and any meaning from our visits was long gone, perhaps an unhappy chapter in her life that was now vague and seemed like a lifetime ago. How often has that happened, where I attached inordinate meaning to a case I had invested in? The client moves on, but I remain stuck in time, the slow learner that I am.

Bernadette leaves a phone message

One month after I saw Charles, I listened to a message left by his wife: "We're doing fine, we're going on a cruise to Alaska. Charles says to tell you the number is down to a three and won't go any lower. I, at least, appreciate all your help. I know my husband can be difficult but he's my husband. Thanks again and good luck. If we need any help down the road, I'll call."

How is it that some of the most unlikeable vets have the nicest wives? I was glad this case was concluded. If five years pass and they call for an appointment, I'll be retired and they can see somebody else. The whole time, I felt chided by Charles and his dismissive attitude. I still wonder about whether I should have pushed my hunch that he was harboring some secret about the war. As narcissistic as he is, I doubt that he would report a lower number just to make the therapist feel good. Or would he? Evidently he never did anything about his big lie and come to think of it, what would it matter? Maybe the whole course of therapy was two narcissists butting heads against each other. I never saw either Bernadette or Charles again and haven't run into them in Tucson since I retired.

CHAPTER THIRTEEN

Employing indirect techniques in various treatment settings, and more

Other indirect techniques

Confederate outside the door

Here's a rather unusual—maybe bizarre is a better word—technique, and its origin is no less strange. About 10 years back I was seeing a Mexican-American man with guilt from service in the Iraqi war in 2004. He and his squad were guarding a "bag farm," an area where huge synthetic bladders of fuel were stored. One of his men was killed there and he could not forgive himself.

He had failed individual and group therapy and was referred for hypnosis. I did three customary sessions of ego-strengthening, and though he was able to achieve deep trance, there was no improvement in the presenting problem. The next session I was about to do a procedure called age regression, abreaction and reframing with him when early in the session two women employees parked themselves outside my office door and held a brief but very loud conversation. I was about to open the door and ask them to talk elsewhere, but they suddenly departed. But before they left, one of them remarked, "You need to get rid of that *big form*."

The disturbance distracted me to the extent that I just stopped after the induction and didn't proceed with the plan, opting for a story instead. When the man returned in two weeks he was markedly improved. No more worry and anguish, no more guilt or insomnia. "What happened?" I asked. He answered, "One night the Virgin Mary visited me in my dream and told me to get rid of that *bag farm*." After he revealed this it took me a few minutes to put two and two together. A month later he remained improved and we scheduled no further sessions. This guy was cured and only because of my dumb luck!

Thereafter, I tried out this technique in our hypnosis training group. With the subject in trance, I slipped a piece of paper under the door and on it was the desired suggestion, such as, "Lydia, you can finish that dissertation," or "Ed, you can do it." The person outside then said the words with sufficient volume, then repeated it, and left. It worked like a charm. We then employed the technique with clients, I think about four times, each time it worked, and not once was there any conscious awareness of it by the subject.

Rustling some papers

Interested in an even sneakier technique? Erickson first reported on having clients change chairs so that their resistance is left in the first chair. The first time I tried it I was amazed at how it worked, and thereafter I used it several times over the years. The pretext need not be really convincing. I simply say something like, "Judy, please be so kind as to humor me a second and just switch chairs for my benefit, simply move over to this chair for the rest of the session, would you?" But that's not really sneaky at all. This one is.

A college class taught me the group equivalent of the "changing chairs" technique. I was lecturing to a class of graduate students and was about to do a group relaxation exercise. When doing so, it's always good to excuse anyone who might not want to participate. I announced that, and a woman at one of the tables nervously and noisily rustled some papers in front of her, quickly rose from her chair, and bolted out of the room. Wow, what a surprise, what a distraction, it seemed to cut the atmosphere with a knife. But it also neutralized anxiety, the rest of the class responded with both shock and relief, and they then responded marvelously to a group induction and story.

"Too good a thing to not use in the future," I thought to myself as the class ended. Accordingly, I used that several times over the years in the first meeting of an anger management group. In the group, people are anxious, wonder if they made a mistake by attending, are reluctant to reveal personal information—all the stuff we see in an initial group therapy session. We pass out some handouts so everybody at the large table has some papers, and when I subtly nod to the confederate, he rustles his papers with a relish and then beats a hasty exit. The effect is often dramatic: there is an immediate release of tension once the atmosphere in the room has been cut. The veteran we used for that, Harry, tired of the rustling-some papers role, so we found a better one for him. Articulate and a bonafide Vietnam PTSD guy, he was the whiskey voice of authority, so we had him attend the first meeting only of group anger management. His only instructions were, "Tell them this is an okay place to be, speak from the heart." So, he casually talked about how "… the stuff they teach here is good, it'll help you with your anger, used to be that somebody would give me a finger in traffic and I'd run them down, I beat them up but sometimes I'd get beat up, and nowadays everybody has a gun in their car … not any more, the tools they gave me here, I keep them sharp … and my wife likes the new me … and they also tell you some stories, I don't know about those …" Worked like a charm, he was a natural. Harry accomplished in ten minutes what would take us hours.

I tried *Rustling Some Paper* twice in family therapy. The first time, it was the second session after an especially angst-ridden first session a week before with parents and children. A student started the session with me and about five minutes into it she did her thing with the papers and burst out. It did not work one bit; in fact, the parents thought we should stop the session so I could go out and check on her, but I said, "Nah, that's how she is, no big deal." With this family, I was unsuccessful in shifting blame from the children to them for the marital woes, and they quit after five times. The second time we used it, with a couple, I asked the student, "Say, tone it down a notch, don't overdo this," which she did, the tension magically drained from the room, and therapy was successful.

An unconventional story application: Strange but true

One time, I was asked to see a woman client in her house. I don't normally do that as I think providing therapy in people's homes has several pitfalls, one of them being that therapists lose important leverage inherent in clients' going to the office. But this case was different. *Real different*, it turned out.

Doctors had delivered the baby of a young mother who went to the refugee clinic at the university, and now the mother was paralyzed from the waist down. The doctors explained to me that there was no medical reason for the paralysis; in other words, this was an hysterical paralysis, something I had never dealt with before. I asked two colleagues, a psychiatrist and a psychologist, what they might do, and their answers involved medication and long-term therapy. I didn't have the time or interest in long-term therapy, and I figured the doctors would have gotten a psychiatric consultation already, or put her on something themselves, if they had wanted to. The mother, age 22, from El Salvador, had had two other children with no complications. Though she and her parents were forced to flee the civil war in her country when she was very young, she had not personally experienced any of that trauma. She took no medication, she was otherwise healthy, and her husband was supportive. She knew almost no English.

Can chickens be incorporated into a treatment plan?

I entered the modest home in Tucson's barrio. Chickens scurried by me in the kitchen as I was shown to the bedroom where (I'll call her) Maria sat up in bed holding the baby. First, I made sure to confirm with her husband that this was okay, and he said yes, eager to have his now-disabled wife walking again. I introduced myself, asked Maria if this was okay, and she said, "Oh, you're from the church, so it's fine." (One of the local churches was instrumental in starting the refugee clinic.)

I asked how I might help and she said, "I need to walk so I can take care of my baby." Simple, straightforward presenting problem, full steam ahead. Except … that I had no idea what to do! Maria endorsed no distress of any kind, no anxiety or depression, nor did she evince a *belle indifference*. I had seen a few of those before. After about 20 minutes I dredged up some enthusiasm and asked, "How about if I come back next Tuesday at the same time and we'll start to work on your walking so you can take care of your baby?" She was absolutely delighted. The brief session was over. I made my way through the kitchen where children playing had now joined the chickens on the floor.

Back to the basics with a story

In a few days a plan surfaced while I was driving home from my regular job at the V.A. I had several stock ego-strengthening stories that I had translated into Spanish, and I took one of those with me. Past the chickens, into the bedroom, and after some brief pleasantries, I pulled out the story and said, "I would like your help with something, plus I think this can help you. I want to read you this story and I would like you to correct any mistakes, I need to make sure I get this right, so you can tell me, okay?" "You bet." Then, I proceeded to read it to her, I think it was The Greenhouse, line by line, slowly, often repeating a sentence over and over again. She would say, "Read that part again, one more time," and I would do so, stopping to insert suggested words or phrasing in the text. It took three visits to complete the first story. Each time a story was finished, I left a redacted copy with her along with instructions to read it once a day. After six more visits spaced out over three months I was no longer able to see her because of my schedule. I left her with three or four stories to read. There had been no change in her functional status.

A month later I saw her at the clinic—walking with a cane. I said "Hi" in passing. A few months after that, I saw her in the parking lot walking unassisted, albeit with a pronounced limp. That was the last time I saw her. I'd like to take some credit for her improvement, but for all I know, time alone can be thanked. I've not used that story technique since, but it's there in my toolbox if I need it.

Hypnotic techniques in hospitals, residential treatment, and correctional facilities

Hospitals and treatment facilities

Hypnotic language, seeding, metaphor, story and anecdote are a natural fit in group and individual therapy for addictions and other problems in hospital settings. One former trainee who now works with clients in psychiatric hospitals and residential treatment told me, "My clients welcome a story because it's a nice respite from the highly structured routine of ongoing evaluation and the expectation of constant self-disclosure." Hospitals have brief stays (three days on average in the U.S.), while in residential treatment the stays can be weeks to months. In both of these, meditation, hypnosis, relaxation and related procedures are practiced, often in a group format, in addition to conventional modalities.

There are many treatment facilities that cater to the wealthy, where the primary focus is addictions. At one facility that I am familiar with, EMDR is the major treatment protocol, but relaxation is also practiced with meditation, yoga and conventional individual and group psychotherapy. In another facility I am familiar with, hypnosis is a major modality.

One thing I've tried to emphasize in this book is that the main utility of this wide range of hypnotic techniques is as *adjunct* to conventional therapy. Certainly this is applicable to all modes of psychotherapy in these facilities, including jails and prisons. In their meta-analysis, Kirsch, et al. (1995) demonstrated that the main utility of hypnosis for various disorders was *as adjunct*, not as a stand-alone treatment. When we market hypnosis—or hypnotic techniques—I think we stand on firm ground if we emphasize this.

Correctional facilities

In the U.S. in general, people are in jail *before* they receive a sentence, and prisons are where they go *after* sentencing. Some one and one-half million adults are in the U.S. prison system. Many are housed in minimum security which has dormitory-style housing where one can walk outside in the prison yard, or watch TV in the day room. Even medium and maximum security prison facilities are generally considered a more favorable place than jail because of more freedom, better food, and the availability of vocational and educational programs along with therapeutic programs, such as individual and group therapy, especially with an addictions focus. Just like the U.S. population *not* locked up, many in prison receive psychiatric medications.

In the past, I worked in a metropolitan jail that housed 1,900 inmates, but often the number was 2,300. This included people— men and women both—awaiting trial or sentencing for murder, along with many for other serious crimes, such as aggravated assault or rape. Many were homeless and many were there for drug-related offenses, especially methamphetamine-related charges. Two psychiatric units (maximum security) housed up to 100 inmates, the majority of whom carried a psychotic disorder diagnosis, or were on suicide watch. As such, the jail was the biggest psychiatric facility in the county. Another 100 or so in general population or segregation received antipsychotic meds, with 600 or so in those areas receiving other psychiatric meds, typically mood stabilizers and antidepressants. Psychiatrists and nurse prescribers liked working at the jail because it was the only place in town where compliance with meds was guaranteed, and where they knew no illegal drugs obfuscated the clinical presentation.

One thing that appealed to me was that the jail was exceedingly interesting—and certainly much different from other places I had worked. For the mental health counselor, much of the work was crisis intervention. For example, a call came in from a unit: "This woman can't stop crying, can you come and check her out?" or "Can you see this older man who seems confused?" Prevention of suicide was a major focus. If an inmate was queried about suicidal thought and the person declined to answer, or answered vaguely, they were placed on suicide watch, where their clothes, any books, tooth brush—everything—was taken away. They were dressed in a green smock, or vest, and they slept on a mattress on the cement floor with a thick blanket for warmth. As such, suicide watch was viewed by some as a punitive albeit necessary measure that could prevent some from endorsing suicidal thought when queried. At any rate, such vigilance reduced the number of suicides to only three or four a year, where formerly dozens occurred. Here are some things I did in a typical day.

Ramon the screamer

Ramon, age 19, is on my list to see in a mental health unit. The corrections officer (CO) opens the slot in the door (food trap) for me, I bend down to introduce myself, but before I can speak the young man looses a terrifying scream. A vicious kick to the door follows. I close the trap and peer through the plexiglass window. He is curled up in the corner, moaning in Spanish.

The next time I see him it is some weeks later. A court-order led to injectable meds and soon after he agreed to oral meds. He is now a different person—calm, articulate, bright mood, and no voices. He feels guilty about stopping his meds, smoking dope, and getting arrested for breaking a window in the family home. He's interested in a story and I tell him one and leave when the crisis phone rings. Two months later, he is back, wildly psychotic again. I don't need to ask why.

Young Indian woman

Anita, 19, is accused of murdering her mother on one of the nearby Indian reservations. I see in the record that she is both psychotic and retarded. She sits on the edge of her bed with an expression of shell shock. On this day, I am able to see her outside her cell because no others are in the day room of the mental health unit. The CO affixes handcuffs and we sit on stark plastic chairs outside her cell. She says she can't read or write and her fund of general information is very limited. She says she'd like to hear a story and I tell her about a grape vine in northern California. This plant and others in the vineyard produce marvelous grapes because they have to struggle to grow in the very rocky soil. I return each week until she goes to prison, continuing with the grape vine story each visit, and each story elicits a wan smile.

Milling around

I go to a unit in the tower where all of them previously have been to prison for at least five years. They're all out in the day room, playing cards, making a call on the public telephone, chatting and laughing—a good time is had by all. I sit down with an inmate in the midst of the din and immediately the others start milling around, trying to pick up on the discussion. One interrupts with, "Are you a lawyer?" "No, I'm from the Lottery, I'll write out your check next," I answer. He laughs and moves away. There is no laughing from the one I'm sitting down with. He's a real charmer, a big swastika tattooed on his forehead, a poster child for sociopathy. "How can I help you?" I ask. "I want pills, I can't sleep in here," he says. He's not interested in sleep hygiene (avoiding naps and caffeine, etc.) or relaxation techniques. "I'll refer you for a sleep study, which means they'll look in at night to see if you're sleeping. Then we'll go from there." "Thanks a lot," he says derisively and leaves. He normally would have said, "Fuck you," which would earn disciplinary action: strict segregation. I head for the sally port. That one was easy.

"I need my meds now!"

I go to a general population unit for women. I stand in a corner out of earshot for the most part and speak with Michele, a distraught and histrionic white female in her thirties. She tells me she has to have her meds NOW "… or, I just don't know, I'll die." "Maybe you need to be on suicide watch," I query, but she assures me she's not suicidal. I explain to her that everybody entering the jail gets put on a "med hold" for three days (save any meds that are part of a detox protocol) so the staff can get some idea of the real person. Community agencies frequently load up these people on confounding combinations of meds, like multiple SSRIs and multiple benzodiazapines. Many also use meth, cocaine, marijuana, heroin or alcohol, therefore the rationale for a med hold. But the inmate naturally suffers until her meds get started, in this case, probably one SSRI and no benzos, which are regarded as an agent of abuse. Michele's been to the jail before, she knows the routine. I rehearse deep breathing and progressive muscle relaxation with her for two minutes and then leave.

She is moderately interested in nonmedical measures, which is more than most inmates.

Offal in the shower

I enter a general population unit for men. The CO explains that he's getting complaints from inmates that "Pete just isn't right in the head," plus he defecated in the shower. I sit down at a table with an edentulous white male with long white hair. He looks 80 but is only 45. "Where are you now?" I ask Pete. He answers, "Well, you should know, this is the Gospel Rescue Mission. I'm still waiting for my food box." He knows his name but has no idea of the date or where he is, and his gait is typical of people with brain atrophy. His liver is probably pickled from drinking and maybe he'll clear up some before he leaves the jail. He probably doesn't have any family and no doubt he lives at a homeless camp in the desert, a typical example of the flotsam and jetsam of society that enter the jail every day. But all that doesn't matter. My only job right now is to assign him a mental health status so he can be housed in more structure. I enter that on the computer. Even before I leave, two correction officers are there to escort him. "Where we going?" asks Pete. "To the Ritz," one of the officers answers, but Pete already forgot.

Enter the "tweakers"

In the jail vernacular, meth addicts, or "meth heads," are tweakers. There is nothing more pathetic than acutely psychotic tweakers and their frightening paranoia. Equally pitiable is the young tweaker, no longer acute, but with brain fried, who asks, "Will I always be this way?" We know the brain can heal, but there may be little hope for this lot. Equally compelling is the guilt of the less impaired tweaker who, now clear-headed in jail, deeply regrets her errors while partying on meth. Such was the case of Kimberly, a divorced white female, age 25, whose children were legally severed from her by the state. Though now on an SSRI for depression and Vistaril for insomnia, she can't sleep due to guilty ruminations.

Like most in jail, she is here for a probation violation. On probation for drug possession, her urine test came up dirty, which means immediate arrest and jail. I sit down with her at a metal table in the day room. She sobs while she tells her story and I begin to contemplate what I can do to reach her with something meaningful. She has two years of college, majoring in psychology, and is articulate. Due to her level of distress I determine she might be a good participant in a little exercise.

Therapist: Kimberly, you can close your eyes or keep them open as I lead you through a little exercise that might indeed help you now when you need it the most … breathing in comfort and relaxation, nothing to know or think about, nowhere to be, no one to please, *don't even* have to listen to the words … and we can begin to *notice* and to *wonder when*, even in a place like this, you'll start to notice relaxation beginning somewhere in your body.

Not knowing/not doing
Hypnotic language
Hypnotic language
Implication

Women start milling around. One asks, "Are you a lawyer?" "No," I answer, "and I'm not a chaplain either, now please leave us alone." They back off. I need to get my mind back on the task. A husky woman corrections officer with a stentorian voice yells, "Hold the noise down, girls!" They go back to playing cards, gossiping and scheming.

Therapist: You can *imagine*, just *imagine*, Kimberly, holding a heavy sack in your hand, out at your side … it's a leather sack of *guilt/gilded* coins, gold coins (she nods her head) and I'd like you right now to *imagine* dropping that sack of *guilt/gilded* coins, and *when* you have done so, you'll know and I'll know because you'll find yourself *taking* one, more deep, comfortable breath …

Suggestion
Suggestion
Misspeak

Suggestion
Suggestion
Contingent suggestion

She breathes deeply after 10 seconds.

Therapist: Now, Kimberly, I can remember … when I was young, lying on the grass … (Tears issue from her eyes, though her eyes remain closed. I should

not have mentioned children) but I've also done so	**Suggestion**
as an adult, looking up at the sky … how those	
clouds never stay in the same place, they inevitably	**Suggestion**
move … and *thoughts* can be the same way …	**Suggestion**

Now, I'm going to tell you a little story called The Three Lessons …

We finish right before the CO shouts that day room is over, time to go back to their cells. She looks more relaxed, relieved. "Did you say guilt in there?" she asks. "I surely may have," I answer.

"I can't remember much of the story," she says. "That's good, don't worry about it," I say. I quickly explain the use of an anchor, or associational cue, to aid in relaxation. I noticed her relaxing her hand on her stomach during this exercise, so I assigned that as an anchor. She responded very well. I think. She would be a good client in one's private practice.

I check back with her in two weeks. "My meds are finally starting to work." "Good for you," I say. She says she is practicing with her anchor. I make a mental note to see her again in a month, but by then she is gone.

93-year-old pedophile

I get a call from the Infirmary. "He wants to talk to Psych," says the corrections officer. Some, in their bargaining, think seeing Psych will help them legally. I speak through the trap to a 93-year-old man in a wheel chair. He starts right in: "I was framed, I'm no child molester … that Mexican woman wanted me to watch her kids and then she turned on me … I'm a veteran, I fought for my country in the Pacific in World War II." I know the veteran part is true because somebody has already got his record from the V.A.

I review extant coping measures, which consist solely of reading. He's not interested in anything else and is already on various meds. Several months later he is sentenced to 15 years in prison, his third conviction for child molestation.

"I deserve to die"

"Are you still suicidal?" I ask the young man. He wears the green smock and is pacing in the bare cell. "Of course I am, wouldn't you be?" he says. He has been in jail more than three years, as he won't accept a plea agreement of life in prison for raping and killing a 4-year-old girl. "I deserve to die, give me the death sentence," he adds in a soft voice. There is ample remorse in jail.

Blind and deaf

When someone can't safely leave the jail we call it a disposition problem, and I hate those. I see a 75-year-old African American woman in the infirmary. She is a homeless alcoholic. She is also blind and deaf and in a wheelchair, only able to transfer from the wheelchair with assistance. In the past three years she has been to jail 13 times for a probation violation, and each time a community agency gave her a ride to her homeless camp in the desert. Like many, she is not interested in jail substance abuse services. Custody questions releasing her, saying it might not be safe. Doctors above me confer. Success thirteen previous times is compelling. The van arrives and off she goes again. Why can't the police just leave this woman to her beer?

"Maybe I'm interested"

Maude, 63, was arrested because she neglected her animals. Near her trailer in the desert the Sheriff's deputies found 14 emaciated horses, 53 cats, 27 dogs, and a plethora of hamsters, gerbils and reptiles in cages, all in poor condition. The inside of her home was typical of a hoarder's, so clogged from floor to ceiling with tons of junk in every room that one could barely walk in there. She was biting her fingernails, a real Nervous Nellie.

"Ever hear of deep breathing?" I asked. "I don't think anything could help me—and I don't think I've ever heard of deep breathing. Say, do you know what they did with all my babies?" she answered. "How about if I tell you the Tomato story?" I asked. She responded, "Why not?"

Tomato story
Taken from Araoz (1995)

Prior to 1841 no one in the United States had ever eaten a tomato. Then, one spring day in 1841, Robert Gibbon Johnson walked up the steps of the courthouse in Salem, New Jersey, produced a tomato from his sack, and held it aloft so those assembled could see it. Then, Johnson put the tomato to his lips, opened his mouth, bravely took a bite of that tomato, and swallowed it down.

And sure enough, Robert Gibbon Johnson did not die. Thereafter, people in the U.S. gradually began to add tomatoes to their diet.

Then I left. I checked, and a week later she was still there. I visited her a second time, and asked if she was interested in deep breathing, and sure enough, she was.

Organized crime
"What the deuce?! What wishes my interlocutor?" he asks through the trap. This one sure has a dramatic presentation—and diction to boot. I say, "I'm from Psych. You take any pills?" "None whatsoever, and I sleep well." He explains he has been in jail for four years and "... I am accused of 56 deucedly heinous charges, all beneath the rubric of organized crime." This Asian male in his 70s smiles broadly. He has perfect teeth, a true rarity here. "I do have a question for you, sir," he says politely. "Go ahead," I say.

"What do you call this: A schizophrenic in a mental hospital teeters atop a drinking fountain, and then he falls, crashing in a heap on the yellowed tile floor?" "You got me, what's the answer?" I say. "A Freudian slip." He laughs heartily, as do I. Nothing like a little levity behind bars.

Another view behind bars
An odd culture, the jail. As some inmates were personality disordered and scammed and schemed for meds or housing, their only real currencies, staff were suspicious and expected them to lie and

manipulate. This then meant that in any interaction with clients, staff might discount their complaints. Ky, a wise mental health counselor at the jail for many years, put it this way: "All the things these broken people do are *survival skills,* and when we do the same thing on the outside, we have a different name for it: *Social skills.*" As I said, it was a most interesting place. It was well organized and run, kept scrupulously clean, and I never felt unsafe. However, safety and security always came first—and before treatment, if necessary. After all, the corrections officers did not wear stab-proof vests for nothing.

Generating your own material

Most people who use stories and anecdotes in therapy eventually compose their own. This is good because it fits with the idea of adapting therapy to *you.* Sure, we adapt therapy to the unique needs of the client, but what about *you*? As a therapist, you'll probably be doing this work for a long time and you'll need to see what you are comfortable with, what works for you. Clients then immediately notice your confidence.

Balloons may have been a fantasy

I remember when I wrote my first therapeutic story, Balloons. It was the early 1980s on a dark winter morning in Tucson, I was jogging on a street near my house and I suddenly recalled a visit I had with my high school friends on a cold November day in 1964 to the University of Wisconsin football stadium. I had an image of a big net full of balloons and someone opened the net and loosed all the balloons. Now, the balloons part, I don't know if that really happened or not, but it doesn't matter.

People have told me they have creative moments during their morning shower, or when they're drifting off to sleep at night. A productive writing time for me is on airplanes or in airports. I'm very low tech—no tablet computer and the like—but I usually have a pen and note pad with me.

I spend a fair amount of time alone driving and I usually listen to the radio or an audio book, always fiction of some kind. I hear a word or phrase or concept that is noteworthy and I write it down on the notepad next to me on the front seat. The scribbles add up. I'll review them now and then and at some point I'll have what I need for a story, anecdote, induction, etc. I take advantage of quiet moments when my observations and intuition may exploit a given situation. For example, when I was visiting a relative near Grafton in Australia, I spent time on his porch, appreciating the lush natural world of New South Wales. As my brother-in-law worked in his garden he talked about his garden club. Right then I grabbed my pen and pad and wrote an ego-strengthening story in the appendix, Little Cactus.

I was in a restaurant in the early 1980s when I scribbled my first journal article on several paper napkins. There is something about the steady din of a restaurant that is amenable to absorption in contemplation and writing. Since then, I have scoured a wide variety of books and magazines for story ideas. *Smithsonian* magazine, *National Geographic* magazine, and periodicals in the U.S. dealing with nature, like the magazines of the Audubon Society and the Sierra Club, are a few from which I have developed material. A while back, *National Geographic* had an article on the tunnels beneath Paris, and there was an interview with its author on National Public Radio (NPR). We have used an audio file of the interview in training large groups. They listened to the recording as a large group, and then broke into small groups and each group developed a therapeutic story from the recording. On the radio, I listen to the BBC and NPR, to name a few. I wrote the Molasses Reef story right after I listened to a report on NPR about restoring that reef. I mentioned earlier on that I occasionally point to a movie, *The Mission*, when atoning for a guilty deed is part of the clinical presentation. Certainly movies are one medium that can inspire our work. When I watch TV, it's usually sports, news or history, and to date, nothing on TV has inspired me to write anything.

A famous story attributed to Milton Erickson is African Violets, which is appended. Many, including yours truly, have told and re-told the story over the years. Well, about 10 years ago I decided to try and find the origins of this story, so I visited the archives at the Erickson Foundation in Phoenix. On an old audiotape I heard Erickson describe what he said to the depressed woman before he left her house that day in Milwaukee, and there was no indirection involved whatsoever! In fact, he told the woman in no uncertain terms, "Grow a lot of African violets and give them to all your friends." Directive, even authoritarian, and it worked; she had to let light into her house as she grew those flowers, and she had to interact with people, all of which cured her depression. I wonder who first fashioned that encounter into a permissive story, as that's really the only version we have today. And come to think of it, it's one of my favorites that I've used for many years.

Refining your therapeutic voice

Therapists new to hypnotic techniques sometimes listen to themselves telling a story and perhaps pay attention to their voice for the first time. For years I've heard them say things like, "I just don't like the sound of my voice." I say to them, "Well, then, let's practice. This is like anything else. The more you practice, the better you get." People may practice in the shower or with a tape recorder. I know people who get the feel of a script, say a story, by reading it to their spouse, or even their dog or cat. Some work on their hypnotic patter while stuck in traffic. It's all about practice.

Remember Marilyn Monroe's squeaky girlish voice in those old movies? Well, I had an intern once, Kay, whose voice was just like Marilyn Monroe's. The very first day she said, "Just listen to my voice. I can't stand it!" and "What would you do if you had a voice like mine?" I was at a loss for words, just stumped and thought, "Oh, my, this is not good." But even Kay, through tedious practice with a tape recorder, succeeded in developing a fairly good hypnotic voice.

What is a good hypnotic voice?
Generally, a hypnotic voice will be melodic and smooth, and have less pitch and volume. Does this mean you should speak in a boring

monotone? Sometimes, when clients tell me, "You have such a nice voice," I answer with, "Believe me, it took years of practice for me to become this boring!" I have my conversational voice, my therapist voice, and my hypnotic voice. Maybe you have more than three. A conversational voice may be breezy and carefree with little attention paid to enunciation. In other words, it is very casual, maybe even sloppy, and there's nothing wrong with that *except* when it carries over to your other voices. My therapist voice may be casual at times, but in speaking to clients I am careful to pronounce words completely and with sufficient volume. However, when I want to emphasize a point, I speak in a lower pitch and with less volume to lend emphasis to a key point. Then there's my *hypnotic voice*, which is probably the most varied. A psychologist friend, from whom I learned a lot, Bob Hall, reminded us, "Massage them with your words," and in an induction or story I'm always thinking *massage*.

A good hypnotic voice goes with the client

People who have employed hypnotic techniques for a while come to appreciate the need for clear, careful enunciation, and speaking with the front part of the mouth, not strangling words in the throat. I want my voice to be inviting, welcoming, and embracing. Milton Erickson told clients, "My voice will go with you." This is a valuable suggestion, but it is not likely to be a successful posthypnotic suggestion unless your voice is a memorable one. Few of us are born with arresting voices like Jeremy Irons' or Morgan Freeman's. But come to think of it, even famous actors had to work to develop what would eventually become their trademark voice.

I often employ "my voice will go with you" but more indirectly: "From here on who knows if this voice can go with you?" or even more indirectly, "One woman one time imagined, just imagined, a voice accompanying her." Of course, it is even better to tie the suggestion to something that is likely to occur in the natural environment, e.g., "You may find my words to be an ally when you take one deep, satisfying breath."

Contrasts are your friend

It is believed that a subtle vocal alteration is a true unconscious suggestion. So, during formal trance work, or when reading a story at the end of a session, I always speak with lower volume and decreased rate when I deliver a key suggestion: "... and all those balloons, red ones, blue ones, green ones, *she just let them go.*" As I am saying, "... *she just let them go*" I am thinking massage but I am also imagining a gentle breeze blowing across the client's cheek, and a soft pulsing of words emanating from deep within the room. Those are the little tricks I use to try to be effective. I typically begin a session speaking with a louder volume and then gradually lower it as I get into the induction or story. But I also toy with volume, rate and pitch throughout the session. Contrast this variance with a slow, consistent monotone that never alters. That would make ME bored and could put the person to sleep. It's hard enough to keep people awake these days with all the medications they take.

I believe that altering the qualities of our patter is in itself trance inducing in the same way that apposition of opposites is trance inducing. So, "... I don't know if in your hands, or in your feet, you'll begin to notice a coolness or warmth, heaviness or lightness, tingling or numbness." This juxtaposition of opposite hypnotic phenomena helps lull a person into trance. So, too, our alteration of volume, rate and other qualities further hastens the process.

Your voice in a story and other scripts

I have memorized many inductions, stories, anecdotes, and techniques, but some things I simply can't remember and have to rely on reading scripts. Clients come to expect and appreciate reading to them as a natural part of the session. When writers turn in a script for a movie or a play they generally include very few hints on how lines in the script should be delivered. Writers are confident that professional actors will *interpret* the material, bring their experience and intuition to bear on the written word. If the script calls for emphasis or certain feelings to be conveyed to the audience, writers leave it up to the actors to communicate the appropriate emotion. So, too, with an induction or story that I write. I might underscore a key suggestion, but aside from that, I trust that the reader will identify from the context when to speed up or slow down, and when to alter the quality of the voice to fit the clinical situation. For sure, ten different therapists may individualize the reading of a script in many different ways, and that is good. Just as it is desirable to tailor therapy in general to individuals and their particular situation, so, too, it is desirable to adapt your reading of a script to both your particular client and how you are feeling on any given day. I may say, "... and all those balloons, she just let them *go*" with one client, whilst with another client my intuition may dictate that I repeat the phrase, perhaps waiting ten seconds to do so.

I also hope that if you haven't already done so, with practice you will eventually be able to *ad lib* certain material without having to read it. As you become more comfortable with an induction or story, it can become a part of your own repertoire. As you develop your craft you can truly add your own voice by devising your own inductions, stories and anecdotes. By not having to continually glance back and forth between script and client you will be in a better position to both pace ongoing behavior and adapt your voice to the ever-changing clinical scenario.

A few more notions

Check closely for hearing loss. If you have to shout, "... JUST LET YOURSELF DRIFT OFF." Well, you get the picture. Instead, use an audio amplifier. With mine, I speak into the small microphone in the hand-held amplifier whose cord is connected to headphones worn by the client. These days there may be better devices out there. This can also help if you have a noisy hallway outside your office. Save your voice. One benefit of doing hypnosis is that you get to take a break from clients' dumping negative affect into your ears. However, several hypnosis clients in one day may tax your voice. I counter this by employing ample pauses and using periods of silence as a deepening, both of which give me time to rest and collect my thoughts. I also occasionally have clients speak during trance, e.g., "... tell me now, with your words, what are you experiencing deep inside." Clients speaking during trance may lighten trance. After they speak I usually say something like, "Okay, take two deep breaths and let yourself sink even deeper."

Sit erect. If you are slouched, or if your legs are crossed, your breathing may be impeded. Notice your own breathing; breathe deeply and often as you reel out your patter. I keep in mind one image: a *column* of breath. I want to start every so often with a nice *column* of breath. Also, I *always* have a drink of water within reach. Times that I've forgotten to do so I inevitably developed a cough or parched throat. Keep your hands away from your face. If you talk with your chin resting on your hand, or if you have a hand anywhere near your mouth, your voice will be partially blocked. If you find yourself pressing, back off and take a deep breath.

You WILL find your own voice, one that you are comfortable with, and it will serve you well. Practice different voices during day-to-day conversation, in therapy, or when you're alone. For therapists who are still unable to find their voice, I developed a story about Samuel Edgar, who, after much travail, succeeded in finding his voice (Gafner, 2004).

A version of this appeared both in the *Newsletter of the American Society of Clinical Hypnosis*, in *Clinical Applications of Hypnosis* (Gafner, 2004, and in *Techniques of Hypnotic Induction* (Gafner, 2010)).

CHAPTER FOURTEEN

Favorite inductions and stories

Story inductions

Glen Canyon induction

Taken from Gafner (2010)

In a moment I will read to you an account of floating down the Colorado River in 1963 before the gates of Glen Canyon dam closed and water from the river began to fill in this 200-mile-long expanse. I call this account My Journey of Discovery and some listeners of this story have indeed discovered something of importance in their own lives. You may sit back, close your eyes if you wish, and let yourself travel in your own way, as I read to you the following account.

I want to tell you about time, both clock time and geologic time, *rapidly occurring time* like the shutter	Time distortion
speed of my camera, and *timeless time*, like when	Time distortion
the photo of shimmering sandstone cliffs remains in my mind's eye, or, when the camera's tripod waits on the soft sand of the river's shore, *time standing still*, awaiting ephemeral light and shadow for	Time distortion
the next photograph, milliseconds blending into minutes amidst millennia's majesty. How delight-	
ful when my *unmoving body* and *steady gaze*	Eye fixation / Catalepsy
are *arrested* by vermilion cliffs, or when an *hour*	Time distortion
escapes my grasp, and the sun descends in mere	Time distortion
seconds, when mid-afternoon *hurdles* into night-	Time distortion
time as my eyes briefly close. I remember well *the*	Fluff
grave of the Confederate soldier near Pick Axe Canyon, and how each year I would pause there and *see new pieces* of gray uniform that were	Fluff
brought up by pack rats. Wherever we stop for the night along the river the stars are so bright I can	
read by them, but after a few words *sleep* comes	Suggestions

quickly and the images of the day are woven into my *dreams*.

Dreaming by night and journeying as if in a dream by day, therein my travels through Glen Canyon. One minute my body is *heavy*, warmed by the sun, though my mind is *light*, and the next minute alternating air currents—*moist, dry, cool, warm*—enliven my body as my mind is seized by the vibrant *green* of a *red*bud tree, and behind that green the delicate lavender of the walls gives way to slate gray and powder blue sky, and then to black because a crow has cawed somewhere. I can hear my breathing in that narrow canyon, and my footfalls produce an echo on the crackling shale, but soon my feet, *way down there*, are back on soft river sand.

Apposition of opposites
Apposition of opposites
Opposites
Opposites
Opposites

Dissociation

It is time to leave this lovely canyon, knowing I will return, if only in my dream. My body moves on, *disconnected* from my mind way back there, as the ever-beckoning river awaits and my journey continues. I most appreciate this trip late in the year when long shadows and subdued light make the best photos. Late in the year the sun drops quickly behind the walls and the *chill* of my body is embraced by the *warmth* of the camp fire. Driftwood burns hot and fast, as do rock-hard chunks of juniper—spiraled, twisted, ancients. *Sleep* descends rapidly, as we are lulled by the waves lapping the shore, the crackling fire, and then comes the stillness.

Dissociation

Apposition of opposites
Apposition of opposites

Suggestion

We embark at Mexican Hat and we float between gray limestone walls and towering cliffs of Navajo sandstone. At Rosebud Canyon a spring, high above, cascades down, giving life to a hanging garden of trees, flowers, mosses and ferns. It is a good place to stop for the night. We leave the raft, stretch, and briefly explore petroglyphs left by the ancients. We see something we have found in many canyons, Kokopelli, the hunchback flute player. *Sleep* arrives even earlier this evening, and soon we *drift and dream*. I awake in the middle of the night—what time could it be? I do not know, as no one wears a watch—and I *walk woodenly* into a canyon. I hear a chorus of frogs that I did not notice before. The moonlight casts a blue scrim over the petroglyphs, and the jagged cliffs now appear soft and as if in motion. *Is that* a human figure up ahead? I look back to where I remember the river to be, and I see a sheet of molten silver. Did *someone* call my name? *I hear* a lilting flute above the canyon. Many feelings and images reverberate within me now as I write this account, memories resurfacing from an unknown stimulus. Now at home the morning sun's kiss is *warm* on my face as I gaze out the kitchen window, and the *cold* tap water brings back *burning* sun on my bare shoulders as we wade through trenches of *chilly* water near Rainbow Bridge, my body as heavy as the boulders around me. The *coldness* disappears as I glimpse the ancient sand dunes up ahead, inviting, *warm*, embracing.

Mystery Canyon was so named because steps carved into the wall end half-way up, and no one knows what can be found way up at the top. The falling water echoes softly in the pools at the bottom where we lie by the campfire, playing a guessing game. "It is the remnants of a lost civilization, the Mystery People of Mystery Canyon," someone ventures. "When I close my eyes I can hear their words, way up there," says another. "It's the Sand Man, that's who is up there," I whisper, and soon we are fast *asleep*.

Twilight Canyon leads to a large amphitheater that could accommodate a thousand people. All around the bottom are pictographs: mountain goats, the sun, and stick figure people whose *feet are absent*. "Where did the feet go?" someone asks. *"Disconnected, off somewhere,"* I answer.

Margin annotations:

Suggestion
Suggestion

Catalepsy

Positive

Hallucinations

Apposition of Opposites
Opposites

Opposites

Opposites

Opposites

Suggestion

Dissociation

Dissociation

Another responds, "It reminds me of the unseen hand, or maybe one hand not clapping," as we move deeper into the vast amphitheater, an awesome and incredible place. At the exit near the back we pass through a narrow aperture and gaze up at a *beautiful smooth wall* with a natural design in the rock. With a little imagination *we see* a chariot pulled by horses, their manes flying in the breeze.

Positive Hallucination

Some time later we find ourselves at Music Temple. "J.W. Powell, 1869," is among the names we find inscribed on the wall. I remember reading the 1871 account of John Wesley Powell, who *lost an arm* in the Civil War. He wrote about the "sweet sounds" of Music Temple, a vast hollow space where this night we light a candle. We close our eyes and *hear* in 1957 the water dripping—I know not from where—and *imagine* in this great cathedral the same symphony heard by Powell nearly a century ago. Before the candle burns down I take my party to a recess in the wall. I reach in and extract a pot. I hold it in my hands and say, "Notice the distinctive whorl of the corn flower. Anthropologists say this was made by someone they call Corn Woman in the late Anasazi period. Her design has been found on similar pots from Chaco Canyon to northern Mexico." The others caress the pot before I return it to its ledge. The candle is now extinguished and our feet barely touch the ground as we glide out of Music Temple, *forgetting* if day or night *amnesia* awaits us on the exterior.

Dissociation

Positive Hallucinations

That night by the campfire someone says, "I now know what it means when 'scientists can see through time'." Late that night I steal from my sleeping bag. In the lemon glow beside the river a stick finds its way to my hand. The stick moves *of its own accord* in the sand. Whether my hand *drew* a corn flower or something else, or if this in fact occurred in my dream, I do not know.

Automatic Drawing

Rumination Induction (for insomnia)

Taken from Benson (2001) and Gafner (2006)

In a moment I'm going to count slowly from 25 to one, just like this, "25 … 24 …" and while you hear those numbers descending down, I would like you to imagine your relaxation deepening, ever so gradually. I remember one person, one time he told me later that as he listened to the numbers going down, he imagined comfortable warmth going all *down* his body. Another person said that as she heard the numbers she had an image of soothing coolness beginning at her feet and going *up* her body just a bit at a time. 25 … 24 … (continuing to count slowly to one).

When Dee was a kid she was fascinated by her mother's big jewelry box that had multiple tiers with drawers and small box sections on the top. There was a place to hang necklaces in a door that swung out. Each small box held one pair of earrings while the stacked drawers held larger items such as bracelets or watches. *Each piece of jewelry had a specific place to rest*. Dee never ceased to marvel at the detail and organization of the box. "Everything had its place," she recalled.

Her brother, Sloan, an avid fisherman, had a tackle box that served a similar purpose, and even though he thought everything had its place, Dee knew that in her mother's jewelry box everything was just right.

Let your mind sleep now. Sleep very deeply, as there's nothing you need to know, or do, or think about. This is your time to enjoy and appreciate the pleasantness and comfort of deep relaxation.

Everyone talks during the day, and sometimes we even talk to ourselves in our minds, mulling over this or that. This serves a useful purpose when we're awake, but you don't need that self-talk at night when you're going to sleep. Don't you deserve a pleasant and relaxing sleep?

Some people call it a garage sale, others call it patio sale, rummage sale, or any variety of names, but you know what I mean. Many people may bring a large assortment of goods together and arrange them in orderly fashion, men's clothing here, women's over there, furniture here, stuffed animals over there. Perhaps color coded labels designate who owns what, blue dots were put on by the Jones, orange by the Garcías, and the *Dozers*, who knows what color they had?

You can take any random thoughts that drift through your mind, consolidating them into just one space. As they are placed in their compartment they can dissipate from your mind, as quickly as predicted rainfall that never really happened. You can enjoy a nice, deep refreshing breath and *let that mind clear*. Sleeping deeply now, but sleeping even deeper at home.

One person one time, I forget her name, she quickly mastered the technique of compartmentalization by lying down at night and imagining her thoughts flying into a small drawer. The very first session she said, "I'm looking forward to the time when I can look back," and from right then she began to appreciate a really *good night's sleep*. Another person, who also achieved a pleasant night's sleep, he said, "I don't mind storing my evening thoughts away, but I choose to compartmentalize only 80 percent of them." He had a good reason for doing so, but I forget what it was. The same man said, "Once I let go and slept, checking the perimeter wasn't necessary, as I realized it would still be there in the morning."

I can remember when someone would read me bedtime stories, preparing me for a nice, restful sleep. You may recall such a story now, or maybe all you can think about is Dee and her jewelry box. It really doesn't matter at all. Beginning now, I would like you to slowly move that right hand, letting your thumb and first finger come together, forming a little circle. That's right, as heavy as that right hand may feel right now, it can move the thumb and first finger so they make a little circle. That circle is your anchor, or reminder; it is your connection between here and home, as it can initiate *slowing down* and *heaviness* in your body, and doing what you need to with random thoughts, as you prepare to sleep. You may wish to combine your anchor with a deep, refreshing breath. That's the way.

The Magic Theater: A guided imagery induction
Taken from Young (2007) and Gafner (2010)

Let those eyes close now and allow yourself to begin to appreciate the wonderful comfort that can develop when both your body and your mind really *slow down*. No doubt you can recall other times in the past when you *let go* and drifted off into another state, not a state like Indiana or Texas, but a state of mind where the deepest part of you was *open* and *receptive* to new experience.	Suggestions Suggestions
	Suggestions Suggestions

In a moment I will invite you to accompany me on *a most interesting journey* of discovery … which can happen *all by itself*. For one person it might be letting go *effortlessly*, for another *freeing up* one's self, *independent* of conscious deliberation, and for someone else it just occurs *automatically*. "Mental *cruise-control*" was how one woman put it. Effortless, independent, automatic, unconscious: they all may point in the direction trance. Going down a real road requires conscious attention, while none is required on this journey.

Suggestion covering
All possibilities
All possibilities
All possibilities
All possibilities
All possibilities
All possibilities

But first, I want your experience to *deepen* as I count backward, down from 20 to one, 20 …, 19 …, 18 …, imagine now, just imagine yourself in a building, any building you like, perhaps one you've been in before, a familiar place. There you are, on the first floor, walking down the hall, and you pass a door that you paid little attention to previously. You pause at the door and see that it is a service elevator. You touch a button that opens the door, you enter, and the door gently closes. You think to yourself, "Should I go up or down?" Of its *own accord* your hand extends out from your body and you touch the down button. The elevator descends rapidly and in a moment the door opens. You step out and gaze upon a small theater. It is the Magic Theater and you take a seat in the back row.

Deepening

Dissociation

It is very quiet in the theater, and glancing around, you see that you are alone. A profound *fatigue* comes over you, your eyes close all by themselves, and you enter a most pleasant *sleep*. In your sleep you *dream*, drift and dream, for what seems like the *longest time*. In your dream the curtain on stage opens and you see a movie screen. On the screen you see various nature scenes. One is Alpine Spring and you drink in the most inviting and peaceful setting you have ever seen. Then, your eyes move to the other scenes, one entitled Desert Solitude, another called River Raft Trip through the

Suggestion

Suggestion
Hypnotic dreaming
Time distortion

Grand Canyon, one a visit to a South Seas Island and yet another entitled Canadian Wilderness.

Your eyes move back and forth from one to another. Each is most appealing, one more captivating than another. You then hear a woman's voice that says, "Select one and only one NOW." In your mind you choose Alpine Spring, and suddenly the whole screen fills with Alpine Spring. You see yourself standing beside a bubbling spring high in a lovely mountain wilderness. Is this Switzerland? Are you in the Himalayas? You do not know, and it really doesn't matter. The woman's voice is heard again, this time in a mere whisper. She says, "That's right, there's *nowhere* you need to be, *nothing* to think about, *no one* to please, *nothing* to do or change, all you have to do is just sit there and breathe." | Not knowing/not doing
Not knowing/not doing

The wildflower blossoms are yellow, some are white. Some in the distance are blue. Your eyes drink in a riot of color. The scents are most invigorating. The warm sun and refreshing mountain air envelop you. "I feel absolutely wonderful," you think to yourself.

"Your *journey begins*," says the voice one more time, and you begin to walk down the trail. The scents you experience, the sounds, the breathtaking vistas, all are of such indescribable clarity. There is a spring in your step as you move along briskly, confidently, occasionally stopping to appreciate something that holds you in its embrace. Has a *minute* passed, or several *hours*? You do not know, and it is of no import whatsoever. Never before, have you known such *comfort and well being*. | Suggestion

Time distortion
Time distortion
Suggestion

The voice appears again. That voice is out there, but it is as if it reverberates from deep within you. It says, "In a moment you will *experience* something most meaningful to you. *Will it be* an evergreen epiphany?" "A what?" you ask yourself. | Suggestion
Question

"An epiphany of any hue would be most welcome indeed!" you think. You wish the voice would speak to you again. All is now very quiet, inside and outside. You continue on the trail for what may be a short time or a long *duration*, you have no way of determining *time*, clock time, time on a calendar, *seconds* or *hours* within a dream. In your dream you speak to yourself: "Why can't this last forever?" are the words.

Time distortion
Time distortion
Time distortion
Time distortion

You know that you can *come back* to Alpine Spring any time you want, simply by closing your eyes. There is a mountain goat in the distance. It is *unmoving*, as of *stone*, its gaze on you is unwavering. These lovely flowers, by my feet, what are they called? Color, texture, and meaning tumble in your mind. Pine trees in the distance, moss by your feet, shades of green about you, and deep inside yourself. Blue sky in the distance deepens your reverie.

Posthypnotic suggestion

Catalepsy
Catalepsy

You continue your journey. Isn't it highly *curious* what percolates deep within? (Pause for several seconds.) Your eyes open. You are back in the theater, the curtain on stage is closed and you arise from your seat, *woodenly* at first, as you make your way back to the elevator.

Question

Catalepsy

I will be quiet for a few minutes while your unconscious mind contemplates today's experience. During this deepening, who knows what else will surface from deep within?

Ego-strengthening stories

The Maple Tree

I've often thought about how many different kinds of trees there are, but it really doesn't matter at all if we wonder or imagine about their number; because we go on experiencing many things without knowing the specifics. There are many trees in different parts of the world: short, stubby trees in the desert, or tall trees in the mountains and rain forest, evergreen trees like pines, or trees that drop their leaves and display bare branches in winter. Those bare branches are soon covered by the green leaves of spring and summer, and during the crisp days of autumn those leaves gradually change—the red sugar maples, rainbow-colored sumacs and purple sweet gums, a patchwork of brilliant and fiery colors. Then the leaves begin to fall, in all the forests, billions of tons of leaves all over the world, one gigantic transfer of energy. Where the leaves fall and decompose, the soil is deep and fertile.

Some years back it was a blustery autumn day in the forest, in a grove of ordinary maple trees, where the crows cawed up above and lower down squirrels jumped from tree to tree, and way down below leaves were blowing on the ground. Seeds were blowing down from the maples trees, and like most seeds, the vast majority didn't sprout or take root but got eaten, or just decomposed on the forest floor. But one seed that day landed on an old log and just lingered there, and eventually it became covered by the snows of winter, and there it stayed, unnoticed by deer and rabbits, nestled deep in a crack in the decaying log, snug and protected. Deep inside, it didn't matter to the seed that outside, there was freezing cold, howling winds and great drifts of snow.

In the spring, the seed was still there. It swelled with moisture and sprouted, and a tiny root crept down into the damp, rich rotting wood of the old log. And slowly it grew, a seedling with scrawny branches and little green leaves that reached for available sunlight, while down below a strong root system started to develop and spread out. It continued to grow and grow, and soon it was a good-sized tree, and as the years passed the rich and fertile soil allowed it to survive drought, and two times it endured fires that left its bark scorched and blackened.

The seasons came and went and the maple tree continued to grow and grow. One winter day the unbearable weight of the snow broke off several large branches. For three summers precipitation was barely measurable, and while some nearby trees didn't make it, the maple survived this devastating drought and continued its growth. One summer day a bolt of lightning crashed into the tree and split it up near the top, but the tree survived this direct hit and that year produced a modest quantity of leaves and seeds. Despite various adversities it continued to grow, roots deep in the soil, roots intermingled with other roots.

The Little Cactus

Mrs. Strongton came out to her sun porch and greeted the gardener down below. "G'day, to you, Samuel." "Good mornin', ma'am," he mumbled. Mrs. Strongton was animated early this day, with her customary energy and verve. "Samuel, behold my wonderful subtropical garden, doubtless one of the finest in our part of New South Wales. Who would ever imagine such flamboyant foliage in this place, where one's house must be elevated off the ground due to frequent floods? Behold, young man, my magnificent African tulip trees and resplendent camellias and poinsettias; the glistening wands of the glossy-leafed—I forget its name."

"Yes, m'am," he answered, knowing that she might just be warming up, such was her enthusiasm for her garden. "My good man, behold the limpid orange blossoms of my crucifix orchid, the flamboyant foliage of the philodendra; the delicate blossoms of the calliandria— powder puff bush to you, young man. Oh, and notice the shiny quilted leaves of the loquat."

"The what?" asked Samuel. "Loquat tree. I presented you with a bag of the juicy fruit just last week, and then we have a backdrop of climbing vines and a foreground of blazing bromeliads and thick-fleshed aloes, and when you touch the satiny petals of the tibouchina, how can you not be overwhelmed with emotion?" she said breathlessly. "Yes, ma'am," he answered. Pretty soon she would wind down and he could begin his work. It was already hot at 7:00 a.m.

Mrs. Strongton jabbed a finger in his direction before adding, "And then we have one lone mammillaria supertexta, the cactus, if you will, there by your right foot, where sufficient sunshine embraces it.

The little fellow will attain no more than five inches in height, such a contrast it is with its fine white hair and circle of miniature red blossoms. How in the world it can survive here is beyond me."

"I try my best to take good care of 'em all," said Samuel. The lady quickly followed with, "You do much more than try, Samuel. I regard you as my garden's physician, as resourceful as the finest specialist in Sydney who restores to good health the most debilitated of patients." "Thank you, ma'am," he responded. "At any rate, I am hosting the Northern Rivers Garden Club here next week and I want you to trim everything back just right. Don't hold back," she said. Before he could answer she turned on her heel and disappeared inside the dark house.

He gazed at rainbow lorikeets fluttering in a eucalyptus tree. The sugar cane field in the distance offered the eye a different shade of green. He heard the tinkling of bellbirds as he brushed aside a bothersome tree fern by his cheek. As he contemplated where to begin today's work, he saw something inside a tangle of vines. He parted the vines and discovered another little mammillaria cactus, its cottony haze still white despite growing in the shade. "What's this thing doing here? She'll never miss it," he thought, and with a deft swipe of his foot the little plant was uprooted. He grasped it with his gloved hand and hurled it into the blackness beneath the house.

Ten years passed. Mrs. Strongton was long gone and now a young family lived in the house by the Clarence River. The ensuing years had seen drought along with floods and beneath the house churning water had tossed about the little cactus. Still, there it lay as an unrecognizable brown chunk of matter, covered with grime, spider webs, leaves and other debris. One day, the current gardener discovered the cactus in a pile of trash he had raked up beside the walk. As he examined it closely he heard a voice inside his head. "It lives, yes, it lives," whispered the voice, and right then he thought, "Let's stick this thing in the ground."

He planted it in the mostly sunny part of the garden. As the days and weeks passed, he observed the cactus. One day he glimpsed the beginnings of white hair, and several weeks later he saw a ring of red blossoms near the top. Inside his head he heard it again, one time, and then again. "It lives, yes, it lives," said the voice.

The Lighthouse

A story was told to me one time by a man (or woman) who was old, very old. He had had a long life of adventures, and he had many stories to tell, as he had enjoyed various travels around the world. As I listened to him, I reflected upon my own experiences, although my own were pretty bland by comparison.

One summer, this man had visited several lighthouses on the Atlantic coast of the U.S. He learned that sailors journeying in total darkness may feel like a black liquid is swirling about them, and the dizzying disorientation can make it difficult to tell up from down, or right from left, or east from west. Sailors came to *deeply appreciate* these light stations that were still in operation after many years of service. He remembered speaking with ships' pilots who continued to rely on these familiar fixtures, even though they also had radar and satellites for modern guidance. "I like something I can see with my own eyes," said one pilot, who could close his eyes and still experience a lighthouse's powerful white flashes that blazed every ten seconds, and were visible from as far away as 20 miles.

One such lighthouse, located at Discovery Point, on a rocky island, two miles off the coast, had a 70-foot tower made of massive granite blocks that dovetailed in such a way that the walls grew *even stronger* when pounded by the waves. Discovery Point had seen more than 200 years of duty, and countless ships, alone in dark or fog, came to appreciate the special way Discovery warned sailors of notorious sea hazards. In 1760, Discovery began as a mere lantern on a pole, which gave way to a whale oil lantern and reflector, once the granite tower was built. Several years later, no one knew precisely when, someone put in a 2,000-pound fog bell that was rung by a mechanical device powered by the waves. Years later, some time in the early

1800s, a first-order Fresnel lens was imported from France. This lens was replaced briefly in the 1920s by an electric fog horn, but in the 1930s, a second-order Erickson lens was inserted, which continues in operation to this day.

Now, Discovery encountered a good deal of adversity and change over the years. On four occasions in 1778, it was fired on by a British frigate. The cannonballs bounced off the rocks down below, and one found its mark half-way up the tower, but Discovery survived this direct hit. Three similar blows were endured during the Civil War, but the damage was quickly repaired, and the lighthouse continued on, doing its job year after year, vigilant, strong, and reliable. Originally, a lighthouse keeper lived in Discovery, but soon they realized that this wasn't necessary, as way up on top, way up the tight spiral staircase, the durable lens required only minor maintenance every month or so.

There were other things that happened with the passage of time. For a period, the county didn't have enough money in its budget, and the lighthouse suffered some neglect, which was soon remedied by the repair of mortar between the granite blocks. Vandals in the early 1940s turned out to be minor, just a one-time occurrence.

However, the greatest adversity faced by Discovery was the relentless pounding of the waves, year after year, strong and continuous one season, less so the next year, but persistent and severe nonetheless. Repair from erosion was necessary every once in a while due to the fierce weather, the biting seas, the battering waves, the surging water, and the tenacious cold foam and swirling green. The man remembered scaling the staircase of Discovery late one afternoon, which soon had him gasping for breath. He realized after going from ground level to up at the top, that the structure felt really *solid* beneath his feet. If someone could have seen him up there, gazing out, they would have observed the twilight flooding the sea, and when the coast dropped behind the horizon, only the lighthouse remained.

The Balloons

Maria grew up in Texas, and because of excellent grades and test scores she was offered a scholarship by the University of Wisconsin in Madison. During her freshman year she worked at various jobs to make ends meet: busing tables in dormitories, picking sweet potatoes on the university farms, and selling concessions at university sporting events: hot chocolate, coffee, popcorn, caramel apples, and soft drinks. It was now early November and she found herself dispensing Coca-Cola at the homecoming football game. Her boss appeared suddenly and said, "Maria, come with me, I have a special duty for you down on the field."

She followed him to a corner of the end zone where she encountered a massive net that contained thousands of small balloons—red ones, blue ones, green ones, different colors—all those balloons straining against the massive net. The boss said to her, "Your one job is this: When those players run back on the field to start the second half, you yank HARD on this cord right here and *let all those balloons go.*" "Sure enough," she answered, definitely an easy job.

It was cold down there on the field and Maria had to stamp her feet and rub her hands together to keep them warm. She regarded the net and then moved closer and examined it. "I'll let one balloon go," she mused to herself, and she did just that, maneuvered the net and released one balloon, a blue one, and watched as it sailed up and away, disappearing over the city. She became so absorbed in the balloons that she continued releasing them, one here, two over there; red ones, white ones, blue ones, *just letting them go.* She didn't hear the roar of the crowd as the players streamed back on the field to start the second half of the game, and just then her boss approached and yelled, "Pull the cord!" and she snapped back to her senses, grasped the cord, gave it a hard pull, and all the remaining balloons, thousands still beneath the net, she *just let them go.*

Instigative stories

African Violets

It was still cold and rainy outside as Milton Erickson finished a speaking engagement in Milwaukee, Wisconsin one day in the 1950s. One of the doctors in the audience asked Erickson if he would be kind enough to pay a visit to an elderly shut-in, a depressed woman who had not left her house in several weeks.

Erickson labored up the steps of the three-story Victorian house, was introduced to the woman and then asked, "Madam, would you please give me a tour of your house?" On the first floor it was dark, curtains drawn and very little lighting, and the same on the second and third floors. As Erickson was about to descend the stairs on the top story he glimpsed light coming in a south-facing window. In the windowsill was a tray of beautiful African Violets. Erickson made a mental note of this and then followed the others down the stairs.

He bid farewell to the woman and never saw her again. However, before he left, he said to her, "Madam, wouldn't it be nice if your friends could also enjoy those beautiful African Violets?" A year or so later, Erickson inquired about the woman and learned that as she started to grow the flowers for her friends, she had to open curtains on one window after another, and soon light filled the entire house. She became so well known for her flowers that she was known as the African violet queen of Milwaukee.

Sonja Benson was working with a woman, Josie, whose difficulties interpersonally and "being way too hard on myself" had not been helped by several sessions of CBT. Sonja wrote this story (Gafner & Benson, 2003) for Josie, who then made great strides in both areas.

Pauly the Pufferfish

I've often wondered about the thousands of kinds of fish in the ocean and rivers and lakes and ponds of the world, and tried to imagine the sheer number of total fish in those waters. How many billions could there be? That's why the story of one single fish arrested my attention, the story of Pauly the Pufferfish.

Now, you may know puffer fish as blowfish, those marvelous little creatures that have no ribs, which allows them to puff themselves into balloons much bigger than their usual selves. Puffer fish only inflate when they consider themselves to be in some kind of danger. They can also release poison into the water nearby. The problem with inflating is that it slows them down to half their usual speed, and then they can't maneuver so effectively in the water. All these protective devices can be very limiting.

Now, Pauly was a "map" puffer—a most interesting and curious looking puffer fish, with a short nose and a body with dark lines radiating out from around his eyes. You might think that such an interesting puffer would have all kinds of friends, and that he might draw other fish to him like pilot fish to a whale. But that wasn't the case at all. Pauly happened to be one of those rare puffers that actually released some of his poison out into the water around him when you least expected it. You see, usually puffers only emit poison when they are in extremely stressful situations, like when they are about to be eaten. One of the reasons that puffers only release poison under such dire circumstances is that, amazingly, that very same poison has fatal consequences for the puffer that released it.

Now, of course, Pauly didn't ever release so much poison that he died. But you have to wonder if those little bits of poison here and there in the water around him didn't have some sort of adverse effect on him. Certainly, it kept his friends and admirers to a minimum, which was very unfortunate, given how interesting and cool a fish Pauly truly was. All of this added up to a dilemma for Pauly. He really wanted to connect with other fish, as it's a lonely life when you drive others away. However, he didn't know how to control the poison he released. After all, wasn't it an instinct, or at least automatic?

Well, late one afternoon, while swimming near the moss-covered hulk of a long forgotten Spanish galleon, Pauly met a porcupine fish, a very close relative to blowfish, with sharp spines that also can inflate its body to fend off attackers. The porcupine fish's name was Harold. For whatever reason, Harold wasn't much affected by the poison Pauly slowly released into the water around them, and the two of them became friends. Harold talked to Pauly about all the ways fish can be in danger, and feel stressed out enough to either inflate or release poison. "How do you see it?" asked Harold.

"I don't know, I just don't know," responded Pauly, taken aback and confused. But as they continued to talk, Pauly came to realize that for his whole life he had been more than a little nervous about getting too close to other puffers, even though deep down, he really wanted to connect. Harold continued, "What if someone accidentally inflates, and another gets caught in their spines?" he asked. Pauly just nodded. He was beginning to understand. Harold knew exactly what Pauly was talking about because getting close to either puffer fish or porcupine fish always carries some risk. He helped Pauly realize that what he feared was really fear itself—the fear of getting too close and getting hurt. Harold further helped Pauly to see that loneliness and disconnection was much more hurtful than the possible pain that can go along with being close to someone.

Pauly slowly got accustomed to having Harold around. In fact, before he realized it, he began to *enjoy* Harold, and that was a very comfortable feeling. At about the same time, the slow release of poison from Pauly's body stopped, and he soon found other fish swimming closer to him. Now, Pauly, still occasionally inflated unnecessarily when he got nervous, but it happened less and less all the time.

Silver Fox

It was cold, oh-so cold, as I waited patiently in the dark. That winter night in 1983 in Prudhoe Bay, Alaska, the thermometer read 45 degrees below zero. I knew he would arrive soon, just as he had visited me many times before.

Then he emerged from the ice fog like a wounded ghost, the silver fox hobbling on his three legs. I kneeled and ever so gradually extended the morsel of sandwich in my hand. As he inched closer I could see the fear in his eyes, but hunger and survival propelled him to within three feet of me. I fumbled with my arctic mittens and proceeded to tear off piece after piece of the sandwich. And then he was gone.

Each meeting with the fox left me more connected to him and his passion for survival. Each encounter with the fox had made me painfully aware of my own limitations. While I was not physically disabled like the fox, I was devoid of understanding. I was stuck in life and could not move ahead.

We were both struggling to survive in a harsh environment where we had to deal with circumstances beyond our control. The fox became my soul mate. He remains so to this day. (Anderson, 2007.)

Eating Dirt
Taken from Gafner & Benson (2003)

Let me tell you about a client I had one time who was in the habit of eating dirt. Yes, eating dirt. While this may seem extraordinary to you, this man certainly didn't think it was anything to take lightly. Now, this man, he knew that eating dirt wasn't particularly good for his body, as it could throw his digestive system out of whack, and on occasion it even made him feel sick. He was embarrassed about this habit, yet he felt like it was beyond his control most of the time. He tried rationalizing to himself: "It's only dirt, and all kids eat dirt at one time in their lives, so it can't be THAT bad." Or, he would say, "It's a natural substance so it can't be so bad, certainly not as bad as taking drugs."

He ate dirt by himself, then he ate dirt to amuse his friends, who, of course, thought he was quite the kidder, and they egged him on repeatedly. Then, he realized that he didn't need his friends' approval, at least not in that way, and he wasn't going to eat dirt anymore to get it. After a time, he went to the doctor who, after several tests, told him that he must be driven to eat the dirt because his body was missing some sort of mineral he wasn't getting from his diet. With that explanation, the man felt relieved, as at least there was an answer in sight that would allow him to stop eating dirt forever. When he asked the doctor what mineral he was seeking by eating dirt, the doctor told him that if he listened to his *inner voice*, he would know what good things to give himself, so he wouldn't need to eat dirt anymore.

And you know, all by himself, with a bit of *introspection and quiet time* with himself, he realized what the dirt was doing for him, and how he could get it in healthier ways. With that knowledge, he was able to provide himself with the appropriate substitution, and to this day, he has never had a need or a desire to eat dirt again.

In the Freezer

It was way out in the country, in some state in the Midwestern U.S. I forget if it was Ohio, Indiana, or some place else. It was an old two-story, clapboard house, way out in the middle of nowhere, a rather ancient dwelling that had been there as long as nobody could remember.

Various families had lived in the house since the 1930s, and probably even before that. Not much had changed in that house over time, except that no doubt they had to replace the roof now and then, or at least patch up the holes. The house was set back from the road, barely visible through the trees and across the fields that perhaps had produced corn or soybeans in previous decades. But now, the fields lay dormant, having been untilled for a long, long time.

Inside the house, on the first floor, way in back in a room that now served as a crowded laundry room, there was an old freezer, a big old appliance that was like a chest, tucked away in a corner of the room. The freezer currently shared the room with a dog dish and the washing machine and drier. From the rest of the house, you just forgot about it back there in that room, and if you were in the kitchen, you might hear the tumbling of the washer, or the hum of the drier. But the big freezer you just forgot about. Any time people moved out of the house they just left the freezer. "It goes with the house," was what a succession of owners and tenants had been told over the years.

When children fetched something from the freezer, they had to strain to lift the heavy lid, and they had to stand on a stool in order to reach way down into it, peering through the frosty fog, in search of a popsicle amidst the frozen turkeys, gallons of orange juice that had been bought on sale, containers of spaghetti sauce, and who-knows-what else in unmarked, frost-covered containers that lay down in the icy depths. Magic marker tends to wear away with the passage of time, and on other containers, the labels simply curled off and deteriorated amidst the years and years of unrelenting freeze. In there, way down in the dark, jammed under a package of hot dogs that had been there for many years, was a container of frozen strawberries. No one could remember the last time someone had defrosted the freezer, and the inside walls were thick with ice. It was a wonder that it continued to function with such remarkable efficiency.

The laundry room was rather barren except for a weathered picture of a tranquil winter scene, a page torn from some magazine and tacked to the wall. Some hardcover books with yellowed pages lay in the dust behind the drier. They may have been poems of Robert Service, or a Jack London novel. No one knew for sure, as no one had swept back there for several years. A pencil on a string hung from the wall, close to dozens of lines marked on the wall, "January ten, three feet eight inches, February third, three feet nine inches." The once-white linoleum melded with the sagging floor.

Over the years, someone had taken out that container of strawberries and let it thaw for a couple of hours. But they invariably put it back without consuming it. If you examined its contents, you could see evidence of the repeated partial thawing and refreezing of that block of sugary crimson. The container was always put back, deep inside, and somehow it retained its crystallized integrity, despite years of being jostled about, squashed, dented, and nicked, not to mention the thawing that occurred during summer electric storms, when power went out in the whole house.

From the window in the room, you could look out over the freezer and see the snow banks of winter, the summer rains, and the brilliant autumn leaves. Some time back, an occupant of the house had hung a prism in the window, one of those curious little glass objects, that you could turn this way and that, and depending on how you turned it, and depending on the time of day, a person could see quite a kaleidoscope of colors.

Glossary of Terms

absorption of attention   Part of the induction phase and necessary for successful trance, the client's attention is focused on, for example, a story, a bodily sensation, a spot on the wall, or something else. Eye fixation, eye closure, diminished bodily movement, facial mask and other signs may indicate a successful absorption of attention.

age progression   Essentially the opposite of age regression, in trance clients are asked to imagine themselves in the future, perhaps feeling or behaving confident, strong, or in control. Therapists often tend to provide more structure for age progression than necessary, e.g., imagining pages of a calendar flipping forward, or imagining one's self in a time tunnel, or similar device, when often all that is necessary is for the therapist to wait for a few seconds while clients take themselves to a future time. Typically clients are asked to signal, e.g., with a head nod, "when you are there." The most famous example is Erickson's crystal ball technique. Also a hypnotic phenomenon.

age regression   A technique useful in hypnosis for accessing resources during problem solving and other applications, age regression is a naturally occurring phenomenon whenever we have a memory or reminiscence. In hypnosis, age regression, like other therapeutic applications, follows the induction and deepening phases. It may be guided and structured, for example, "Beginning now, I want you to ride a magic carpet back through time to age 15, and when you're there, in your mind, you may signal with your YES finger ..." If the therapist's intention is to implement the age regression, abreaction and reframing technique to treat an incident of abuse at age 15, the therapist waits for the client to signal before continuing. Sometimes we don't have a target age and we "go fishing" for important data. To do this, a general and permissive age regression is usually sufficient, e.g., "Starting now, I want you to go back in time, in your own way, taking as much time as you need, to *any time* in the past that might be important for the problem at hand, and when you get there, let me know by nodding your head." When the client nods her head she may have gone back in time to 10 minutes ago or 10 years ago, and the only way we will know is by asking for a verbal report. Following the verbal report we will customarily ask her to continue her unconscious search until the process is completed. As with other techniques, we never want to surprise clients, and should tell them our intentions when setting the agenda during pre-trance discussion. Also, if relevant, it is important for us to remind clients that all memories, including those accessed through hypnosis may not be valid, as they could be distortion or fantasy. Also a hypnotic phenomenon.

age regression, abreaction and reframing   This eminently useful technique (Hammond, 1990) is very helpful for trauma, especially one-time incidents. After getting the client's permission for same, induction and deepening are followed by age regression to the time of the event. We then ask them to abreact, or fully express, any feelings associated with the event, e.g., "Tell me now all the anger you have inside you ..." and do the same with fear, sadness, guilt, shame, or any other emotions. Have a box of Kleenex handy, as clients will typically cry, moan, blow their nose, or do other things associated with abreaction. When we feel there has been complete abreaction, we move on to reframing, e.g., "It is wonderful how you've released these pent-up feelings. I know that now, with the perspective of time and maturity you can move on and do well in your life." We can then seek unconscious commitment for same, e.g., "Let me ask a question of your unconscious mind ... and that question is this, 'Are you willing to put this in the past, move on and do well in the future? You may answer with one of those fingers on your right hand.'"

amnesia   Some practitioners believe that in some cases facilitating amnesia is necessary for later problem resolution, as amnesia allows unconscious processing to proceed without conscious interference. Amnesia can be suggested directly, e.g., "Beginning now, you may just forget anything from today that you wished to remember," or,

"The material today, will you remember to forget it, or just forget to remember?" A more indirect suggestion is, "Last night when I slept I had a dream, and when I woke up I could not remember the dream." Distraction may also facilitate amnesia, e.g., the client is re-alerted and immediately the therapist launches into an irrelevant story. Many clients will have amnesia for some portion of the trance experience even if it is not facilitated. Also, in many cases partial—not complete—amnesia may be a more realistic goal. Amnesia along with other hypnotic phenomena may be helpful in treating chronic pain.

amplifying the metaphor This technique is especially effective with anxiety and anger. In pre-trance discussion "the problem" is agreed upon and following induction and deepening the therapist permissively elicits a symbol or metaphor (e.g., a color, an object, or anything concrete) for both the problem and the absence of the problem. Then, the problem is amplified, e.g., "Now, whatever symbol or representation you have for the problem, I want you to make it very strong, amplified. If it is the color red, intensify it, feel the red in all its brilliance beginning now, while I count to three, one, two, three, and now, just let it go." Then, the same is done for the problem's absence while the therapist ties its absence to an anchor, e.g., "... make a circle with your right thumb and index finger and similarly make that symbol strong while I count, one, two, three, very good, and just let that hand relax."

apposition of opposites Hypnotic language such as this is believed to be trance inducing. This technique juxtaposes opposites such as near-far, up-down, and inside-outside, e.g., "Another person one time noticed a *heaviness* developing in that *right* hand, while a *lightness* was detected in the *left* hand ..." Hypnotic language can be a major tool of the therapist in talk therapy as well as in hypnosis.

arm catalepsy Catalepsy means suspension of movement, and a cataleptic or rigid arm is employed in the arm catalepsy induction (Gafner & Benson, 2000), a highly directive but brief and effective means of inducing trance. It is contraindicated in people with cervical pain, peripheral neuropathy and related conditions and some clients may appreciate a conversational or story induction instead.

authoritarian approach Such an approach in psychotherapy may involve telling clients in no uncertain terms what to do. A therapist who employs directive or authoritarian language in hypnosis may say, "You *will* now drop off into deep trance and you *will* lose your desire for cigarettes." Certainly some clients will respond better to this approach and I advocate a place for it in the therapist's toolbox. In a permissive and more indirect approach the operative word is *may* instead of *will*, e.g., "In a few moments you *may* begin to find yourself drifting off into trance, and I wonder when you will start to experience the pleasure of life without cigarettes."

automatic process This refers to mental functioning that is outside of a person's conscious awareness. Synonymous with unconscious process, a few of the techniques that access this process are metaphor, misspeak, and subtle vocal shift. Much of a person's mental functioning is unconscious and not governed by conscious intent and purpose. In this book, the unconscious is a vital target in hypnotherapy.

bind of comparable alternatives An example of hypnotic language, this technique appears to offer the client a choice between two or more alternatives, offering the illusion of choice, e.g., in hypnosis, "This session would you like to go into a light trance, a medium trance, or a deep trance?" Or in talk therapy, "The material we covered today might be pertinent to your personal life, useful at work, or maybe you can simply incorporate it into your overall experience."

confusion A broad category of techniques that are used to counter unconscious resistance, confusion typically distracts, interrupts, or overloads. One common confusional technique involves the non sequitur , e.g., during the induction or deepening, the therapist says, "At that store the shopping carts always seem to stick together." The therapist then pauses briefly while the client's conscious mind tries to make sense of this out-of-context statement, and then the therapist follows with a way out of the confusion, and in the desired direction, e.g., "And you can go deep," or, "You can let go." Confusion is generally indicated only when straightforward techniques have failed, and should always be used judiciously and respectfully. When clients don't respond to directive, guided imagery or story inductions, a confusional induction is often successful.

contingent suggestion　Also known as chaining, this type of suggestion connects a suggestion to an ongoing or inevitable behavior, thus making it more likely to be accepted, e.g., "... and as you begin to notice that familiar heaviness in your hand, you can let that comfort spread all throughout your body." A dentist who employs hypnosis may use contingent suggestion as a posthypnotic suggestion, e.g., "... and the next time you return here and settle into the chair, the moment I turn on this light you can begin to develop pleasant numbness in your mouth." (See also *truism, linking word*, and *leading*.)

debriefing　A very important phase in the hypnotic process, this follows the re-alerting and is where the therapist ratifies hypnotic phenomena, answers questions, and elicits subjective experience. The therapist may learn important data, especially in the early sessions, e.g., "I couldn't hear you," or "... that story you told me today about a lake, didn't you know I almost drowned in a lake?"

deepening　Following the induction phase and before the therapy phase of hypnosis, trance is deepened in many varieties of ways, often by counting down from 10 to one. In this book, for instructional purposes I break down a hypnosis session into pre-trance discussion, induction, deepening, therapy phase, re-alerting and debriefing. Many who practice hypnosis roll these phases into one, or use no formal deepening.

displacement　Used in pain management, the locus of pain is imaginally displaced to another part of the body, or outside the body, e.g., "... the discomfort in your knee, why should one knee hog all the pain ... you can allow 30% of it to be shared by the little finger on your left hand ..." The client typically will continue to experience the sensation, but hopefully with less pain in the target area. It is important for the therapist to think pattern interruption and diminution of the pain rather than the elimination of it. Anxiety and other symptoms can also be imaginally displaced.

dissociation   Dissociation is a hallmark feature of trance as well as an excellent ratifier or convincer of trance. The more clients experience dissociation, e.g., hands or feet separated from the body, the richer the hypnotic experience. Encouraging dissociation is recommended even with clients who experience dissociation pathologically, e.g., with PTSD, and the strategy may be explained to such clients as capitalizing on a natural ability. The same is true for other pathological features, such as psychological numbness and spacing out. Employing dissociative language, e.g., *that* hand instead of *your* hand, facilitates dissociation.

ego-strengthening   Self-efficacy or ego strength is defined as believing that one's behavior will lead to successful outcomes. To many, ego strength is also seen as the ability to cope with environmental demands. This book describes two types of hypnotic ego-strengthening, short-burst and metaphorical. The author posits that major therapeutic gains may be made with hypnotic ego-strengthening for anxiety, mood, and chronic pain disorders even without employing corrective or abreactive measures. Hypnotic ego-strengthening techniques are explained to the client as "a mental building up," something appreciated by persons with chronic problems. Of course, consciously directed ego-strengthening, such as coping skills training and other skill building and similar measures, should be applied as well.

embedded suggestion   An exquisitely useful tool in hypnosis, this is also referred to as embedded command or embedded meaning. An inward focus can be encouraged, for example: "Going *inside* can be very *interesting* ... *in* there where you have your imag*in*ation, *in*tuition ..." A psychologist in Phoenix was working with a client on weight loss and wanted to encourage walking. He mentioned another client who bought a *wok* ... and *wokking* became his preferred manner of food preparation. The client lost 80 pounds, kept it off, and is still walking.

eye closure   This can be suggested by phrasing such as, "… your eyes may blink and those eyelids might feel heavy, and those eyes can close whenever you wish …" Eye closure can also be seeded through rehearsal prior to the induction, e.g., "Close your eyes very briefly while I count to three … now how did that feel?" However, some clients, especially those with PTSD, may not wish to close their eyes during hypnosis. It is best for the therapist to not push eye closure if a client is reluctant to do so, as sufficient depth may occur by fostering absorption of attention in eye fixation alone.

eye fixation   For clients who fear loss of control, the therapist may ask them to focus their gaze on a spot of their choice, e.g., on the wall, or the back of the hand. Most clients eventually become comfortable enough to close their eyes.

fluff   Therapists often think that every word in an induction or story should be purposeful or didactic. However, meaningless, meandering detail, or fluff, may deepen absorption and serve to increase receptivity to key suggestions. A few well-placed suggestions amidst the fluff may be very effective.

hidden observer   This is a phenomenon experienced by nearly everyone in trance and it is good to point it out to the client, e.g., "You have your conscious mind, your unconscious mind, and your hidden observer, the part of you that observes what's going on." People's hidden observer usually diminishes after the first session or two; however, if it remains active it may impede the client's letting go. Then, a confusional induction may be indicated.

hypnotic language   Hypnotic language is thought to fascinate, connect with the unconscious, and to foster absorption. In this book, bind of comparable alternatives, implication, power words and other concepts are subsumed under hypnotic language.

hypnotic phenomena   This term refers to catalepsy, dissociation, time distortion, amnesia, automatic writing and drawing, arm levitation, anesthesia, positive and negative hallucination, and other phenomena that are both naturally occurring phenomena as well as phenomena that may occur in trance. Suggestions for hypnotic phenomena may be delivered in an induction or story. Debriefing will yield the client's experiencing these phenomena, and the therapist should then ratify or reinforce it.

ideomotor finger signal   To avoid the client's becoming a passive recipient, and in order to learn important data, it is important for the client to communicate during hypnosis. This dance or back-and-forth communication can occur via a head nod, verbal report, or finger signal. The author typically asks clients to put their hands out on their lap so they can be observed, and then, in trance, the therapist elects preferences for fingers—usually on the preferred or dominant hand—that can signify YES, NO, and I DON'T KNOW/NOT READY TO ANSWER YET. Then, say, you've processed a particular symptom and want to know if the client is ready to let go of it, you ask, "Now, I want to ask a question of your unconscious mind, and the question is this, 'Are you ready to put X behind you and move on?' Taking as much time as you need, you may answer with one of your fingers." It is believed that a mere twitch of the finger represents a true unconscious communication (and a response that is available on the finger before it is available on the tongue), whereas a deliberate lifting of the finger is a conscious response. Sometimes a finger signal is not evident and during debriefing the client says, for example, "I thought my YES finger moved."

implication   With implication, the operative word is *when*, not *if*, e.g., "I wonder *when* you'll notice heaviness in your hands?" or "Which one of your hands feels heavier?" In accessing unconscious resources, the therapist may say, "... *when* the back part of your mind has selected some strength or resource that served you well in the past, your YES finger can move all by itself."

indirection   Indirection generally refers to an unconsciously directed approach. To tell a client an anecdote or story about someone else who successfully managed her anger is an indirect suggestion, while a directive approach for the same problem would involve straightforward instruction. The higher the reactance or resistance, the more indirection is indicated.

induction   The phase of hypnosis where trance is induced. As described in this book, the other parts of the process include pre-trance discussion, (induction), deepening, therapy, re-alerting and debriefing.

instigative anecdote or story   Useful for clients who are stuck, this metaphorical approach is designed to be self-referenced by the client in order to stimulate unconscious problem solving.

interspersal   First described by Milton Erickson, this invaluable indirect technique involves interspersing the therapist's hypnotic patter—or induction, deepening, or story—with key suggestions, such as "just let go," or "you can do it." If this random insertion is preceded by a pause, attention is riveted. If the client is analytical, it is useful to lead away after the suggestion, e.g., "... *just let go*—and I can't stop thinking of that barking dog yesterday." Then, the suggestion may percolate in the unconscious without analysis. The author usually informs clients that he may be saying things that don't make sense in order to "get in underneath the radar." The therapist's approach is always framed as helping.

law of parsimony   This law holds that the therapist should do only what is necessary to achieve the desired effect. For a client who is experienced with trancework, a lengthy induction may not be necessary, and all that need be done is "... just sit back now, let those eyes gently close, settle into that chair and taking as much time as you need, let a deep trance develop all on its own ... and when you're sufficiently deep in order to do the work we need to do today, your YES finger will rise."

lead away   This is a confusion technique that is used to distract the conscious mind from a preceding suggestion by saying something irrelevant, e.g., "... *you can overcome this problem—and* let me tell you how those shopping carts stuck together at the grocery store." Such techniques are useful with clients who show unconscious resistance.

leading   Pacing and leading are important in communication to show understanding. The word *and* has been called the most important word in psychotherapy because it links and leads to suggestions or directives. So, in discussion following hypnosis, we might say, "I know how nervous you feel in social situations, *and* I think it's important for you to regularly practice your anchor that we covered in hypnosis today."

linking word   We may offer the client a series of truisms followed by *and* before a suggestion. Similarly, "... you exhale *and* you can feel tension leaving your body." (See also *leading, truisms* and *contingent suggestion*.)

metaphor   We listen for metaphors offered by clients so they can be utilized in therapy. "There is a wall around me" is a therapeutic invitation to "loosen the mortar between the bricks, knock a hole in the wall, lower the wall for one hour in the morning," or any variety of pattern interruption. The most common types of metaphors in hypnosis are story and anecdote.

misspeak   This elegant indirect technique should be used sparsely to be most effective in communicating a suggestion to the unconscious. For example, "The man changed his behavior across the *board/ border* down up in Canada." The therapist appears to misspeak, the first word is the suggestion and the second word serves to lead away. The author may prepare misspeak for clients by asking himself the question, "What do they need to hear in order to be well?"

naturalistic trance states   Discussion prior to hypnosis should ask when a client normally drifts off or becomes pleasantly absorbed in something like a movie or song. Many experience "highway hypnosis" while driving. By comparing hypnosis in the office to natu-rally occurring behavior there may be less fear of loss of control.

non sequitur   Used for distraction or interruption, this is a brief, out-of-context phrase used to interrupt conscious mental sets. When the therapist offers a non sequitur, the client strives to make sense of it, and the therapist offers a way out—and in the desired direc-tion, e.g., "Why did it rain last week?" followed by a suggestion such as, "you can go deep." Employed in short-burst ego-strengthening.

not knowing/not doing   Clients find this device quite liberating in that it fosters unconscious responsiveness and dissipates con-scious effort. This suggestion tends to free up the untrained trance subject who is trying very hard to "get it right." It is also thought to assist in discharging anxiety or resistance. In an induction the author usually adds, "There's absolutely nothing at all that you need to know, or do, or think about, or change, in fact, all you really need to do is just sit there and breathe. There's nowhere you need to be, nothing to accomplish, and you don't even have to listen to the words, which can drift in and drift out."

pattern interruption   First described by Milton Erickson and further developed by Cade & O'Hanlon (1993), among others, this elegant and wide-ranging technique is a major tool in the toolbox of practitioners of strategic and other brief therapies. Clients often come to us and desire to *eliminate* their problem, and when thera-pists approach the goal in this way both parties often end up disap-pointed. It is eminently easier—and more realistic—to aim instead for *altering* one aspect of the problem which in turn often results in problem resolution. To effect this, we work with the client to alter the intensity, frequency, duration, location or some other aspect of the problem. For example, for a father and daughter who typically argue in the kitchen in the morning, the therapist asks them, "I want you to indulge me in a little experiment, which is this: I would like you to limit your arguing to only Monday, Wednesday and Friday in the living room. Are you willing to do that?" Thus, the location and frequency are altered. Pattern interruption is a wonderful technique for virtually any individual problem as well as relational problems. Rationales presented to clients are either an experiment, or to try and bring the problem under voluntary control.

pause   Believed to be a form of indirect suggestion, the therapist pauses for a couple of seconds during, say, an induction or story. A pause causes the listener to begin an unconscious search, and clients may at that moment be receptive to suggestion. For example, in a story, "... he was searching for something and in the afternoon she found it when (pause) *he saw a flash of light*." Or, used after a suggestion, "... he made a significant discovery (pause) which *came as a total surprise*." The author also used pause as a suggestion, though less indirectly: "During the session you may hear a pause (pause), or a period of silence, and I don't mean the paws on a cat or dog, and you may use these times to let your experience deepen."

permissive suggestion   Many clients respond better if given a wide range of choice: "You may begin to notice sensations, feelings, experiences or even something else peculiar or curious in your hands, feet, or elsewhere in your body." This may also be expressed with less verbosity: "Beginning now and taking as much time as you need, let yourself experience anything at all in your body or your mind."

perturbation   The author's simple rule of thumb: when stuck, perturb. This helps clients break out of rigid points of view or dysfunctional behavior. Your target for perturbation is always the unconscious, and instigative anecdotes or stories are a major way to perturb. If you, as a therapist, are stuck, try reading an instigative story or several anecdotes to yourself, move on to doing something else, let them percolate in your unconscious for a few days, and then see what spontaneously might spring to mind.

posthypnotic suggestion   This is a suggestion presented in trance for a behavior to occur outside of trance. For example, "When you return here next time and sit down again in that chair, the comfort of the chair will be a signal for you to begin to drift off." The author employs this suggestion for subsequent sessions, as above; to trigger relaxation outside the office by use of the *anchor*, and in *unconscious problem solving*.

power words   Certain words in hypnosis may enhance the trance process, as they are believed to access the unconscious, or at least a sense of wonderment or curiosity. Examples are story, imagine, wonder, notice, curious, explore, intriguing, appreciate, and interesting. Authors such as Gilligan (1987) and others frequently combine notice and appreciate, e.g., "... when you *notice* that familiar sensation in your hand, you may begin to *appreciate* the pleasantness of trance." In this book, power words are subsumed under *hypnotic language*.

pre-trancework discussion   This is the initial part of a hypnosis session where the therapist checks in with the client and sets the agenda.

question   Deceivingly simple yet quite elegant, a direct question asked during trance can rivet attention, stimulate associations, and facilitate responsiveness. During the induction, we may ask, "... a highly curious sensation in one hand, do you notice it yet?" The author often reaches for: "What is beginning to percolate *now* in your unconscious mind?" When the therapist senses resistance, which is usually *un*conscious, such a question may bring it to the fore, where it can be discussed and problem solved once the client is re-alerted.

re-alerting   This is a part of the hypnosis session that follows the therapy component. The author typically uses, "Beginning now, I'm going to count from one up to five and by the time I reach five you can resume your alert, waking state, as if waking up from a nice, pleasant, refreshing nap, (increased volume), 1, 2 ..." Many clients are not eager for trance to end, or may require a few minutes to re-alert, so be patient.

reframe   Reframing is a vital technique in most methods of psychotherapy, as the therapist's conveyance of new information provides the client with a new understanding or appreciation of a behavior or attitude. The client may see something in a new light, or be given hope, after a problem is given a positive connotation. "Just coming to this first session has to take some *courage* and that tells me there is hope," the author is prone to say. Virtually any problem or attitude can be reframed with a value thought dear to the client: closeness, duty, protectiveness, love, strength, loyalty, caring, are but a few. Therapists should be judicious with their reframes, as most clients are accustomed to hearing politicians and others say things like, "This is both a challenge and an opportunity," about some dreadful problem. In talk therapy, we can tell immediately from non-verbals whether the reframe is accepted. In hypnosis, a reframe is most commonly effected via metaphor, e.g., a story or anecdote about *someone else* who gains a different understanding or appreciation.

repetition Anything that is important, such as a suggestion or directive, should be repeated—but not too much. The author may repeat "breathing in comfort and relaxation" in an induction, and suggestions may also be repeated differently, e.g., "... a cool, refreshing breath can be most enjoyable."

reactance Resistance is to reactance as tide is to ocean, or guilt is to shame, a behavior or attitude that may be part of a larger whole. A reactant individual fears loss of control and in the author's experience most clients who have high reactance will not accept a referral for hypnosis.

resistance Many times what we perceive as resistance to hypnosis may simply be anxiety about a new experience. "I don't want to go into trance" is probably high reactance and, of course, hypnosis will not be pursued further. However, "I *want* to go into trance but just *can't*" is likely unconscious resistance, which may be an indication for a confusional induction, but which also may be successfully discharged by a *clarifying discussion, permissive suggestions, a suggestion covering all possibilities, not knowing/not doing, metaphor,* and similar devices. Resistance can also be discharged by having clients change chairs (so the resistance is left in the first chair), or by asking them questions which must be answered by "no," e.g., (in Tucson), "It's not hot out today, is it?" Most clients are keenly aware of their resistance, which will abate through reassurance, or as they become more comfortable with the process.

restraint   Let's say you've conducted a couple of sessions with a person and he doesn't practice using his anchor or listen to the CD made for him, the author usually restrains, or holds them back from moving ahead, e.g., "… change may mean uncertainty … we may be moving too fast … you may not be ready for this … or, perhaps you should think about it for a few weeks before we reschedule." When the author has clients who are anxious or resistant, the first session or two he typically begins an induction, re-alerts, asks them how they are doing, then resumes the induction. If necessary, he will re-alert and re-induce more than once. Holding back something pleasant or potentially helpful builds responsiveness and enhances client control.

seeding   A suggestion may be more successful if it has been seeded beforehand. To do this, the target suggestion is mentioned (seeded) early on, and later, by mentioning the target again, the "seed" is activated. If the problem is anxiety and in the therapy component the author's target is slowing down, he may say to the client, "The traffic on the freeway sure was *slow* this morning." To seed this non-verbally, the author may *slowly* get up from his chair to retrieve a pen, and *slowly* return to his chair. Later on, when *slowing down* is mentioned in a story, the seed is activated. Seeding is akin to fore-shadowing in literature when, say, dark, foreboding clouds presage tragedy. It is also similar to priming in social psychology. This unconsciously directed technique is well worth the little preparation required ahead of time.

short-burst   As used in this book, short-burst is employed in ego-strengthening. A *non sequitur* is offered … and followed shortly by a suggestion, e.g., "Why do dogs bark? … you can go deep." When not used with a confusional suggestion such as a non sequitur, it is the same as *interspersal*. In addition to short-burst the author employs metaphorical ego-strengthening.

story   The story is a vital metaphorical approach and a primary means for offering suggestions in hypnosis. As an indirect technique, a story goes in "underneath the radar," meaning that it cannot be defended against or consciously analyzed. Essential to a story is *embedded suggestion*.

suggestion covering all possibilities   When the therapist mentions several suggestions, the likelihood of the client's accepting one or more may be more likely, e.g., "... as a person goes deeper into trance various sensations may begin to develop in the hands or feet ... a tingling or numbness in one hand or that hand on the other side ... coolness or warmth in one or both feet ... maybe a heaviness up here, a lightness down there, or some other intriguing sensation in the extremities or elsewhere in the body." The author often reaches for metaphor in this situation: "... one woman one time, she detected, just noticed, an itching in her right earlobe, and in the left ..."

therapy component   As described in this book, a phase of the hypnosis session that may consist of a story or stories, age progression or age regression, unconscious exploration or problem solving, or a highly structured technique such as *amplifying the metaphor*. Some practitioners have no clear phases.

time distortion   A hypnotic phenomenon that is important to elicit and ratify, especially early on. In this book suggestions for time distortion are embedded in many of the inductions. Time expansion and time contraction are contained in "In trance, time may seem to speed up or slow down." After re-alerting the person the first session it may be relevant to ask, "How much time do you think passed here today?" All hypnotic phenomena experienced by the client should be reinforced.

truism   This is an undeniable statement of fact. A series of truisms leads to a "yes-set" and acceptance of suggestions. In talk therapy, the author may say, "Okay, we've met three times now, all sessions were at 3:00, we've explored your anger and feelings about your ex-wife ... *and* between now and next time I'd like you to do X." In hypnosis, he may say, "Coming in here today on this rainy day, having to wait five minutes extra in the waiting room, and finally coming in here, sitting down there, you know and I know that today especially you can drift off into the deepest of trances."

unconsciously directed therapy   A cornerstone of this approach in hypnosis or psychotherapy is metaphor and story, whose purpose is to influence the unconscious mind. Cognitive-behavioral therapy is primarily concerned with conscious mechanisms, whereas other approaches—like Gestalt, psychodrama, or psychodynamic—employ techniques directed at both the conscious and unconscious mind.

unconscious mind   Milton Erickson and others believed that much of a person's mental functioning is governed not by conscious intention and deliberate choice, but by features that operate outside of conscious awareness and control. Findings in psychological research have confirmed this (Bargh & Chartrand, 1999). Some clients may mean unconscious when they say subconscious or back part of the mind. The author may describe it to clients as "that part of you that takes over when your dreaming, or daydreaming."

unconscious problem solving   The hypnotherapist may instigate problem solving on an unconscious level with a variety of techniques including directives or other suggestions to the unconscious, with instigative anecdotes or stories, or with, for example, a permissive suggestion that is tagged to a behavior known to occur in the natural environment. With the latter, the therapist knows, say that the client drives by Broadway and Fifth nearly every day. The therapist offers the suggestion that "you will learn something important to help you with your problem" when he passes through that intersection, followed with a suggestion for amnesia. Next session the client returns with a new resource but has no awareness of how or why. This technique works best with clients in whom amnesia is easily fostered.

unconscious process   In psychology literature this is more often referred to as automatic process, or that which lies outside of one's immediate awareness. Techniques such as *metaphor, pause,* and *misspeak* are believed to access this process.

utilization   If they give you lemons, make lemonade. That is an example of utilization in daily life, as is this: The U.S. war in Vietnam left thousands of bomb craters, which many people converted to duck ponds after the war. In psychotherapy, or hypnosis, the client's behavior, however problematic, is accepted, embraced, and utilized, or employed, to transform the problem. A treatment philosophy more than a mere technique, "utilization dictates that whatever the patient/family brings to the sessions can be harnessed to effect a psychotherapeutic result" (Zeig & Geary, 2000). This is a fundamental principle of Ericksonian therapy, as interpretation is to psychoanalysis, or desensitization is to behavior therapy. For a client who is very rigid, the therapist may reframe the behavior as steadfast *purpose* and say, "Let's start to make some *purposeful* changes with which you can feel comfortable." For hypervigilant clients who are reluctant to close their eyes, the therapist may encourage attentional absorption with eye fixation on a spot on the wall.

References

Allen, S.N., & Bloom, S.L. (1994). Group and family treatment of posttraumatic stress disorder. *Psychiatric Clinics of North America*, 17, 426–430.

Anderson, R. (2007). Unpublished story.

Araoz, D.L. (1995). *The new hypnosis in sex therapy*. Northvale, NJ: Jason Aronson.

Bandura, A. (1997*). Self-efficacy: the exercise of control*. New York: W.H. Freeman.

Banks, L.W. (1999). Searching for the good spirit of Begashabito Canyon. *Arizona Highways*, 75 (3), 4–9.

Bargh, J.A., & Chartrand, T.L. (1999). The unbearable automaticity of being. *American Psychologist*, 54 (7), 462–479.

Beahrs, J.O. (1971). The hypnotic psychotherapy of Milton H. Erickson. *American Journal of Clinical Hypnosis,* 14 (2), 73–90.

Benson, S. (2001). Unpublished story.

Blanchard, E.B. (2005). A critical review of cognitive, behavioral, and cognitive-behavioral therapies for irritable bowel syndrome. *Journal of Cognitive Psychotherapy: An International Quarterly*, 19 (2), 101–123.

Blanchard, E.B. (2001). *Irritable bowel syndrome: Psychosocial assessment and treatment*. Washington, D.C: American Psychological Association.

Bleich, A., Dycian, A., Koslowsky, M., Solomon, Z. & Wiener, M. (1992). Psychiatric implications of missile attacks on a civilian population: Israeli lessons from the Persian Gulf War. *Journal of the American Medical Association*, 2681, 613–615.

Cade, B. & O'Hanlon, B. (1993). *A brief guide to brief therapy*. New York: W.W. Norton and Co.

Davis, P. (2003). Efforts underway to restore Florida's Molasses Reef. *All thing Considered*, National Public Radio, Aug. 25.

Diamond, M.J. (1983). The veracity of ideomotor signals. In Zilbergeld, B., Edelstien, M.G., & Araoz, D.L. (Eds.), *Hypnosis: Questions and Answers*. New York: W.W. Norton and Co.

Edgette, J.H., & Edgette, J.S. (1995). *The handbook of hypnotic phenomena in psychotherapy.* New York: Brunner/Mazel, Inc.

Edmunds, D. & Gafner, G. (2003). Touching trauma: Combining hypnotic ego-strengthening and zero balancing. *Contemporary Hypnosis*, 20 (4), 215–220.

Ehlers, A., & Clark, D.M. (2000). A cognitive model of posttraumatic stress disorder. *Behaviour Research and Therapy*, 38 (4), 403–415.

Engel, C.C., Engel, A.L., Campbell, S.J., McFell, M.S., Russo, J., & Katon, W. (1993). Posttraumatic stress disorder symptoms and precombat sexual and physical abuse in Desert Storm veterans. *Journal of Nervous and Mental Disease,* 181, 683–688.

Erickson, M.H. (1966). The interspersal technique for symptom correction and pain control. *American Journal of Clinical Hypnosis*, 8 (3), 198–209.

Erickson, M.H., Rossi, E.H., & Rossi, S.L. (1976). *Hypnotic realities*. New York: Irvington.

Fass, R. (No date). Hypnotherapy in the treatment of noncardiac chest pain of presumed esophageal origin: A randomized clinical trial, unpublished study.

Fatali, M. (1991). Symphony in stone. *Arizona Highways*, 67 (1), 22–27.

Gafner, G. (2010). *Techniques of hypnotic induction*. Carmarthen, Wales: Crown House Publishing Ltd.

Gafner, G. (2006). *More hypnotic inductions*. New York: W.W. Norton and Co.

Gafner, G. (2004). *Clinical applications of hypnosis*. New York: W.W. Norton and Co.

Gafner, G. & Benson, S. (2003). *Hypnotic techniques*. New York: W.W. Norton and Co.

Gafner, G., & Benson, S. (2001). Indirect ego-strengthening in treating PTSD in immigrants from Central America. *Contemporary Hypnosis*, 18 (3), 135–144.

Gafner, G. & Benson, S. (2000). *Handbook of hypnotic inductions*. New York: W.W. Norton and Co.

Gafner, G., & Duckett, S. (1992). Treating the sequelae of a curse in elderly Mexican-Americans. In *Hispanic Aged Mental Health* (T.L. Brink, Ed.). New York: Haworth Press.

Gardner, R. (1971). *Therapeutic communication with children: The mutual story-telling technique*. New York: Science House.

Geary, B.B. (1994). Seeding responsiveness to hypnotic processes. In J.K. Zeig (Ed.), *Ericksonian methods: The essence of the story* (pp. 315–332). New York: Brunner/Mazel.

Gilligan, S.G. (1987). *Therapeutic trances: The cooperation principle in Ericksonian hypnotherapy*. New York: Brunner/Mazel.

Gonsalkorale, W.M. (2006). Gut-directed hypnotherapy: The Manchester approach for treatment of irritable bowel syndrome. *International Journal of Clinical and Experimental Hypnosis*, 54 (1), 27–50.

Haley, J. (1973). *Uncommon therapy: The psychiatric techniques of Milton H. Erickson, M.D.* New York: W.W. Norton & Co.

Hammond, D.C. (1990). *Handbook of hypnotic suggestions and metaphors*. New York: W.W. Norton and Co.

Hartland, J. (1971). *Medical and dental hypnosis and its clinical application*. New York: Macmillan.

Holmes, E.A., Grey, N., & Young, K.A.D. (2005). Intrusive images and "hotspots" of trauma memories in posttraumatic stress disorder: An exploratory investigation of emotions and cognitive themes. *Journal of Behavior Therapy and Experimental Psychiatry*, 36, 3–17.

Jacobs, I. (2005). Unpublished anecdotes.

Kirsch, I., Montgomery, G., & Sapirstein, G. (1995). Hypnosis as an adjunct to cognitive-behavioral psychotherapy: A meta-analysis. *Journal of Consulting and Clinical Psychology*, 63 (2), 214–220.

Koetting, M.G., & Lane, R.C. (2001). Therapeutic metaphor as barrier to the self: A case of an older adult. *Journal of Clinical Geropsychology*, 7 (3), 245–250.

Kroger, W.S. (1963). *Clinical and Experimental Hypnosis in Medicine, Dentistry and Psychology*. Philadelphia: Lippincott.

Lavertue, N.E., Kuman, V.K., & Pekala, R.J. (2002). The effectiveness of a hypnotic ego-strengthening procedure for improving self-esteem and depression. *Australian Journal of Clinical and Experimental Hypnosis*, 30 (1), 1–23.

Liquid Mind (1995). *Ambience Minimus,* Music compact disk, Sausalito, CA: Real Music.

Litz, B.T., & Blake, D.D. (1990). Decision-making guidelines for the use of direct therapeutic exposure in the treatment of posttraumatic stress disorder. *Behaviour Therapy*, 17, 91–93.

McCarroll, J.E., Ursano, R.J., & Fullerton, C.S. (1993). Symptoms of post-traumatic stress disorder following recovery of war dead. *American Journal of Psychiatry*, 150, 1875–1877.

McCarroll, J.E., Ursano, R.J., Fullerton, C.S., & Lundy, A. (1995). Anticipatory stress of handling human remains from the Persian Gulf War: Predictors of intrusion and avoidance. *Journal of Nervous and Mental Disease*, 183, 698–703.

McMullen, L.J., & Conway, J.B. (2002). Conventional metaphors for depression. In S.R. Fussell (Ed.), *The verbal communication of emotions: Interdisciplinary perspectives* (pp. 167–181). Mahwah, New Jersey: Lawrence Erlbaum.

Mlodinow, L. (2012). *Subliminal: How your unconscious mind rules your behavior,* New York: Pantheon.

Nijdam, M.J., Gersons, B.P., Reitsma, J.B., de Jongh, A., & Olff, M. (2012). Brief eclectic psychotherapy versus eye movement desensitization and reprocessing therapy for post-traumatic stress disorder: A randomized controlled trial. *British Journal of Psychiatry*, 200, 224–231.

Papp, P. (1983). *The process of change*. New York: Guilford Publications.

Pekala, R.J., Maurer, R., Kumar, V.K., Elliott, N.C., Masten, E., Moon, E., & Salinger, M. (2004). Self-hypnosis relapse prevention training with chronic drug/alcohol users: Effects on self-esteem, affect and relapse. *American Journal of Clinical Hypnosis*, 46 (4), 281–297.

Pitman, R.K., Orr, S.P., Altman, B., & Longpre, R.E. (1996). Emotional processing and outcome of imaginal flooding therapy in Vietnam veterans with chronic posttraumatic stress disorder. *Comprehensive Psychiatry*, 37 (6), 409–418.

Pollan, M. (1994). Secret world of a pond. *New York Times Magazine*, July 24, 35–37.

Powers, M.B., Halpern, J.J., Ferenschak, M.P., Gillihan, S.J. & Foa, E.B. (2010). A meta-analytic review of prolonged exposure for posttraumatic stress disorder. *Clinical Psychology Review*, 30, 635–641.

Prochaska, J.O., DiClemente, C.C., & Norcross, J.C. (1992). In search of how people change. *American Psychologist*, 47, 1102–14.

Rosen, S. (1982). *My voice will go with you: The teaching tales of Milton H. Erickson*. New York: W.W. Norton and Co.

Scott, A., & Gafner, G. (2007), Metaphor in anger management, paper presented at the annual meeting of the American Psychological Association, Washington, D.C.

Shoham-Salomon, V., & Rosenthal, R. (1987). Paradoxical intervention: A meta-analysis. *Journal of Consulting and Clinical Psychology*, 55 (7), 22–27.

Siegelman, E.Y. (1990). *Metaphor and meaning in psychotherapy*. New York: Guilford Publications.

Sopory, P., & Dillard, J.P. (2002). The persuasive effects of metaphor. *Human Communication Research*, 28 (3), 382–419.

Southwick, S.M., Morgan, C.A., Darnell, A., & Bremner, J.D. (1995). Trauma-related symptoms in veterans of Operation Desert Storm: A 2-year follow-up. *American Journal of Psychiatry*, 152, 1150–1155.

Stanton, H.E., (1997). Increasing internal control through hypnotic ego-enhancement. *Australian Journal of Clinical and Experimental Hypnosis*, 7, 219–223.

Sutker, P.B., Davis, J.M., Uddo, M., & Ditta, S.R. (1995). War zone stress, personal resources and PTSD in Persian Gulf War returnees. *Journal of Abnormal Psychology*, 104, 444–452.

Sutker, P.B., Uddo, M., Bailey, K., Vasterling, J.J., & Errera, P. (1994). Psychopathology in war zone deployed and nondeployed Operation Desert Storm troops assigned graves registration duties. *Journal of Abnormal Psychology*, 103, 383–390.

Taylor, M. (1992). Secret pass. *Arizona Highways*, 68 (3), 40–45.

Wallas, L. (1985). *Stories for the third ear*. New York: W.W. Norton and Co.

Whorwell, P.J. (2008). Hypnotherapy for irritable bowel syndrome: The response of colonic and noncolonic symptoms. *Journal of Psychosomatic Research*, 64, 621–623.

Yapko, M. (1990). *Trancework: An Introduction to the Practice of Clinical Hypnosis* (2nd ed.). New York: Brunner/Mazel, Inc.

Young, C.A. (2007). Unpublished story.

Zeig, J.K., & Geary, B. (2000). *Letters of Milton H. Erickson*. Phoenix, AZ: Zeig, Tucker & Theisen.

For Further Training and Reading

For Further Training

You read an ad on the internet where you can "become a hypnotist" with online training or by attending a few classes, no education is required. These are ads obviously aimed at lay hypnotists, not professional clinicians, and should be avoided. Others are not so apparent. There may be many reputable places where you can get training, but I would investigate it carefully. I once asked Dr. Chuck Mutter of the American Society of Clinical Hypnosis (ASCH), what was his litmus test. He said, "Ask them if they are endorsed by either ASCH or the International Society of Clinical and Experimental Hypnosis (ISCEH)" (personal communication, 2002). So, that's my advice to you when you're deciding on training. Besides trainings by ASCH or ISCEH, I would highly recommend training, sponsored by the Milton H. Erickson Foundation, or one of its component societies in the U.S. and other countries.

As far as reading goes, I regularly read the *American Journal of Clinical Hypnosis* (www.asch.net) and the *International Journal of Clinical and Experimental Hypnosis* (ijceh.educ.wsu), as well as *Contemporary Hypnosis*, a publication of the British Society of Experimental and Clinical Hypnosis (www.bsech.com). Another fine journal is the *Australian Journal of Clinical and Experimental Hypnosis* (www.ozhypnosis.com.au). Additional resources are the British Society of Medical and Dental Hypnosis (www.bsmdh.org) and the Royal Society of Medicine, Section for Hypnosis and Psychosomatic Medicine (www.rsm.ac.uk/academ/smth_p.php). Some newsletters, such as those of the International Society of Hypnosis (www.ishhypnosis.org) or the Milton H. Erickson Foundation (www.erickson-foundation.org), can help you keep abreast of developments in the field.

For Further Reading

I continue to learn a great deal from many books on hypnosis. Some of these are listed below:

Hypnosis: Questions and Answers, by Bernie Zilbergeld, M. Gerald Edelstien, and Dan Araoz

The Letters of Milton H. Erickson, by Jeffrey Zeig and Brent Geary

Brief Therapy: Myths, Methods, and Metaphors, by Jeffrey Zeig and Stephen Gilligan, Eds

Ericksonian Methods: The Essence of the Story, by Jeffrey Zeig, Ed

Ericksonian Psychotherapy, Vols I and II, by Jeffrey Zeig, Ed

Treating Depression with Hypnosis, by Michael Yapko

Trancework: An Introduction to the Practice of Clinical Hypnosis 4th ed, by Michael Yapko

Resolving Sexual Abuse, by Yvonne Dolan

Handbook of Hypnotic Suggestions and Metaphors, by D.C. Hammond

The Handbook of Hypnotic Phenomena in Psychotherapy, by Janet Edgette and John Edgette

Hypnosis and Suggestion in the Treatment of Pain, by Joseph Barber

Psychological Approaches to Pain Management, by Robert Gatchel and Dennis Turk, Eds

The Psychobiology of Mind-Body Healing, by Ernest Rossi

Mind-Body Therapy, by Ernest Rossi and David Cheek

Therapeutic Metaphors for Children and the Child Within, by Joyce Mills and Richard Crowley

Therapeutic Trances and the Legacy of Milton H. Erickson: Selected Papers of Stephen Gilligan, by Stephen Gilligan

A Brief Guide to Brief Therapy, by Brian Carle and Bill O'Hanlon

My Voice Will Go With You, by Sidney Rosen

Assembling Ericksonian Therapy, by Stephen Lankton

The Answer Within: Clinical Framework of Ericksonian Hypnotherapy, by Stephen Lankton

Tales of Enchantment: Goal-Oriented Metaphors for Adults and Children in Therapy, by Stephen Lankton and Carol Lankton

and, last but not least, the valuable works of Milton H. Erickson, two of which are:

Hypnotic Realities, by Milton Erickson, Ernest Rossi and Sheila Rossi

The Collected Papers of Milton H. Erickson on Hypnosis, Vols I–IV, by Ernest Rossi, Ed

Index

curanderismo, 195, 204
curandero, 194, 195, 204, 205
curse, 189–202, 204, 215

debriefing, 28, 76, 102, 119, 271,
    274, 275
depression, 2, 13, 22, 31, 33, 69, 73,
    74, 79, 109, 141, 143, 153, 154,
    164, 227, 232, 239
directive techniques, 71, 75
dissociation, 27, 28, 37, 40, 41, 43, 44,
    99, 246, 247, 248, 251, 272, 274
dissociative identity disorder, 44
dissociative language, 25, 40, 272
distraction, 53, 130, 224, 269, 277
double negative, 43, 99

ego-strengthening, 2, 7, 11, 25, 35,
    39, 52, 55, 56, 69–86, 87, 120,
    155, 184, 223, 227, 253, 272,
    277, 282
embedded suggestion, v, 25, 44, 46,
    80, 168, 183, 184, 272, 282
EMDR, 6, 143, 149–152, 228
Erickson, Milton, 9, 40, 41, 52, 70, 72,
    73, 83, 97, 103, 107, 108, 109,
    110, 112, 129, 224, 238, 239,
    240, 258, 260, 267, 277, 283, 284
experiment *see* pattern interruption,
    rationales
exposure, 95, 146, 149, 151, 153,
    154, 160, 181, 219
exposure, prolonged, 150, 192

facial mask, 20, 27, 41, 267
family therapy, 4, 8, 65, 79, 94, 134,
    148, 154, 157, 164, 225
finger signals *see* ideomotor finger
    signals
fluff, 184, 245, 273

Gafner, George, 21, 45, 46, 61, 65, 71,
    73, 79, 80, 110, 114, 116, 126,
    133, 136, 139, 157, 174, 178,
    181, 182, 193, 196, 220, 243,
    245, 249, 250, 260, 263, 269

gain, secondary, 8
Glen Canyon induction, 245
Greek Chorus technique, 189, 200
green poultice, 14, 76, 121
guided imagery induction, 250

Hall, Bob, 117, 240
hallucination,
    negative, 38, 274
    positive, 37, 248
hand levitation, 28, 71
hands, 6, 16, 17, 23, 26, 35, 57, 72,
    89, 96, 108, 115, 116, 121, 125,
    126, 137, 138, 165, 175, 182,
    190, 196, 218, 241, 243, 248,
    249, 259, 272, 274, 278, 282
hidden observer, 273
hypnosis, 2, 4, 9, 10, 14, 19, 21, 25,
    27, 28, 36, 39, 42, 55, 58, 70,
    71, 73, 74, 75, 78, 84, 96, 113,
    117, 129, 143, 146, 148, 151,
    156, 160, 164, 180, 186, 187,
    198, 223, 224, 242, 267–284
hypnosis training, 4, 117, 160, 224
hypnotherapist, 283
hypnotic language, 1, 10, 35, 36, 38,
    53, 108, 228, 233, 269, 270,
    273, 279
hypnotic phenomena, 27, 37, 38, 41,
    42, 44, 241, 269, 271, 274,
    282

IBS-specific suggestions, 87
ideomotor finger signals, 102
IED, 2
implication, 72, 233, 273, 274
impotence, 2
indirect technique, 10, 37, 52, 72,
    223, 275, 276, 282
indirection, 27, 52, 53, 70, 75, 76, 80,
    239, 275
instigate, 9, 283
instigative anecdote, 114, 116, 136,
    139, 275, 278, 283
interspersal, 49, 52–53, 58, 63, 83,
    85, 181, 184, 275, 282